Teacher's resource

150 Numeracy Hour Lessons

YEAR 3

Contents — Page

First published 2001
exclusively for WHSmith by

Hodder & Stoughton Educational,
a division of Hodder Headline Ltd.
338 Euston Road
London NW1 3BH

Reprinted 2002

A CIP record for this book is available from the British Library.

Author: Howard Byers
Series editor: Paul Broadbent

ISBN 0340 79005 9

Typeset by Techset Ltd.
Printed and bound in Spain by Graphycems

Summary of objectives

	Theme	Topics	Objectives – children will be taught to:
Autumn Term			
1	Addition and subtraction	Understanding + and − Mental calculation strategies (+ and −)	Extend understanding of the operations of addition and subtraction. Read and begin to write related vocabulary. Use +, − and = signs. Recognise that addition can be done in any order. Put larger number first in order to count on. Identify near doubles. Bridge through a multiple of 10 and adjust.
2	Money	Money and 'real life' problems Making decisions, checking results	Recognise all coins and notes. Understand £p notation (e.g. £3.06). Find totals, give change and work out how to pay. Choose appropriate number operations and calculation methods to solve word problems. Explain and record methods informally. Check sums by adding in different order.
3	Time	Measures, including problems	Read time to 5 minutes. Choose an appropriate number operation and calculation method to solve word problems. Explain and record method informally.
4	Measuring length	Measures, including problems	Use ruler to draw and measure lines to nearest half cm. Read and begin to write the vocabulary related to length. Measure and compare using *m*, *cm*. Know relationship *m*, *cm*; *km*, *m*. Use decimal notation for *m* and *cm*. Suggest suitable units and equipment to estimate or measure lengths, including *km*. Read scales. Record to nearest whole / half unit, or as mixed units (e.g. 3 m 20 cm).
5	Shape	Shape and space Reasoning about shapes	Classify and describe 3-D and 2-D shapes, referring to reflective symmetry, faces, sides/edges, vertices, angles. Read and begin to write the vocabulary of position. Use spaces on square grids. Identify right angles in 2-D shapes and in the environment. Investigate general statements about shapes.
6	Counting	Counting, properties of numbers Reasoning about numbers	Count larger collections by grouping them in tens, then other numbers. Count on/back in 10s/100s, starting from any two-/three-digit number. Count on or back in twos, starting from any two-digit number and recognise odd and even numbers to at least 100. Solve number puzzles. Explain methods and reasoning orally and in writing.
7	Multiplication and division	Understanding × and ÷ Mental calculation strategies (× and ÷) Money and 'real life' problems Making decisions, checking results	Understand multiplication as repeated addition and as an array. Read and begin to write related vocabulary. Recognise that multiplication can be done in any order. To multiply by 10/100, shift the digits one / two places to the left. Choose an appropriate number operation and calculation method to solve word problems involving money and 'real life'. Explain and record method informally. Check multiplication in a different order.
8	Fractions	Fractions	Recognise unit fractions $\frac{1}{2}, \frac{1}{3}, \frac{1}{4}, \frac{1}{5}, \frac{1}{10}$, and use them to find fractions of shapes and numbers. Begin to recognise fractions that are several parts of a whole $\frac{2}{3}, \frac{3}{4}, \frac{3}{10}$.
9	Subtraction and time	Understanding + and − Mental calculation strategies (+ and −) Time, including problems Making decisions, checking results	Understand that subtraction is the inverse of addition. Say a subtraction statement equivalent to an addition statement and vice versa. Find a small difference by counting up from the smaller number. Read and begin to write the vocabulary related to time. Use units of time and relationship between them. Choose appropriate number operations and calculation methods to solve word problems. Explain and record method. Check subtraction with addition.
10	Handling data	Handling data	Solve a given problem by organising and interpreting data in frequency tables, and in pictograms with the symbol representing two units.

Summary of objectives

	Theme	Topics	Objectives – children will be taught to:
Spring Term			
1	Comparing, ordering and rounding	Place value, ordering, estimating, rounding Reading numbers from scales	Read and write the vocabulary of comparing and ordering numbers, including ordinal numbers to 100. Compare two three-digit numbers and say which is more or less. Read and begin to write the vocabulary of approximation. Round any two-digit number to nearest 10. Read scales and dials.
2	Mental addition	Understanding + and − Mental calculation strategies (+ and −)	Add three then four single-digit numbers mentally. Add three or four small numbers by putting the largest number first and/or finding pairs that total 10. Partition into 5 and a bit to add 6, 7 or 8.
3	Money problems	Money and 'real life' problems Making decisions, checking results	Choose appropriate number operations and calculation methods to solve money or 'real life' word problems with one or more steps. Explain and record method. Check with an equivalent calculation.
4	Shape	Shape and space Reasoning about shapes	Make and describe shapes and patterns. Relate solid shapes to pictures of them. Read and begin to write the vocabulary of direction. Make and use right-angled turns, and use the four compass points. Solve shape problems or puzzles. Explain reasoning and methods.
5	Measures	Measures, and time, including problems	Read time to 5 minutes on analogue and 12-hour digital clocks (e.g. 9:40). Read and begin to write the vocabulary related to mass. Measure and compare using kilograms and grams, and know the relationship between them. Suggest suitable units and equipment to estimate or measure mass. Read scales. Record measurements using mixed units, or to the nearest whole/half unit (e.g. 3.5 kg). Choose appropriate number operations and calculation methods to solve measurement word problems with one or more steps. Explain and record method.
6	Number sequences	Counting, properties of numbers Reasoning about numbers	Count on in steps of 3 or 4 or 5 from any small number to at least 50 and back again. Create and describe simple number sequences. Investigate general statements about familiar numbers, and give examples that match them. Solve number puzzles. Explain methods and reasoning orally and in writing.
7	Mental calculation Understanding + and −	Mental calculation strategies (+ and −) Understanding × and ÷ Mental calculation strategies (× and ÷)	Add three two-digit numbers using apparatus or informal methods. Partition into tens and units and recombine. Understand division as grouping or sharing. Read and begin to write the related vocabulary. Recognise division is inverse of multiplication. Use doubling and halving, starting from known facts. Say or write division statement corresponding to multiplication statement.
8	Solving problems	Money and 'real life' problems Making decisions, checking results	Choose appropriate number operations and calculation methods to solve money or 'real life' word problems with two steps. Explain and record method. Check results, e.g. check division by multiplication, halving by doubling.
9	Equivalent fractions	Fractions	Begin to recognise simple equivalent fractions, e.g. $\frac{5}{10}$ is equivalent to $\frac{1}{2}$, $\frac{5}{5}$ to 1 whole.
10	Bar charts	Handling data	Solve a given problem by organising and interpreting data in bar charts – intervals labelled in ones then twos.

Summary of objectives

	Theme	Topics	Objectives – children will be taught to:
Summer Term			
1	Comparing, ordering and rounding	Place value, ordering, estimating, rounding Reading numbers from scales	Compare two three-digit numbers, say which is more or less and give a number that lies between them. Round any three-digit number to the nearest 100. Order a set of whole numbers to 1000; position them on a number line. Identify unlabelled divisions on a number line or measuring scale.
2	Mental addition and subtraction	Understanding + and − Mental calculation strategies (+ and −)	Extend understanding of addition and subtraction. Add several small numbers. Add or subtract a near multiple of 10 to a two-digit number, by adding or subtracting the nearest multiple of 10, and adjusting. Use patterns of similar calculations.
3	Solving problems	Money and 'real life' problems Making decisions, checking results Pencil and paper procedures	Choose appropriate number operations and calculation methods to solve money or 'real-life' word problems with one or two steps. Explain and record method. Check results. Use informal pencil and paper methods to support, record or explain TU + TU, HTU + TU and HTU + HTU
4	Measuring capacity	Measures, including problems	Read and begin to write the vocabulary related to capacity. Measure and compare using *litres* and *millilitres*, and know the relationship between them. Suggest suitable units and equipment to estimate or measure capacity. Read scales. Record measurements using mixed units, or to the nearest whole/half unit (e.g. 3.5 litres). Choose appropriate number operations and calculation methods to solve measurement word problems with one or more steps. Explain and record method.
5	Symmetry and angles	Shape and space Reasoning about shapes	Identify and sketch lines of symmetry, recognise shapes with no line of symmetry. Sketch reflection of simple shape in a mirror. Read and begin to write the vocabulary of position, direction and movement. Recognise that a straight line is two right angles. Compare angles with a right angle, saying whether they are more or less. Investigate general statements about shapes, and suggest examples to match them. Explain reasoning.
6	Properties of number	Counting, properties of numbers Reasoning about numbers	Recognise two-digit and three-digit multiples of 2, 5, and 10 and three-digit multiples of 50 and 100. Solve number puzzles. Explain methods and reasoning orally and in writing.
7	Multiplication and division	Understanding × and ÷ Mental calculation strategies (× and ÷) Money and 'real life' problems Making decisions, checking results	Begin to find remainders after division. Round up or down after division. Use known facts and place value to multiply and divide mentally. Choose appropriate number operations and calculation methods to solve money or 'real-life' word problems with one or two steps. Explain and record method. Check results.
8	Fractions	Fractions	Compare two familiar fractions. Know that $\frac{1}{2}$ lies between $\frac{1}{4}$ and $\frac{3}{4}$. Estimate a simple fraction (proportion) of a shape.
9	Subtraction and time	Understanding + and − Mental calculation strategies (+ and −) Pencil and paper procedures Time, including problems Making decisions, checking results	Add using pencil and paper methods. Use known number facts and place value to add/subtract mentally. Use informal pencil and paper methods to support, record or explain TU – TU and HTU – TU. Use a calendar. Choose appropriate number operations and calculation methods to solve time word problems with one or two steps. Explain and record method. Check results.
10	Venn and Carroll diagrams	Handling data	Solve a given problem by organising and interpreting data in Venn and Carroll diagrams – one criterion.

Year 3

Mental maths starters

1. Show me

Children hold up number cards or fans to show addition or subtraction facts to 10. '*Show me 8 take away 2*' and '*Show me 7 plus 3*'. Use a variety of words for addition and subtraction.
Extend to facts to 20.

2. Thigh Clap Snap Snap

Start this clapping rhythm going then introduce counting on just the snaps of the fingers. Count on or back in ones or twos from any number less than 100.

3. Counting stick

Point to one end of the stick and name it zero. Name the other end 20 (for counting in twos), 50 (for counting in fives) or 100 (for counting in tens). Point to the different positions counting on or back. Point to random positions and ask for the multiplication fact.

4. Arrow cards

Ask children to use a set of arrow cards to make 2-digit numbers. Use the language of comparison and ordering. '*Make a number greater than 50*'. '*Make a number between 65 and 70*'. The children can work in small groups to put their numbers in order.
Extend to 3-digit numbers.

5. Doubling and halving

Recall doubles up to 10 and doubles of 5, 10, 15..... 50.
Call out a number to be doubled. Children show the double on number cards. Repeat by calling out a doubled number so that children can show the halves.
Extend by including doubles of whole numbers to 20 and multiples of 50 to 500.

6. Rounding

Each child needs a number line 0 to 100 with divisions of 10 marked on it. say a number up to 100 and the children round up the number to the nearest 10 and point to the position on the number line. Talk about rounding numbers up or down.
Extend the activity by using a number line to 1000 and rounding 3-digit numbers.

7. Cover ups

Provide each child with a 4×4 grid showing a different multiple of 5 to 100 in each of the squares. Ask the children to cover numbers with counters to make different totals. Ask them to cover numbers to make 100. How many different ways can they find?
Extend the activity by providing a grid with multiples of 100. Ask them to make totals of 1000.

8. Ordering

Make a set of sticky labels with a selection of numbers to 100. Ask a group of children to wear the labels and put themselves in order. They then show their position on a number line.
Extend the activity to include 3-digit numbers.

9. Fact families

Give a multiplication fact for the 2×, 5× and 10× table. The children make three related facts, e.g. *5 × 3 = 15, 3 × 5 = 15, 15 ÷ 3 = 5 and 15 ÷ 5 = 3.*

10. Target numbers

Write a number on the board and ask children to give you calculations for which this is the answer. Encourage them to use addition, subtraction, multiplication and division. Group them on the board to show the different types of questions.

Theme 1 Addition and subtraction

Objectives

- To extend understanding of addition and subtraction
- To begin to read and write the related vocabulary and use +, − and = signs
- To recognise that addition can be done in any order
- To put larger number first in order to count on
- To identify near doubles
- To extend understanding that subtraction is the inverse of addition
- To practise rapid recall of addition and subtraction facts

Vocabulary

more, add, sum, total, plus, minus, equals, altogether, sign, addition, subtract, subtraction, take away, how much more than…, how much less than…, difference between…, + *(plus)*, − *(minus)* and = *(equals)* signs

Resources

Number cards 0–9 for pupils' use, or number fans or similar.
Cards with mathematical symbols +, −, =
Large cards with the highlighted words from the vocabulary list.
Copymasters 1 and 2, Homework 1.

Assessment

At the end of this theme is the pupil able to:

- Add two or more two-digit numbers with the help of apparatus or pencil and paper;
- Mentally recall all whole number addition and subtraction facts to 20;
- Use addition facts to find subtraction facts and vice versa;
- Use appropriate mathematical vocabulary?

Mental maths starter 1

Lesson 1

Introduction

Each pupil needs a set of number cards 0–20 or similar *e.g. number fan.*
Practise mental recall of addition and subtraction facts to 20 by asking pupils to hold up the answers to:

- *Simple addition problems with answers up to 10*
- *Simple subtraction problems from numbers up to 10*
- *Simple addition problems up to 20*
- *Simple subtraction problems from numbers up to 20*

Vary the mathematical language you use, *e.g. Add 3 and 7, what is 3 and 5, subtract 6 from 10.* Pay particular attention to the highlighted words. Check that pupils understand the appropriate vocabulary and have a good recall of number facts. Ask pupils what methods they are using to find the answers mentally.

Activities

Introduction/revision of mathematical vocabulary linked to addition (whole class/group)

Give the pupils an addition sum on the board, ask them what sort of sum it is, elicit the answer 'addition'. Write the word addition on the board (or stick up the card with that word on). Hold up the other vocabulary cards in turn (or write them on the board). Allow pupils to decide which words and symbols are linked to addition and write or stick these around the word 'addition'. Write up examples on the board *e.g. 8 plus 4 equals 12* using both words and symbols for maths vocabulary.

Addition vocabulary (individuals/pairs)

Demonstrate the first 3 problems on Copymaster 1. Complete Copymaster 1 by filling in missing word or symbol as requested. Partners to check each other's work.

Differentiation

Low Attainers – Use practical equipment to complete addition problems
High Attainers – Work in pairs to set each other addition problems, which they then write out in three different ways using words or symbols.

Plenary

Recap the vocabulary used. Check understanding by asking pupils to suggest different ways of saying or writing an addition problem.

Lesson 2

Introduction

Each pupil needs a set of number cards 0–20 or similar *e.g. number fan.* Practise mental recall of addition and subtraction facts to 20 by asking pupils to hold up the answers to:

- *Simple addition problems with answers up to 10*
- *Simple subtraction problems from numbers up to 10*
- *Simple addition problems up to 20*
- *Simple subtraction problems from numbers up to 20*

Vary the mathematical language you use, *e.g. Add 3 and 7, what is 3 and 5, subtract 6 from 10.* Pay particular attention to the highlighted words. Check that pupils understand the appropriate vocabulary and have a good recall of number facts. Ask pupils what methods they are using to find the answers mentally.

Activities

Introduction/revision of mathematical vocabulary linked to subtraction (whole class/group)

Give pupils a subtraction sum on the board, ask them what sort of sum it is, and elicit the answer 'subtraction'. Write the word 'subtraction' on the board (or stick up the card with that word on) Hold up the other vocabulary cards in turn (or write them on the board). Allow pupils to decide which words and symbols are linked to subtraction and write or stick these around the word 'subtraction'. Write up examples on the board *e.g. 8 minus 4 equals 4* using both words and symbols for maths vocabulary.

Subtraction vocabulary (individuals/pairs)

Demonstrate the first 3 problems on Copymaster 2. Complete Copymaster 2 by filling in missing word or symbol as requested. Partners to check each other's work.

Differentiation

Low Attainers – Use practical equipment to complete subtraction problems
High Attainers – Work in pairs to set each other addition problems, which they then write out in three different ways using words or symbols.

Plenary

Recap the vocabulary used. Check understanding by asking pupils to suggest different ways of saying or writing a subtraction problem.

Lesson 3

Introduction

Each pupil needs a set of number cards 0–20 or similar *e.g. number fans*. Practise mental recall of addition and subtraction facts to 20 by asking pupils to hold up the answers to:

- *Simple addition problems with answers up to 10*
- *Simple subtraction problems from numbers up to 10*
- *Simple addition problems up to 20*
- *Simple subtraction problems from numbers up to 20*

Vary the mathematical language you use, *e.g. Add 3 and 7, what is 3 and 5, subtract 6 from 10.* Pay particular attention to the highlighted words. Check that pupils understand the appropriate vocabulary and have a good recall of number facts. Ask pupils what methods they are using to find the answers mentally. If it isn't mentioned, remind pupils of 'counting on' as a strategy for mental addition. Go over a couple of examples. Explain that it may be easier to put the larger number first because then there will be fewer numbers to count on. For example, it is easier to count on from 12 if you are adding 3 and 12.

Activities

Reinforcing the understanding that addition can be done in any order (whole class/group)

Towards the end of the mental activity, give the pupils a mental addition sum such as $8 + 4 = ?$; and follow it immediately by the 'reverse' sum. Repeat this two or three times. Point out the pattern – that addition can be done in any order. Confirm the pupils have understood by writing up some addition sums with two digit numbers, working them out together, and ask them to give you the answer to the same sum in a different order.

Addition practice (pairs, equal ability)

Pupils should devise and complete five addition sums using two two-digit numbers. Each pupil then passes them to his/her partner who rewrites them in a different way and checks the answer. Repeat if necessary and if time allows.

Differentiation

Low Attainers – Use single-digit numbers in the addition problems.
High Attainers – Use three two-digit numbers in the addition problems.

Plenary

Revisit the theme of the lesson by asking for the answers to pairs of addition sums. Remind pupils of strategies for counting on. Give some seemingly 'difficult' ones *e.g.* $123 + 456 = 579$, *so what is* $456 + 123$?

Lesson 4

Introduction

Each pupil needs a set of number cards 0–20 or similar *e.g. number fan*. Practise mental recall of addition and subtraction facts, using a range of vocabulary for both addition and subtraction. Phrase some questions to give pupils practice in problem solving, *e.g. If you had fifteen collectors' cards and you gave away twelve, how many would you have left?* Check pupils' understanding of vocabulary and addition and subtraction facts. Lead into the whole class activity below.

Activities

Recognising and using near doubles in addition and subtraction (whole class/group)

Ask the pupils to double a range of numbers, *e.g. double 8, double 3* and also to halve numbers, *e.g. what is half of 18?* Stress the importance of remembering these and link to the two times table. Write up a problem using near doubles such as $5 + 4 = ?$ Ask the pupils how they found the answer. If it isn't mentioned, explain the strategy that *5 is one more than 4. $4 + 4$ is 8, so $5 + 4$ is one more than $4 + 4$, so the answer is 9.* Repeat this, checking that pupils are using the appropriate strategy.

Practising using near doubles (individuals/pairs)

Ask pupils to identify and write down the 'near double' pairs that can be added to make a range of numbers that you have written on the board or on a worksheet. Then they should write out the addition sum to explain the method. For example, 19 is one of the numbers. The pupils should write:
$19 = 10 + 9$, 10 is one more than 9, $9 + 9 = 18$, so $10 + 9 = 19$.

Differentiation

Low Attainers – Find the answers to problems using actual rather than near doubles.
High Attainers – Use near doubles that have differences of 2 and 3, *e.g. 9 and 7.*

Plenary

Check pupils' understanding of near doubles through questioning. Remind them that other methods using near doubles such as *$19 = 10 + 9$, 9 is one less than 10, $10 + 10 = 20$, so $10 + 9$ is 19 (one less than 20)* are equally valid.

Lesson 5

Introduction

Each pupil needs a set of number cards 0–9 or similar *e.g. number fan*. Practise mental recall of addition and subtraction facts. Use a range of vocabulary and strategies for both addition and subtraction.

Activities

Subtraction as the inverse of addition

Ask pupils to start with a given number and count on a specific amount *e.g. Start with 18 and count on 5. What number do you arrive at?* Start with the same number and ask pupils to count back the same amount. Through questioning, elicit the idea that counting back is the same as subtraction. Stress that subtraction is the **inverse** (opposite) operation to addition.

Addition and subtraction 'sentences' (pairs/individuals)

Each pupil sets him/herself (or their partner) an addition problem. The pupil then solves the problem and finds as many ways as possible to restate the problem, *e.g.* *$18 + 5 = 23$, therefore $5 + 18 = 23$; $23 - 5 = 18$; $23 - 18 = 5$.* Continue as necessary.

Differentiation

Low Attainers – Set initial problem suitable for pupils' ability and allow use of practical apparatus.
High Attainers – Use 2- and 3-digit numbers for addition.

Plenary

Check pupils' understanding of subtraction as inverse of addition. Ask individuals/pairs to share their examples with the class.

Theme 2 Money

Objectives
- To recognise all coins and notes in use
- To understand £p notation *e.g. £3.06*
- To find totals, give change and work out how to pay
- To choose appropriate number operations and calculation methods to solve word problems
- To explain and record methods informally
- To check sums by adding in any order

Vocabulary
money, coin, note, penny, pence, pound, £, p, price, cost, buy, bought, sell sold, spend, spent, pay, change, dear, costs more, more/most expensive, cheap, costs less, cheaper, less/least expensive, how much, how many, total, amount, value

Resources
Enough real or toy money for each pupil to have a few of each denomination of coin and note.
Number cards 0–9 for pupils' use, or number fans or similar.
Large 'coins' on card for whole class work.
Copymasters 3 and 4, Homework 2.

Assessment
At the end of this theme is the pupil able to:
- Recognise all coins and notes in common use;
- Add and subtract sums of money;
- Work out the correct amount of change involved in simple transactions;
- Check their calculations by writing sums in a different order?

Lesson 1

Introduction
Each pupil needs a set of coins and notes.
The teacher should have a large 'coin' or 'note' of each denomination.
Hold up each coin, showing each face. Ask pupils to hold up:
- *matching coin*
- *coin of greater value*
- *coin of lesser value*

Activities
Guess my coins (whole class group)
A pupil selects 3 different coins and tells the class the amount. Others take turns in naming the three coins and the whole class then check with their own coins.
This can be repeated as necessary to check recognition and understanding.

Coin recognition (pairs/individuals)
Each pair needs a pair of dice.
The pupils throw the dice, record the number and make that number of pence in as few coins as possible.
They then record the coins by drawing around them and the amount made.
The pupils can compare how many coins they each need to make a particular amount.

Differentiation
Low Attainers – Use a single dice.
High Attainers – Multiply the numbers on the dice.

Plenary
Go through one or two totals and check coins used.
Set one or two problems such as *I have 3 coins and the total is 17p. What coins have I? What is the fewest number of coins I need to make 27p?*

Lesson 2

Introduction
Ask and confirm how many pence in 1 pound (100).
Write up and explain 100p = £1.00. Explain notation.
Repeat for 100p, 200p, 300p etc.
Write up amounts such as 150p, explain that this is £1.50.
Check understanding by writing up different amounts.

Activities
Adding pounds and pence (whole class)
Two pupils to take turns in writing up a number of pounds and pence, one below the other. Teacher demonstrates addition of these two amounts. Repeat, but ask third pupil to carry out addition, supporting if necessary. Check by reversing order of amounts. Repeat to reinforce and check understanding.

Shopping (pairs/individuals)
Each pupil needs Copymaster 3.
Select two items, state which is the cheaper and find the cost of both together, recording their work in their own way.
Ask pupils to think of and use suitable way of recording their work.

Differentiation
Low Attainers – Select amounts below £5.00; use practical apparatus.
High Attainers – Find the totals of more than two items, but continue to check by putting amounts in different orders.

Plenary
Ask pupils to demonstrate how they have recorded their work. Discuss them and ask pupils which they think are the most suitable.

Lesson 3

Introduction

Each pupil needs a set of notes and coins.
Check pupils' understanding of amounts to £10.00 by asking them different ways to make whole numbers of pounds e.g. *£7.00 could be made from 1 five pound note and 2 one pound coins or 3 two pound coins and 1 one pound coin.*
Write up each amount mentioned and check understanding of notation e.g. *in £7.00, £ is the symbol for pound, 7 is the number of pounds, . is the separator and 00 is the number of pence.*

Activities

Subtracting pounds and pence (whole class)

Two pupils to take turns in writing up a number of pounds and pence, the smaller below the larger. Teacher demonstrates subtraction of these two amounts. Use appropriate language e.g. *What is the difference between these two amounts? Which is the smaller?* Repeat, but ask third pupil to carry out subtraction, supporting if necessary. Check by adding answer to one of the original amounts. Repeat to reinforce and check understanding.

Subtracting continued (pairs/individuals)

Each pupil needs Copymaster 4. Select two items, state which is the more expensive and find the difference in price, recording their work in their own way. Check by adding answer to one of original amounts. Ask pupils to think of and use suitable way of recording their work.

Differentiation

Low Attainers – Select items that are below £2.00; use practical apparatus.
High Attainers – Work out the total cost of two items and find the difference in price between the total cost of another two items.

Plenary

Ask pupils to demonstrate how they have recorded their work. Discuss them and ask pupils which they think are the most suitable.

Lesson 4

Introduction

Each pupil needs a set of number cards and a set of money. Ask pupils to imagine they have one pound and work out and hold up the amount of change when they spend certain amounts of money, e.g. *How much change would you have if you spent 27p? How much would you have left if you bought a comic for 24p and a lollipop for 36p?* Continue, checking understanding and asking pupils to explain the strategies they use.

Activities

Calculating change (whole class)

A pupil suggests an amount of money below £1.00. Teacher demonstrates how to find change for this amount. Then an amount below £5.00, £10.00. £20.00. Work through examples on board, using appropriate strategies and language for subtraction. Demonstrate checking by addition
(£5.00 − £1.56 = £3.44; £3.44 + £1.56 = £5.00).

Shopping lists (pairs/individuals)

Ask pupils to find the cost of three items on Copymaster 4 and find out how much change they would get from the next size of note up (£5.00, £10.00, £20.00, £50.00). Check by addition. Work individually or in pairs on problems they set themselves from the copymaster.

Differentiation

Low Attainers – Find change for amounts below £5.00; use practical apparatus
High Attainers – Use larger sums of money from larger amounts.

Plenary

Revisit addition and subtraction of money. Link to giving and working out change. Check understanding by simple mental calculations such as *If I spend 65p in one shop and £1.00 in another, how much change will I have from £5.00?*

Lesson 5

Introduction

Start by asking pupils 'simple' mental problems, e.g. *Add 4 and 5; subtract 6 from 12; what is the difference between 17 and 9?*
Say you are going to make the problems more difficult, but the pupils don't have to answer them yet. Make the problems more difficult, e.g. *Add 37 and 29; how many more than 16 is 45?* Ask pupils how they might go about solving these using pencil and paper methods. Write suggestions on the board; try each out.

Activities

Solving word problems in money (whole class)

Read out a simple word problem such as *John bought a newspaper for 50 pence, a packet of sweets for 36 pence and a comic for 55 pence. How much change will he get from £2.00?*
Work through the stages required to solve this problem *(addition of 50 pence, 36 pence and 55 pence, followed by subtraction of total from £2.00).* Show how this could be set out using pencil and paper methods. Continue with similar examples, using a range of addition and subtraction vocabulary.

Addition and subtraction of money, giving change and word problems (pairs)

Pupils take turns to create a word problem from two prices on Copymaster 4 and both work out and record the answer using pencil and paper methods. The pair then compare and check their answers. Continue as necessary.

Differentiation

Low Attainers – Use amounts up to £1.00; use practical apparatus.
High Attainers – Use larger amounts of money; buy more than two items.

Plenary

Revisit and check understanding of objectives of theme including recognition of coins and notes, £p notation, adding and subtracting money, finding change.

Theme 3 Time

Objectives
- To read time to 5 minutes
- To choose an appropriate number operation and calculation method to solve word problems
- To explain and record method informally

Vocabulary
time, clock, digital, analogue, hour, minute, second, a.m., p.m., earlier, later

Resources
Copymasters 5 and 6, Homework 3.
Individual settable clock faces.
Large analogue clock faces for demonstration.
1 dice per pupil.

Assessment
At the end of this theme, is the pupil able to:
- Tell the time to 5 minutes;
- Select appropriate calculations and recording methods to solve word problems involving time?

Lesson 1

Introduction
Using a clock face, set time to whole hours. Ask pupils to give time displayed on demonstration clock, e.g. *What o' clock is it?* Pupils to show answers using number cards or number fans. Continue as necessary to check understanding. Ask children how many minutes in one hour, in half an hour, in one quarter of an hour. Set time on demonstration clock face; ask pupils to set time half an hour before, half an hour later and read time.

Activities
Quarter past, quarter to (whole class)
Use board/prepared cards to display/demonstrate numbers of minutes in one hour, half, quarter and three quarters of an hour.
- *60 minutes in one hour*
- *30 minutes in half an hour*
- *15 minutes in one quarter of an hour.*
- *45 minutes in three quarters of an hour*

Ask pupils to set their clocks quarter of an hour before and after given times (whole hours). Check results. Ask pupils to take turns in suggesting times for others to set their clock faces to. Check understanding.

Setting clocks to quarter to and quarter past (pairs/individuals)
Each pair needs two six-sided dice and Copymasters 5 and 6 (clock faces). Ask pupils to work in pairs, throw two six-sided dice, draw 'quarter past…' that number o'clock and write time below. Repeat until all hours covered. Repeat exercise with 'quarter to…'

Differentiation
Low Attainers – Pupils to draw in o'clock and half-past.
High Attainers – Pupils to draw in o'clock, half past, quarter past, quarter to.

Plenary
Check recall of numbers of minutes in above fractions of an hour.
Ask pupils to set a range of times involving these fractions as well as whole hours on demonstration clock.

Lesson 2

Introduction
Question pupils to elicit how many minutes there are in different fractions of an hour, including whole, half, quarter and three-quarters of an hour. Using demonstration clock face, show that there are five minutes between each consecutive number and that the 'big hand' moves from one number to the next every five minutes. Count in 5s around the clock face to 30, pointing out that these are five past, ten past, quarter past (15 minutes past), twenty past, twenty-five past and half past (30 minutes). Check understanding through appropriate questioning.

Activities
Telling the time (whole class)
Ask pupils to move the big hand on their own clock faces to given times between the hour and half past in five minute intervals:
- *5 past…*
- *10 past…*
- *5 minutes after quarter past and so on.*

Ask pupils in turn to say what time it is to check understanding.

Telling the time to within 5 minutes (past the hour) (pairs/individuals)
Each pupil needs Copymasters 5 and 6 (clock faces).
Pupils work in pairs and give each other a time up to 25 past an hour – in 5 minute intervals. Their partner draws the hands on a clock face to show the time five minutes later and writes the time below.

Differentiation
Low Attainers – Use practical apparatus (clock face) and draw in the actual time given.
High Attainers – Draw in and write time 5, 10 and 15 minutes later.

Plenary
Check pupils' understanding by setting the time on the demonstration clock face and asking them to read it. Ask pupils to set given times and 5, 10, 15 minutes after given times and to read these.

Lesson 3

Introduction

Revisit the numbers of minutes in different fractions of an hour, including whole, half, quarter and three-quarters of an hour. Using demonstration clock face, remind pupils that there are five minutes between each consecutive number and that the 'big hand' moves from one number to the next every five minutes. Count in 5s around the clock face from 30 (half past), pointing out that these are twenty-five to, twenty to, quarter to (15 minutes to), ten to, five to and the next hour. Check understanding through appropriate questioning.

Activities

Telling the time (whole class)

Ask pupils to move the big hand on their own clock faces to given times between the half past and the hour in five minute intervals:

- *25 to...*
- *10 to...*
- *5 minutes after quarter to and so on.*

Ask pupils in turn to say what time it is to check understanding.

Telling the time to within 5 minutes (to the hour) (pairs/individuals)

Each pupil needs Copymasters 5 and 6.

Pupils work in pairs and give each other a time between half past and five to – in 5 minute intervals. Their partner draws the hands on a clock face to show the time five minutes later and writes the time below.

Differentiation

Low Attainers – Use practical apparatus (clock face) and draw in the actual time given.

High Attainers – Draw in and write time 5, 10, 15 and 20 minutes later.

Plenary

Check pupils' understanding by setting the time on the demonstration clock face and asking them to read it. Ask pupils to set given times and 5, 10, 15 minutes after and before given times and to read these.

Lesson 4

Introduction

Ask pupils to read various times both past the hour and to the hour, in intervals of five minutes, set up on the demonstration clock face. Repeat, this time giving the pupils the times and asking them to set the hands.

Activities

Working out the time before and after (whole class)

Ask pupils to move the big hand on their own clock faces to any given time at five minute intervals:

- *25 to...*
- *10 to...*
- *5 minutes after quarter to...*
- *and so on*
- *20 past*

Check understanding by asking pupils in turn to say what time it is.

Telling the time to within 5 minutes (pairs/individuals)

Each pupil needs Copymasters 5 and 6.

Pupils work in pairs and give each other a time with multiples of 5 minutes to and past the hour. Their partner draws the hands on a clock face to show the time five minutes later and writes the time below.

Differentiation

Low Attainers – Use practical apparatus (clock face) and draw in the actual time given.

High Attainers – Draw in and write time 5, 10, 15 and 20 minutes later.

Plenary

Check that pupils can set and read time to 5 minutes.

Lesson 5

Introduction

Ask pupils how many minutes there are in between each consecutive number on the clock face (5). Ask pupils how many minutes between non-consecutive numbers, for example:

- *between 10 past 3 and 25 past 3,*
- *between 25 to 4 and 5 to 4,*
- *between 5 past 3 and 5 to 4.*

Use clock face to demonstrate practical method of finding this out.

Activities

How long does it take? (whole class)

Each pupil needs a clock face. Ask pupils to work out the answers to word problems such as *A TV programme starts at quarter past 5 and lasts for 30 minutes – what time will it finish?* Explain strategies for finding answer:

Quarter past 5 is 15 minutes past five, 15 + 30 = 45, 45 minutes past 5 is the same as quarter to 6, so the programme finishes at quarter to 6.

(Pupils may suggest other strategies: these could well be legitimate.) Repeat for similar problems. These could involve lengths of TV programmes, journeys and other events.

How long does it take? (pairs/individuals)

Each pupil needs a copy of a TV listings page from a magazine or newspaper. Ask pupils to find the length of time each programme appears to last and explain their reasoning. Pupils working in pairs could set each other questions as in the whole class activity.

Differentiation

Low Attainers – Make sure that these problems do not span an hour.

High Attainers – Use travel timetables (bus, train, etc) and work out the lengths of journeys.

Plenary

Check understanding of methods used through questioning and asking pupils to discuss their strategies. Ask higher attainers to talk about their task and how they solved it.

Theme 4 Measuring length

Objectives
- To use a ruler to draw and measure lines to nearest half centimetre
- To read and begin to write the vocabulary related to length
- To measure and compare using metres and centimetres
- To know the relationships between metres and centimetres, metres and kilometres
- To use decimal notation for metres and centimetres
- To suggest suitable units and equipment to estimate and measure lengths, including kilometres
- To read scales
- To record to nearest whole/half unit, or as mixed units *e.g. 3 m 20 cm*

Vocabulary
millimetres, centimetres, metres, length, longer than, shorter than, more than, less than.

Resources
Trundle wheels, metre sticks, tape measures and rulers marked in centimetres.
Copymasters 7 and 8. Homework 4.

Assessment
At the end of this theme, is the pupil able to:
- Measure and draw lines to a half centimetre;
- Make sensible estimations of lengths and heights of everyday objects;
- Know there are 100 centimetres in a metre and 1000 metres in a kilometre;
- Record lengths using decimal or mixed notation?

Lesson 1

Introduction
Each pupil needs a metre ruler or a piece of string one metre long knotted in the middle.
Discuss the metre as a unit of length. Explain that it is one hundred centimetres long and that centi- in this context means one-hundredth part, so there are 100 cm in a metre.
Ask what objects they can see that they think are longer (or higher or wider) than a metre.

Activities
Estimating length to the nearest half-metre (whole class)
Put up three headings:

Object	**Estimated length (to nearest half metre)**	**Actual length (to nearest half metre)**

Write up the names of some objects in the classroom, *e.g. bookcase, door, windowsill.* Ask pupils to estimate and write in the length or height of the object. Explain how to record lengths to half-metres, *e.g.* $1\frac{1}{2}$ *m or 1.50 m (50 cm is* $\frac{1}{2}$ *metre)*
Then use string or metre ruler to find length to the nearest half metre; write result in.

Measuring length to nearest half metre (pairs/individuals)
Each pupil needs Copymaster 7.
Each pair to decide on a number of objects to estimate and measure. They then write in their estimates *before* measuring. Pupils then use own string to measure to nearest half metre and complete table.

Differentiation
Low Attainers – Look for ten things that are longer than one metre.
High Attainers – Find five things that are less than one metre but not less than $\frac{1}{2}$ metre.

Plenary
Compare estimates and actual lengths that pupils have found. Remind pupils of units of length. Discuss what lengths may be measured in metres (cloth, buildings, room widths/height/lengths, themselves, playgrounds, racetracks).

Lesson 2

Introduction
Show pupils a metre rule and remind them that this is one metre. Ask how many centimetres make one metre and ask pupils to remember or estimate various lengths in classroom. Discuss suitability of using centimetres or metres for measuring (depends on length, shorter objects in centimetres, longer in metres and so on).

Activities
Measuring to nearest centimetre (whole class)
Show pupils an ordinary classroom ruler marked in centimetres. Use Copymaster 8 (with section of ruler) to remind pupils how to use a ruler to measure to 1 cm:
- *Place 0 on ruler next to beginning of line/object.*
- *Note number nearest to where line/object ends.*
- *Record reading as length to nearest centimetre.*

Check understanding by measuring lengths of first four objects on Copymaster 8.

Measuring to nearest centimetre (pairs/individuals)
Each pupil needs Copymaster 8.
Estimate length in centimetres of classroom object less than the length of class rulers (pen, pencil, rubber, exercise book etc.) and write estimate in table. Then measure object and write in length to nearest centimetre. Repeat for a number of different objects.

Differentiation
Low Attainers – Omit estimation, measure to nearest centimetre.
High Attainers – Measure to nearest centimetre.

Plenary
Go through pupils' findings. Discuss whether or not estimations are becoming more accurate; why it is important to measure accurately. Remind pupils of conventions of recording measurements they have already met.

Lesson 3

Introduction

Ask pupils how many centimetres in one metre.
Lead on to centimetres in fractions of a metre (half, quarter, three quarters, tenths) and that there are 100 centimetres in a metre. Display results. Check that pupils have understood there are 100 cm in one m. Demonstrate notation e.g. *1 m 50 cm or 1.5 m ($1\frac{1}{2}$ m), 0.34 m or 34 cm.*

Activities

Measuring in metres and centimetres (whole/class)
Demonstrate use of tape measure to measure to nearest centimetre. Ask pupils to estimate and measure various objects around classroom and write results on board. Check understanding and accuracy.

Estimating and measuring (pairs/individuals)
Each pupil needs Copymaster 7 and a tape measure.
Pupils estimate lengths of objects longer than 1 metre to nearest centimetre and fill in table. They measure and put in actual length, using *both* types of notation, e.g. *2 m 34 cm and 2.34 m; or 0 m 26 cm and 0. 26 m*

Differentiation

Low Attainers – Measure more everyday objects in whole centimetres.
High Attainers – Measure to nearest cm.

Plenary

Discuss how many centimetres in $\frac{1}{2}$ metre, $\frac{3}{4}$ metre etc.
How many metres and centimetres in 1 m 50 cm, 2 m 25 cm etc.

Lesson 4

Introduction

Discuss the use of metres and centimetres as units of length and what they are most useful for measuring.
Discuss equipment and suitability of this equipment for measuring length:

- *'Classroom ruler' in centimetres suitable for straight lines less than length of ruler.*
- *Metre rule in centimetres useful for lengths longer than above but less than 1 m – at a pinch for objects longer (but point out possible inaccuracies).*
- *Tape measure, metres and centimetres for a variety of lengths, depending on length of tape measure.*

Explain that there is a longer unit of length: the kilometre, which is 1000 metres (*kilo means 1000*).

Activities

Measuring longer distances with a trundle wheel (whole class)
Demonstrate use of trundle wheel to measure longer distances. Explain that the **circumference** of the wheel is 1 metre, so that a single turn of the wheel describes a line 1 metre long and that the wheel clicks once per metre travelled. Discuss when this might be most suitable, for example for long distances when accuracy to within a few centimetres is not necessary. Explain that trundle wheels are also used in surveying.

Using a trundle wheel (small groups/pairs)
Each group needs a trundle wheel and Copymaster 8.
Each group measures and records various distances around school, e.g. *length and width of playground, width and length of hall, length of corridor and so on.*

Differentiation

Low Attainers – Low attainers could be placed in groups with higher attaining pupils.
High Attainers – Use their findings to complete scale drawings of the areas they measure.

Plenary

Share and tabulate findings on board. Discuss differences between different groups' measurements of the same distance when these occur. Discuss use of different measuring apparatus for different purposes.

Lesson 5

Introduction

Explain that 1 centimetre can be divided into 10 parts and that each part is a millimetre (explain that millimetre means one thousandth of a metre). Ask pupils how many millimetres are in $\frac{1}{2}$ centimetre *(5)*; this can be written as 0.5 cm as well as $\frac{1}{2}$ cm. Ask pupils to convert one style of recording fractional lengths to the other, e.g. $10\frac{1}{2}$ cms = 10.5 cm; 2.5 cms = $2\frac{1}{2}$ cm.

Activities

Measuring to nearest half centimetre (whole class)
Show pupils an ordinary classroom ruler marked in centimetres and millimetres (or cm and $\frac{1}{2}$ cm). Use Copymaster 8 (with section of ruler) to remind pupils how to use a ruler to measure $\frac{1}{2}$ cm:

- *Place 0 on ruler next to beginning of line/object.*
- *Note number nearest to where line/object ends.*
- *Record reading as length to nearest $\frac{1}{2}$ centimetre, e.g. $1\frac{1}{2}$ cm or 1.5 cm.*

Check understanding by measuring lengths of first four objects on Copymaster 8.

Measuring to nearest centimetre (pairs/individuals)
Each pupil needs Copymaster 8.
Estimate length in centimetres of classroom object less than the length of class rulers (pen, pencil, rubber, exercise book etc.) and write estimate in table. Then measure object and write in length to nearest $\frac{1}{2}$ centimetre in both ways e.g. *$1\frac{1}{2}$ cm or 1.5 cm.*
Repeat for a number of different objects.

Differentiation

Low Attainers – Omit estimation; measure to nearest $\frac{1}{2}$ centimetre.
High Attainers – Measure to nearest millimetre.

Plenary

Collate lengths of objects to nearest $\frac{1}{2}$ cm.
Ask pupils for two ways these lengths may be written (*accept 5 mm instead of 0.5 cm or $\frac{1}{2}$ cm*). Check pupils' understanding of the units of length:
There are 100 cm in a metre and 1000 metres in 1 kilometre.

Theme 5 Shape

Objectives
- To classify and describe 2- and 3-dimensional shapes referring to reflective symmetry, faces, sides, edges, vertices and angles
- To read and begin to write the vocabulary of position
- To use spaces on square grids
- To identify right angles in 2-dimensional shapes and in the environment
- To investigate general statements about shape

Vocabulary
shape, triangle, quadrilateral, rectangle, square, pentagon, hexagon, heptagon, octagon, circle, cube, cuboid, triangular prism, sphere, angle, right angle, face, side, edge, vertex

Resources
Copymasters 9 and 10, Homework 5.
Large shapes as above on card.

Assessment
At the end of the theme, is the pupil able to:
- Recognise and name a range of 2- and 3-dimensional shapes;
- Describe some of the properties of these shapes;
- Identify right angles in 2-dimensional shapes and in the environment;
- Locate objects by single-figure (or letter/number coordinates)?

Lesson 1

Introduction
Each pupil needs a set of two-dimensional shapes including square, rectangle, circle, triangle, pentagon, hexagon, octagon (Copymaster 9). Ask pupils to hold up:
- named shapes
- shapes with particular characteristics, e.g.: *less than 3 sides, with curved edges, with more than four corners.*

Check understanding and repeat as necessary.

Activities
Quadrilaterals and vertices (whole class)
Ask pupils to hold up four-sided shapes. Explain that all 2-dimensional (flat) shapes with four sides are called quadrilaterals. Name known quadrilaterals (square, rectangle) and draw or display irregular quadrilaterals, explaining that because they have 4 sides, this is what they are called. Point out that each has 4 corners and introduce the word **vertex** meaning 'corner' as mathematical vocabulary they need to remember. Explain that the plural is **vertices**.

Relationships between sides and vertices (pairs/individuals)
Each pair/pupil needs a set of 2-D shapes and Copymaster 9. Draw and complete table to show these properties of 2-D shapes:

Name of shape	Sketch of shape	Number of sides	Number of vertices

Differentiation
Low Attainers – Provide pupils with named 2-D shapes.
High Attainers – Provide pupils with irregular and regular 2-D shapes.

Plenary
Discuss findings – elicit the relationship that in 2-D shapes, the number of sides is equal to the number of vertices.

Lesson 2

Introduction
Each pupil needs a set of two-dimensional shapes including square, rectangle, circle, triangle, pentagon, hexagon, octagon (Copymaster 9).
Ask pupils to hold up:
- named shapes
- shapes with particular characteristics, such as: *less than 3 sides, with curved edges, with more than four corners.* This time include the numbers of vertices as a property.

Check understanding and repeat as necessary.

Activities
Classification and properties of 2-D shapes and reflective symmetry (whole class)
Remind pupils of **reflective symmetry** (line symmetry) – where one half of the shape is a reflection and the **axis of symmetry** is where the mirror would be. Ask pupils to suggest where lines of reflective symmetry are on large or drawn shapes, both regular and irregular. Check understanding.

Symmetry in shapes (pairs/individuals)
Each pair/pupil needs a set of regular shapes (equilateral triangle, square, pentagon, hexagon, octagon) and a mirror. Ask pupils to draw around shape and find and draw all lines of symmetry in these shapes. Pupils to record, as they think appropriate, which shapes show reflective symmetry.

Name of shape	Number of sides	Number of lines of reflective symmetry

Differentiation
Low Attainers – Look at shapes given to record reflective symmetry (regular shapes).
High Attainers – Explore irregular shapes for reflective symmetry.

Plenary
Elicit rule that a regular shape (all sides the same length) has the same number of lines of symmetry as sides (and vertices). Check understanding of 2-D shapes as at the start of the lesson but include symmetry as a property in questioning *e.g. Hold up a shape that shows reflective symmetry and has four sides.* Ask pupils for everyday examples of 2-D shapes *e.g. rectangular doors and windows.*

Lesson 3

Introduction

Hold up a range of 3-D shapes including cube, cuboid, pyramid, cylinder, triangular prism, sphere, hemisphere and ask pupils to name these. Tell pupils the names of any they are unfamiliar with. Ask pupils what they think parts of these shapes may be called, i.e. *faces, edges, vertices*.

Activities

Vocabulary of 3-D shapes (whole class)

Remind pupils of names of 3-D shapes and associated vocabulary. A pupil names a shape and another finds that shape and names a part of the shape and another pupil points out that part. That pupil then names another shape and so on.

Classification and properties of 3-D shapes (pairs/individuals)

Each pair/pupil needs a set of regular 3-D shapes.

Ask pupils to examine shapes and record number of faces, edges and vertices.

Name of shape	Number of faces	Number of edges	Number of vertices

Differentiation

Low Attainers – Provide table with names of shapes written in.
High Attainers – Ask pupils to check Euler's Formula (*number of vertices + number of faces = number of edges + 2*).

Plenary

Ask pupils to name a range of 2- and 3-D shapes according to the properties you give them, such as:

- *A flat shape with five sides*
- *A 3-dimensional shape with a square face.*

Discuss difficulties in fitting spheres, hemispheres and cylinders into this table. What makes it difficult (curved edges and faces)? Ask pupils for everyday examples of 3-D shapes *e.g. dice, boxes.*

Lesson 4

Introduction

Use a 2 lengths of card fixed at one end with a paper fastener (or similar) to remind or demonstrate that the angle between two lines is a measurement of turn. Point out that a full turn is a complete circle. Fold a large paper circle in half and then in half again so that the folds divide the circle in quarters. Look at the angle between the two intersecting folds. Ask pupils what fraction of a whole turn this is ($\frac{1}{4}$). Remind/tell pupils this special angle is called a **right angle**.

Activities

Identifying right angles and making an angle checker (whole class)

Show pupils a setsquare and point out the right angle. Demonstrate how this can be used to check right angles on shapes and figures. Ask pupils where they can see right angles around the classroom (corners etc.). Point out that the corners of pages are usually right angles and that these could be used to check right angles if required. Show pupils how to make a right-angle checker by folding a piece of paper once and then folding it again to match up the folded edges. The folded corner is a right angle.

Measuring and finding right angles (pairs/individuals)

Each pupil makes a right-angle measurer and uses this to find:

- 2-D shapes that have right angles (Copymaster 10).
- Right angles in and around the classroom.

Ask pupils to find suitable ways of recording their findings.

Differentiation

Low Attainers – Sort 2-D shapes into those that have right angles and those that don't. Stick onto a simple Carroll diagram.
High Attainers – Use a protractor to measure right angles.

Plenary

Make a class list of shapes that contain a right angle – check with class that those mentioned do. Continue the list with places and shapes in the classroom that contain right angles. Remind pupils that angle is a measurement of turn and that a right angle is $\frac{1}{4}$ of a full turn.

Lesson 5

Introduction

Play a couple of games of noughts and crosses on the board with a couple of pupils. Ask others to keep a record of who played what when – let them choose how. After the games, ask pupils to say how the game was played. Discuss methods used.

Activities

Number/letter coordinates (whole class)

Display a large 5 × 5 grid (no reference letters or numbers) with a few shapes in different squares. Ask pupils to say where, for example, the triangle is. Label the columns A to E along the bottom of the grid and the rows 1 to 5 upwards. Ask the question again. Point out that the shapes can be located by giving the **grid reference**, or **co-ordinates** of the square, horizontal (letter) first and number (vertical) next, *e.g. B6.*

Battleships (pairs)

Provide each pupil with two 5 × 5 grids. Pupils should shade in 1 lot of three squares (battleship) and 2 of two squares (destroyers), in a horizontal or vertical pattern and not let their partner see it. They take it turns to call out a grid reference and the partner marks this on his/her grid. If the reference corresponds to a shaded square, the partner must say what has been hit. When all squares representing a ship have been hit, that ship is sunk and the owner must say so. The game continues until all ships are sunk.

Differentiation

Low Attainers – Use a 4 × 4 grid and fewer ships.
High Attainers – Use a larger grid and allow diagonal ships.

Plenary

Repeat introductory exercise – list moves in order

e.g	**Mrs Smith (X)**	**Lisa (O)**
	B2	C3
	C2	etc

Remind pupils of important convention in using grid references – horizontal axis (letters) first, vertical axis (numbers) second.

Theme 6 Counting

Objectives

- To count larger collections by grouping them in tens, then other numbers
- To count on or back in 10s/100s, starting from any two-digit or three digits number
- To count on or back in 10s/100s, starting from any two-digit number
- To recognise odd and even numbers up to 100
- To solve number puzzles and explain methods used orally and in writing

Vocabulary

grouping, counting on, counting back, odd or even

Resources

Counting materials, different 2-D shapes, 1–100 number squares. Copymasters 11 and 12, Homework 6.

Assessment

At the end of this theme is the pupil able to:

- Group larger numbers in tens and use this to calculate larger numbers;
- Count on or back in 10s or 100s from any two- or three-digit numbers;
- Count on or back in twos starting from any two-digit number;
- Recognise odd and even numbers up to 100;
- Explain methods used to solve number puzzles?

Mental maths starter 1

Lesson 1

Introduction

Tell the children that they will be estimating, then counting, collections of things in different ways. Practise counting forwards and backwards in groups of 2, 5 and 10. Show the class a box containing a large number of interlocking cubes (at least 300). *What would the best way to find how many there are? Why do you think that way is best? Would you suggest the same method if there were fewer/more cubes?* Record some estimates.

Activities

Counting on and back in 2s, 5s and 10s (whole class/group)

Using small items that can be joined together (paper clips, centicubes), ask the children to work in pairs to count their collection by grouping them in different ways, starting by counting in 10s. First they should write the number they think is in the collection, then count them, making a tally of the groups as they go along. Then ask them to repeat the counting but group them in a different way, e.g. *grouping and counting in 5s.* Is the answer still the same?

(Individuals/pairs)

The children can continue to work in pairs:

a) Work with tiny plastic bags and collections of buttons or other small items. *How many are there?* Can they count them in tens to make the counting easier?

b) Look at the large collection of interlocking cubes used in the introduction and ask some of the pairs to count them. Make a note of the strategies used and how close any estimates were.

Differentiation

Low Attainers – Give each pair/individual a collection of money consisting of 1p, 2p, 5p and 10p coins. Ask them to count their collections.

High Attainers – Add 20p coins to the collection and asks the group to do the same as *for low attainers* and record their results.

Plenary

Discuss when the children might use different sorts of grouping for counting. When might people count in 100s or even 1000s?

Lesson 2

Introduction

Use a large 100 number square on the board and ask the class to count in groups of 2 starting at number 2 as far as 100 mark off each step. Explore one or two problems e.g. *A class of 20 children is about to have a swimming lesson. They all need two armbands each. Count the number of armbands that are needed in groups of 2.*

Activities

Counting on and back in 2s (whole class/group)

List these activities on the board:

a) Count in twos from 20 to 50 – 20, 22 …
b) Count in twos from 52 to 64 – 52, 54 …
c) Count back from 30 to 10 – 30, 28 …
d) Count back from 44 to 12 – 44, 42 …

Remind the children that counting backwards is just as easy as counting forwards. You take away the same number each time. Use the 100 square if necessary.

(Individuals/pairs)

Work in pairs with a variety of counting materials including cubes, counters, pasta shells, pencils and money. Tell the children to count the materials in twos as quickly as possible. They can use a timer to see who can count the fastest. Work through Copymaster 11.

Differentiation

Low Attainers – Practise 2× table forwards and backwards. Can you beat your best time?

High Attainers – Take part in lots of practical activities of counting in 2s, including:

a) Counting children in from the playground.
b) Children as they go to lunch.
c) House points.
d) Lunch boxes.

Plenary

Discuss how much quicker it is to count in 2s. Check who knows their 2× table at speed.

Lesson 3

Introduction

Use a large 100 number square and start at different points. Ask pupils to count on in 2s, 5s and 10s. Hold up a packet of pasta shapes or similar (dried peas or any large number of smallish objects). Ask pupils to estimate how many peas or shapes there are in the packet. List pupils' guesses. Discuss ways of checking the answer.

Activities

Dividing large numbers of objects into countable groups (whole class/group)

Ask 2 or 3 pupils to count out groups of ten pasta shapes. When this is done, ask how many groups of ten there are. Ask pupils to count in tens as they count the groups *e.g. 10, 20, 30, 40 instead of 1, 2, 3, 4 etc until they have counted the number of shapes.*

(Individuals/pairs)

Working in pairs. Each pair needs a large number of different types of shape. Each member of the pair counts out a large number of shapes and records the number (without partner knowing how many) They then check their partners' number. If there is any disagreement, both count together until they reach agreement. Continue, trying different numbers (2, 5, 10) in the smaller groups.

Differentiation

Low Attainers – Use smaller numbers of objects, count in 5s and 10s.
High Attainers – Use a larger number of objects and a greater range of different numbers.

Plenary

Check findings and discuss problems. Were any particular groupings more successful? Did this depend on the number of objects altogether? For example, counting in twos might be useful for smaller numbers and regrouping 10s into 50s or 100s for very large numbers.

Lesson 4

Introduction

18, 17, 4, 3

The numbers in this shape can be linked. They need +, − and = to link them.

$18 - 17 + 3 = 4$ or
$17 + 4 - 18 = 3$

Can the children find any other ways of linking them?

Activities

Odds and evens (whole class/group)

Working in groups, link the numbers in each of these shapes. They must use +, − and = to link them.

14, 19, 6, 11 | 20, 6, 10, 4 | 23, 11, 5, 7 | 10, 12, 16, 14

(Individuals/pairs)

All these numbers are even – 16, 8, 2 and 10. Can they be linked with +, −, = ?

There are three even numbers and one odd number——
7, 8, 12, 6. Can they be linked with +, −, and = ?
There are three odd numbers and one even number——
7, 5, 2, 9. Can they be linked with +, −, and = ?
Fill in this table by ticking.

	4 even	3 even & 1 odd	2 ev. 2od	1ev. 3 od	4 odd
Can be linked	✓				
Can not be linked		✓			

Differentiation

Low Attainers – Use a 1–100 number square and colour in all the odd and even numbers up to 100.
High Attainers – Answer questions such as *The previous odd number to 33 is? The next odd number to 54 is?*

Plenary

Look at the table from the work done in pairs and discuss the results. Did anyone find out anything unusual?

Lesson 5

Introduction

Draw a number line 0–20 on the board and show a pattern of jumping in twos. Ask the children which number has been landed on each time. Then ask them, without using the number line, to write down the next 4 numbers. Use the number line to check their answers. *If our number line was longer and I carried on jumping in this pattern, which of these numbers would I land on? 20, 21, 27, 24, 37, 38, Why?*

Activities

Number puzzles (whole class /group)

Ask them to use the following patterns –

1) 1, 2, 1, 2, follow it on the number line. Write down the numbers that are landed on. Carry it on without the number line. Check to see if you are right.
2) 1, 4, 1, 4 …
3) 1, 2, 3, 4, …
4) 1, 1, 3, 1, 1, 3, 1 …

Let the children try some of their own patterns.

(Individuals/pairs)

Work through Copymaster 12 in pairs and encourage each pair to explain the methods they use to work out each puzzle.

Differentiation

Low Attainers – Use squared paper to build up their own coloured patterns.
High Attainers – Ask the group to talk about any 'moving' patterns they know of *e.g. traffic lights, birds flying.* Can they record them?

Plenary

Make up a class sequence or pattern that all the children can take part in. Go through Homework 6.

Theme 7 Multiplication

Objectives

- To understand multiplication as repeated addition and as an array
- To read and begin to write related vocabulary.
- To recognize that multiplication can be done in any order
- To understand that the place value shifts one place to the left when multiplying by 10 and 2 places when multiplying by 100
- To choose appropriate number operations and calculations when solving word problems involving money and 'real life'
- To explain and record methods informally
- To check multiplication by repeating in a different order

Vocabulary

addition, multiply, multiplication, array, place value

Resources

Assorted dice, number squares, A4 hexagonal paper, assorted cubes, counting apparatus (Denes).
Copymasters 13 and 14, Homework 7.

Assessment

At the end of this theme is the pupil able to:

- Understand that addition and multiplication are linked;
- Understand that multiplication can be carried out in any order;
- Understand the vocabulary of multiplication;
- Understand problems involving multiplication?

Mental maths starters 2, 9

Lesson 1

Introduction

Explain that this lesson is about multiplication and when we might use it in everyday life. Remind the children that we use multiplication when equal numbers are needed *e.g. 5 children need to bring 10 coloured pencils to school; this is the same as $10 + 10 + 10 + 10 + 10$; it can be written as 10×5 or 5×10; we say '5 lots of 10' or '5 times 10'.*
Show this as counting the same size of step on the number line.

Activities

Real life multiplication (whole class/group)

Ask the children when they might need to use multiplication in real life situations. Display a list of small items they might buy or have some pictures with prices under them. Ask questions about buying multiples of different items for the children to solve mentally. Remind them that doubling is the same as multiplying by 2.

(Individuals/pairs)

Working in pairs the children need 2 dice per pair so that they can pose questions by rolling the dice and use the relevant vocabulary *e.g. $5 \times 6 = 30$ which is '5 lots of 6' or '6 lots of 5' or '5 times 6' or '6 times 5' which is the same as $5 + 5 + 5 + 5 + 5 + 5$ or $6 + 6 + 6 + 6 + 6$.*

Differentiation

Low Attainers – Doubling numbers starting with $2 = 4$, double again $= 8$ etc.
High Attainers – Doubling numbers starting with $15 = 30$, double again $= 60$ etc.

Plenary

Give a mixture of numbers to double twice and multiply by 4 for the children to work out mentally and respond quickly.

Lesson 2

Introduction

Tell the children they are going to work with multiples of 10 and look at the effect of multiplying any number by 10. Initially work with 10 sets of a number, such as 10 sets of 4, and show this on place value columns on the board. Start with other numbers less than 10 but ask the children to predict what the answers might be if they multiplied larger numbers by 10.

Activities

Multiplying by 10 (whole class/group)

Ask the children to model some of the larger numbers on a place value mat using Diene's (cubes, longs and flats) apparatus. This is a good time to use a calculator so that they can see the pattern of multiplying larger numbers by 10. Write some everyday problems together involving multiplication by 10.
e.g. *If there are 10 children sitting in 3 rows at the circus, how many children are there? If there are 10 mice in 4 cages in the pet shop, how many mice are there?*

(Individuals/pairs)

Work through Copymaster 13 which involves everyday problems when multiplying by 10. The children can work individually or in pairs.

Differentiation

Low Attainers – Only multiply numbers less than 10 by 10. Use a place value mat to model each question and answer.
High Attainers – Multiply larger numbers by 10. Can they start to understand the change in value as the number is multiplied by 100? How many times bigger is 300 than 3?

Plenary

Model some rules for multiplying by 10. What have the children found out in their investigations?

Lesson 3

Introduction

Draw an array on the board and ask the children to work in pairs and write some statements describing it. Write the statements on the board, adding any they might have missed out. Use the language of multiplication ('sets of' and 'lots of') as well as $5 + 5 + 5 + 5 = 20$, $4 + 4 + 4 + 4 + 4 = 20$, $5 \times 4 = 20$ and $4 \times 5 = 20$ and so on.

Activities

Multiply means? (whole class/group)

Remind the children that the process described in the introduction is called multiplication and write the symbol. Show how the array can be described using the $\times$ symbol, demonstrating that it can be written as 5×4 and 4×5. Say that in their work they will be using cubes to make rectangles like the one drawn and you want them to use the multiplication symbol to write about the rectangles. Ask one of the children to come to the board, throw a large dice and make a 'stick' that length from cubes, for example 6 cubes long if 6 was thrown. Ask a second child to throw the dice and make that many 'sticks' the same length as the 6, for example 2 'sticks' of 6 if 2 is thrown. Draw the array and write the number statements using multiplication. On a large blank 100 square show how this array could be drawn and coloured.

(Individual/pairs)

Working in pairs with their own dice and number square repeat the dice throws and use a different colour to show these new numbers as an array on the 100 square.

Differentiation

Low Attainers – Give the children some dot-to-dot pictures where multiples are joined instead of consecutive numbers, e.g. *join 2, 4, 6, 8 and so on, or 5, 10, 15, 20 and so on.*
High Attainers – Can the children explain what is happening to the patterns on a calculator if they press 2 × = = = ?

Plenary

Let the children show the number squares that they have coloured in. Can they comment on the patterns?

Lesson 4

Introduction

Prepare a multiplication square on the board and fill in the answers with the children –

	1	**2**	**3**	**4**	**5**
1	1	2	3	4	5
2	2	4			
3	3				
4					
5					

Then model some of the answers using centicubes.

Activities

Rectangles and squares (whole class/group)

Refer to the multiplication square and ask the children in their groups to model the rest of the answers using centicubes. Discuss with the children the shapes that they are making. Why do they think all the models make rectangles and squares? Ask them to take a handful of cubes and try to make them into a square or rectangle, then draw the shape and write about it using words and numbers.

(Individuals/pairs)

Working in pairs and starting with a handful of interlocking cubes they will try to make a rectangle, so that if they pick up 15 cubes these can be made into a 5×3 rectangle or turned so that it becomes a 3×5 rectangle. Ask them to draw and record what they do in number sentences. Repeat this for other rectangles.

Differentiation

Low Attainers – Use a calculator to help fill in a small multiplication square.
High Attainers – Test themselves against the clock when filling in a large multiplication square. Add 5 seconds on for every wrong answer.

Plenary

Explain the link between multiplication and division. If they know 3×4 and 4×3 equals 12, then 12 divided by $3 = 4$ and 12 divided by $4 = 3$.

Lesson 5

Introduction

Using squared paper ask the children, using numbers 1–12 in turn, to make as many rectangles as possible on the paper. e.g. *for the number 12 = 4 × 3, 3 × 4, 6 × 2, 2 × 6 etc.*
Remind the children that some numbers have more/fewer rectangles than others.

Activities

More shapes and products (whole class/group)

Repeat the activity/investigation up to 20 that the class started in the introduction. In small groups the class can play the 'Dice Game' using Copymaster 14. You need to put one number on each car to go with the dice you use, so for the 0–5 dice you need 0, 1, 2, 3, 4, 5, 6, then 8, 9, 10, 12 and so on. Vary the game with different dice and therefore different hat numbers.

(Individuals/pairs)

Using a sheet of A4 paper with hexagons on choose a table and write the multiples on the hexagons. In pairs make up games to practise multiplication facts using the hexagons.

Differentiation

Low Attainers – Write some multiplication stories e.g. *A farmer has 4 fields with 6 sheep in each field. How many sheep does he own?*
High Attainers – Time each other on the speed that they can say their times tables.

Plenary

Explain Homework 7. Ask other children to say their tables as fast as they can. Is there a class champion?

Theme 8 Fractions

Objectives

- To recognise unit fractions $\frac{1}{2}, \frac{1}{3}, \frac{1}{4}, \frac{1}{5}, \frac{1}{10}$ and use them to find fractions of shapes and numbers
- To begin to recognise fractions that are several parts of a whole

Vocabulary

fraction, whole, part, numerator, denominator, words and symbols for unit fractions

Resources

Paper to fold and cut, fraction dominoes, counters and cubes, some everyday objects for finding fractions of.
Copymasters 15 and 16, Homework 8.

Assessment

At the end of this theme is the pupil able to:

- Recognise that a fraction is an equal part of a whole shape or a number;
- Recognise and name common fractions, such as $\frac{1}{2}, \frac{1}{4}, \frac{1}{3}, \frac{1}{5}, \frac{1}{10}$;
- Recognise fractions that are several parts of a whole *e.g.* $\frac{2}{3}, \frac{3}{4}$?

Mental maths starters 2, 5

Lesson 1

Introduction

Each child needs a paper rectangle. Ask them to fold the rectangle in half making another rectangle. Discuss how they know what is half and remind them that both halves need to be the same. Ask them to fold the shape again and open it out. How many pieces are there now? Are they all the same size? Show them how to write a quarter and ask them to write this on each piece.

Activities

Recognising fractions (whole class/group)

Continuing from the introduction fold the paper back into quarters and fold again. Again, count the pieces and ask what these might be called and how an eighth might be written. Ask them to write an eighth on the back of each fraction of the paper.
Play 'Show me the fraction':
Show me half. Fold the paper so you can see that fraction
Continue with other fractions.
Show me two eighths. Show me … etc.

(Individuals/pairs)

Working in pairs tell the children to fold a square in half. Does everyone have the same shape? How many ways can the square be folded in half? (A rectangle and a triangle.) Continue by folding in quarters and eighths.

Differentiation

Low Attainers – Fold squares into halves in two ways. Label each part.
High Attainers – Fold rectangles into halves in as many ways as possible. Does the size of the rectangle matter?

Plenary

Discuss the different ways that shapes can be divided into halves, quarters and eighths.

Lesson 2

Introduction

Fold a circle into $\frac{1}{2}$, $\frac{1}{4}$ and $\frac{1}{8}$ and label each part using different coloured pencils. Discuss the size of each fraction and ask *Which of the fractions is largest and which is the smallest?*
Then look at the fraction notation. *Why is it that the one with the largest denominator (the number at the bottom) is the smallest fraction?*

Activities

Several parts of …? (whole class/group)

Draw a series of shapes on the board (a circle, a square, a rectangle) and divide them into halves quarters and eighths. Then ask the children to come out and colour in firstly 1 part of a shape, then 2 parts etc. Ask them *How many equal parts are coloured and how many equal parts are not coloured?*

(Individuals/pairs)

Use Copymaster 15 so that the children, working in pairs, can get used to recognising $\frac{3}{4}$ of a shape, $\frac{3}{8}$ of a shape etc. This worksheet also introduces finding a third and two thirds of a shape.

Differentiation

Low Attainers – Give the children activities that involve working with halves and quarters. Fraction dominoes or snap games will help them to match pictures of fractions with their notation.
High Attainers – Also use the fraction domino or snap games using halves, quarters and thirds.

Plenary

Return to the shapes on the board and ask more questions about fractions that are coloured and fractions that are not coloured.

Lesson 3

Introduction

Draw a rectangle on the board divided into fifths *How many equal parts is this shape divided into? If I colour in three of the parts, what fraction of the shape has been coloured in? If I colour in four of the parts, what fraction of the shape is coloured in?*

Activities

Fifths and tenths (whole class/group)

Look at the shape on the board again and divide each fifth into two equal parts. *How many equal parts is the whole shape now divided into?* (10) Ask the children to come out and colour in different parts of the shape. *How many equal parts are coloured in and what is each part called?* Ask questions such as *If $\frac{2}{10}$ are coloured in how many tenths are not coloured in?*

(Individual/pairs)

Write a list of different fractions on the board in pairs, *e.g.* $\frac{2}{10}$ *and* $\frac{4}{10}$, $\frac{1}{10}$ *and* $\frac{5}{10}$, $\frac{1}{5}$ *and* $\frac{3}{5}$, $\frac{2}{5}$ *and* $\frac{4}{5}$. What is the bigger/larger fraction in each case?

Continue – $\frac{1}{5}$ and $\frac{3}{10}$, $\frac{4}{10}$ and $\frac{3}{5}$ etc.

Differentiation

Low Attainers – Divide different strips of paper into fifths and tenths

High Attainers – Draw a fraction wall for thirds, fifths and tenths.

Plenary

Revise the different fractions that have been looked at in these first three lessons and their equivalence *e.g.* $\frac{2}{5} = \frac{4}{10}$ $\frac{1}{4} = \frac{2}{8}$ *etc*

Lesson 4

Introduction

Hold up a line of 10 cubes and if possible give each pair of children the same number of cubes. Make sure the children have counted the number of cubes carefully. Ask questions such as *If I take one cube what fraction of the whole strip have I taken? If I take three cubes what fraction of the whole strip have I taken and what fraction of the whole strip is left?*

Activities

Parts of a whole (whole class/group)

Lay out other everyday items in groups of ten. Ask questions such as *How many pencils would I have if I take $\frac{4}{10}$s? How many balls would I have if I played with $\frac{3}{5}$?* (Remind the children that this fraction is equivalent to $\frac{6}{10}$.) Do the same with smaller groups and work with different fractions. *What is $\frac{3}{4}$ of a line of 8×10 pence pieces?*

(Individual/pairs)

Give each pair of children 10 cubes and ask them to find 6 different fractions of the ten cubes.

e.g. $\frac{1}{5}$ of 10 cubes $= 2$ so $\frac{2}{5} = 4$ so $\frac{3}{5} = 6$ etc.

Differentiation

Low Attainers – Let these children use 10 cubes and find just $\frac{1}{10}$, $\frac{2}{10}$ etc of the set of cubes.

High Attainers – Begin to find fractions of numbers e.g. *$\frac{1}{3}$ of 9 and $\frac{1}{5}$ of 5*

Plenary

Discuss how the class can find fractions of numbers without using apparatus.

Lesson 5

Introduction

Explain that to find $\frac{1}{2}$ of a number divide by 2

Arrange some cubes or counters for the children to see and divide them into two equal groups, *e.g.* ●●●●●●// ●●●●●●

so $\frac{1}{2}$ of $12 = 6$

To find $\frac{1}{3}$ of a number divide by 3, *e.g.* ●●●●●// ●●●●●// ●●●●●

so $\frac{1}{3}$ of $15 = 5$

Activities

Fractions of numbers (whole class/group)

Continue using the apparatus from the introduction and find $\frac{1}{2}$ of other numbers by dividing the number into two equal parts. Find $\frac{1}{3}$ of a selection of numbers by dividing the number into three equal parts and taking one of them. Also find $\frac{1}{4}$ of other numbers by dividing them into four equal parts and taking one of them.

If $\frac{1}{4}$ of 12 is 3 what is $\frac{3}{4}$ of 12?

(Individuals/pairs)

Work through Copymaster 16 which will reinforce how to find fractions of different numbers. Emphasise that you are dividing each number into equal parts. To find $\frac{1}{8}$ of a number, divide it into 8 equal parts.

Differentiation

Low Attainers – Make up their own number problems involving halves and quarters

High Attainers – Make up their own number problems involving thirds, fifths and tenths.

Plenary

What did you do today that you found easy?

What was difficult about today's work and why?

Go through Homework 8.

Theme 9 Subtraction and time

Objectives

- To understand that subtraction is the inverse of addition
- To say a subtraction statement that is equivalent to an addition statement
- To find a small difference by counting up from the smaller number
- To use units of time and the relationship between them
- To choose appropriate number operations and calculation methods to solve word problems

Vocabulary

addition, add subtract, subtraction, inverse, operation, second, minute, hour, timetable, calculate, calculation

Resources

Number lines, addition squares, analogue clocks and digital clocks. Copymasters 17 and 18, Homework 9.

Assessment

At the end of this theme is the pupil able to:

- Understand and use the relationship between addition and subtraction;
- Tell the time to the nearest five minutes using analogue and digital clocks and record times;
- Choose the right number operations to solve word problems about time?

Mental maths starters 1, 2

Lesson 1

Introduction

Write a simple number fact on the board, such as 10 + 6 = 16, and ask the children to show another way of writing this as addition, without splitting numbers (6 + 10 = 16). Then go on to show how the three numbers can be changed around to show 16 − 10 = 6 and 16 − 6 = 10.

Activities

There and back (whole class/group)

Take another example, 10 + 5 = 15, 15 − 5 = 10, 15 − 10 = 5. Demonstrate these calculations on a number line, showing clearly how jumping back along the number line 'undoes' the jumping forward.

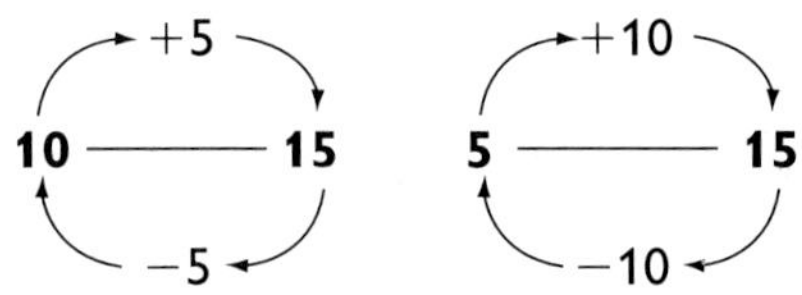

Repeat with other examples.

(Individuals/pairs)

Give the children working in pairs a harder example and ask them to show how this might be done on the number line, reminding them that if they can remember one number fact they can use it to work out three others.

e.g.

+10 +10 +4 +1

36 —— **46** —— **56** —— **60** —— **61**

36 + 25 = 61

Use the number line to show:

61 − 25 = 36

25 + 36 = 61

61 − 36 = 25

Continue with other examples.

Differentiation

Low Attainers – Use number facts below 20.

High Attainers – Use number facts between 20 and 100.

Plenary

Discuss the examples that the children have looked at and ask the children to demonstrate them on the board.

Lesson 2

Introduction

Prepare an addition square to suit the abilities of the class:

+ 5 4 3 2 1

6

7

8

9

10

Ask the children how they will fill in the missing numbers.

Activities

Addition / subtraction (whole class/group)

Once all the spaces have been filled in on the addition square discuss how it can be used for subtraction. *e.g. Find the answer 14 in the square: 14 − 9 = 5, 14 − 5 = 9.*

When the class have got the idea select three more of the numbers and ask them to write as many sentences as they can using addition and subtraction.

(Individuals/pairs)

Let the children work through Copymaster 17. The children, working in pairs, must find one addition fact using three numbers and use this to find another three addition or subtraction facts.

Differentiation

Low Attainers – Make 3 or 4 number facts from 12 + 5 = ?

High Attainers – Make 3 or 4 number facts from 27 + 35 = ?

Plenary

Invite the children to talk about the different words we use to make number sentences e.g., *17 minus 3 is 14* and display these for use during mental maths time.

Lesson 3

Introduction

To aid working out simple subtraction facts mentally the children need to practise finding a small difference by counting up from the smaller number.

Using a number line 0–20: **12 − 4 = 8**

0 1 2 3 **4** 5 6 7 8 9 10 11 **12** 13 14 15 16 17 18 19 20

*** 8 spaces/jumps from 4 to 12**

Activities

Take away more easily (whole class/group)

Repeat what has been looked at in the introduction with other examples. The children can either come out and demonstrate on the board or use their own individual number lines. Emphasise that this is a counting on process starting with the smaller number in the number statement.

15 − 8 = ?

Start at 8 (the smaller number) and count on to 15 = 7 spaces or jumps.

(Individual/pairs)

List ten examples on the board and ask the children to work in pairs and work out the answers by counting on. If they finish quickly then they can set themselves their own examples *e.g. 17 − 9 = ?*

Differentiation

Low Attainers – Work with numbers less than 10.

High Attainers – Work with 2-digit numbers taking away 1-digit numbers *e.g 27 − 9 = 18 still counting on from the smaller number.*

Plenary

Have a competition on how fast the children can work out subtraction facts by using the counting on process. Who can do 10 in one minute?

Lesson 4

Introduction

Review telling the time with the children. Ask questions about the times they are familiar with, such as on the hour, half past, quarter past and quarter to. Remind the class of the position of the hour hand in relation to the minute hand when using an analogue clock. Point out the movement of the hour hand between one number and the next, so that if the time is 10.30 the hour hand is halfway between the 10 and the 11.

Activities

Time 1 (whole class/group)

Use model analogue and digital clocks to demonstrate telling the time at five minute intervals. Try a clock with just the minute hand. Demonstrate the movement of the hand from one number to the next and the movement of the numbers on the digital clock. Choose an hour and move the hands around the clock face again explaining the times as, for example, 10.05, 10.10, 10.15 up to 10.55.

(Individuals/pairs)

Ask the children about the link with telling the time at 5 minute intervals and the 5× table.

Working in pairs get the children to write down what sorts of things they could do in 5 minutes *e.g. Making a cup of tea.*

Differentiation

Low Attainers – Revise o'clock, half past times on analogue clock.

High Attainers – How many minutes between 3.15 and 3.45 etc.

Plenary

What time do you do the following…

a) Get up for school
b) Have lunch etc.

Lesson 5

Introduction

Frequent use of the classroom clock and children's watches to tell the actual time is very important. Have a large clock face in a convenient position in the classroom and encourage children to change the position of the hands frequently to match the classroom clock. If possible, have a clock face which shows digital time as well, so that the children are constantly matching digital and analogue clocks.

Activities

Time 2 (whole class/group)

Discuss with the children the times certain things happen during the day: first of all, the things which happen at the same, time every day; then activities or events which happen on certain days of the week. The children can draw up a timetable for the week which can be put up for the class to refer to.

(Individuals/pairs)

Work through Copymaster 18 in pairs, emphasising to the children the units of time that are being used (minutes and hours).

Differentiation

Low Attainers – Practise reading the time displayed on an analogue clock (15 minute intervals).

High Attainers – Write a story about your day. Put in the times that things happen at home and at school.

Plenary

Use the class clock and go through some analogue times for special parts of the day,

e.g. Games
Story
Home time

Theme 10 Handling data

Objectives

- To solve a given problem by organising and interpreting data in frequency tables, and in pictograms with the symbol representing two units

Vocabulary

pictogram, frequency table, units, record, total, data

Resources

Various dice, large sheets of paper.
Copymasters 19 and 20, Homework 10.

Assessment

At the end of this theme is the pupil able to:

- Solve problems involving collection, sorting and organisation of data;
- Represent data in the form of graphs and charts;
- Interpret graphs and charts and make predictions?

Mental maths starters 4, 5

Lesson 1

Introduction

Draw the following bar graph on the board or enlarge it on the photocopier. Explain to the children that it shows all the different fruits that some children had in their lunch boxes one day. The task is to find out what can be learned by reading the graph.

5	*				
4	*				*
3	*	*		*	*
2	*	*	*	*	*
1	*	*	*	*	*
	a	o	p	b	pch

a = apple
o = orange
p = pear
b = banana
pch = peach

Activities

Graphs and charts (whole class/group)

Ask some focused questions about the graph in the introduction: *How many different fruits were there? How many more children had peaches than pears?* Can the children suggest any other questions? Write some of the questions on the board.

(Individuals/pairs)

Ask the groups if they can work out the total number of children in the class. Change the numbers on the left axis to multiples of 2. How does this change the graph? Work through Copymaster 19.

Differentiation

Low Attainers – Use a simple data collection program on the computer to draw block graphs to discuss and make predictions from.
High Attainers – Write down different ways of collecting data. Decide which might be the most efficient way.

Plenary

Ask the children to explain how the change of numbers (multiples of 2) changes the graph.

Lesson 2

Introduction

Show the children a pictogram showing the same type of data, such as the one below for sales of crisps:

Cheese & Onion * * * * * *
Ready Salted * * * *
Salt & Vinegar * * * *
Tomato Sauce * * * *   *** = 10 packets of crisps**

Discuss what each picture represents and the fact that half a picture means half the number of packets.

Activities

Pictograms (whole class/group)

Count the total numbers of each variety of crisps together and work with the class to help them formulate some questions they could answer using the data. Ask them why this might be an easier graph for finding the total sales than a bar graph. Write how many people actually bought crisps altogether.

(Individuals/pairs)

Work with a partner. Talk about what you do in one day. How many hours are you awake? How many hours are you at school? How many hours do you spend eating? playing? watching TV? Draw a bar graph to show the results.

Differentiation

Low Attainers – Draw their own pictogram using one symbol representing one unit.
High Attainers – Draw their own pictogram using one symbol representing two units, five units etc.

Plenary

Look at the bar graphs that the children have produced. Pose questions about them.

Lesson 3

Introduction

Remind the class about the different types of graph they have used. Draw some very simple examples on the board, such as block graphs, bar graphs with different scales and pictograms. Say that today they will be collecting some data and showing it on one of those types of graph.

Activities

Graphs (whole class/group)

Present the children with the situation that Mr Ice-Cream needs their help because he plans to start selling different flavours of ice-cream. However first they need to find out which is likely to be popular. There is room in their shop for only six flavours. With the children's help write a possible selection on the board. If the list is longer than six options have a show of hands to select the six most popular. Draw a frequency table of the preferred flavours.

(Individual/pairs)

Tell each pair that they are going to decide which drinks Mr Ice Cream should sell. Help them to decide on six possibilities and to make a tally chart in pairs. Show them how to make a tally. Ask for data from a group of children and then use this in pairs to make a graph out of interlocking cubes.

Differentiation

Low Attainers – Repeat the process of making a tally chart with no more than 5 pieces of data.
High Attainers – Draw a graph from the interlocking cubes.

Plenary

Share the graphs with the class. Ask them to explain some of the things they can tell by reading the graph.

Lesson 4

Introduction

Children begin by devising a tally sheet to survey the class's favourite TV programmes. To make their pictograms they need to devise a symbol/motif of each programme. They need to also decide how much each symbol stands for i.e. 2 votes or 4 votes or just 1 vote and what to do with a number of votes that doesn't fit ($\frac{1}{2}$ a symbol = 1 vote?).

Activities

Symbols (whole class/group)

The children can now ask the class in groups their favourite TV programmes and tally them on their chart/sheet. When the information is gathered in they must then decide on the way they want to display their pictogram (either horizontally or vertically).

(Individuals/pairs)

Working in small groups the children can draw their pictograms on large paper to display around the classroom so that the rest of the class can view them.

Differentiation

Low Attainers – Draw the symbols for their programmes on paper to display on the pictogram.
High Attainers – Make sure they use a symbol that stands for an odd number of votes more than one.

Plenary

Look at the display of pictograms and get the children to pose their own questions about them.

Lesson 5

Introduction

To prepare for the class, children need to prepare several copies of a pictogram symbol. These are placed on a pile so that players may take them as they win them. They also each need a sheet of paper and an empty chart with all their names marked on the left-hand side.

Activities

Games (whole class/group)

Children play by throwing a dice and recording their own score as a tally. Each time their tally reaches a new five they may take a symbol card and add it to their row. The winner is the first one to reach a predetermined number of symbol cards.

(Individuals/ pairs)

Now change the dice and play the game again. It is possible to make each symbol card worth 10 instead of 5, and a rule may be introduced so that children must throw exactly the right number to collect their last card.

Differentiation

Low Attainers and *High Attainers* – Work through Copymaster 20.

Plenary

Collect information in about the winners of the pictogram game and make a tally chart/frequency table on the board.

Theme 1 Comparing, ordering and rounding

Objectives

- To read and write the vocabulary of comparing and ordering numbers, including ordinal numbers to 100
- To compare two three-digit numbers and say which is more or less
- To read and begin to write the vocabulary of approximation
- To round any two-digit number to nearest 10
- To read scales and dials

Vocabulary

place value, equal, ten more, one hundred more, ten less, one hundred less, round up, round down, approximate, estimate, estimation, nearest, roughly, nearly, close to

Resources

Copymasters 21 and 22. Homework 11.

Number cards, coloured cubes, newspaper cuttings, hoopla board, number lines, dartboard, hopscotch, scales, containers.

Assessment

At the end of this theme is the pupil able to:

- Use, read and begin to write ordinal numbers (first, second, third) and their abbreviations;
- Make estimates of numbers and measurements in a range of practical contexts;
- Round numbers less than 100 to the nearest 10;
- Read a scale to the nearest marked division?

Mental maths starter 1

Lesson 1

Introduction

Children need their set of number cards 0–9 or similar. Choose 3 of the cards and ask them to make as many three-figure numbers as they can. Ask the children the value of each digit in each number they make. Remind the children how the value of the digit changes when it moves its 'place'.
They can practise the order of numbers by saying the next number before or after *e.g. 89,102,200 etc.*

Activities

Ordering numbers (whole class/group)

Ask 6 children to line up. Ask the children, *Who is 1st, 2nd, 3rd, 4th–6th (last)? What position is (name) in?* Ask the children to swap positions (make sure their new positions are revised). Repeat the original questions. Use a pattern of beads to ask the children questions like – *What position is the 4th red bead? What colour is the 12th bead? What colour would the 15th bead be in the pattern?*

(Individuals/pairs)

Using coloured cubes the children work in pairs to make their own 'strings' of cubes and ask each other questions *e.g. What colour cube is in 10th place?*

Differentiation

Low Attainers – Use different practical equipment to practise ordering numbers.
High Attainers – Predict what colours will be part of different patterns of beads *e.g. What colour would the 19th bead be in this pattern?*

Plenary

Recap the vocabulary used. Check understanding by talking about which teams are 1st, 2nd, 3rd in the football league tables (newspaper cuttings might help here).

Lesson 2

Introduction

The children will need a scoring system *e.g. a hoopla board or a ball with some assorted baskets.* They then take it in turns to make as high a score as possible with 3 balls or 3 hoops. The scores can be recorded on the board and then ordering and comparing activities can take place using suitable vocabulary:
Which score is the highest?
Which score is the lowest?
Is one score more or less than another score?

Activities

More or less (whole class/group)

Using the class number line the pupils can work through examples of 2-digit and 3-digit numbers and fill in the missing numbers (your 'number stick' could be useful here)
e.g. 100———125———? ———175———?
Then ask questions such as *Is 125 more than or less than 150?*
Remind children of < is less than, > is more than signs. Write some examples on the blackboard using the signs. Ask the children to make up some examples of their own and try them out with their partner.

(Individuals/pairs)

Working in pairs each pair writes sets of numbers for each other (3 digits, no more than 8 at a time). They can then join these numbers up using lines that represent 'is more than', 'is less than'.

Differentiation

Low Attainers – Respond to questions such as *What even numbers are less than 20?* and *What odd numbers are more than 20 but less than30?*
High Attainers – Respond to questions such as *How many times smaller is 26 than 260? How many times larger is 150 than 15?* Use Copymaster 21.

Plenary

Recap the vocabulary used. Check understanding by asking children for numbers 'more' or 'less than' 3-digit/4-digit examples on the blackboard.

Lesson 3

Introduction

Children will need examples in front of them that the rest of the class can make estimates from e.g. *lines on a page or pencils in a pot.*
Concentrate on the vocabulary that can be used – **guess how many, round, nearest, roughly, nearly, close to, approximately.**

Activities

Estimation and approximation (whole class/group)
Split the class into groups and label with:

Guess how many **Close to**
Nearest **Approximately**
Roughly

Each group should have items that they can show to the class and ask for sensible estimations using the vocabulary they have been given.

(Individuals/pairs)
Using Copymaster 22, the children, working with a partner, can play the game of estimation highlighting the vocabulary that should be used. The children can be encouraged to use all the vocabulary that they have talked about in the whole class part of the lesson.

Differentiation

Low Attainers – Children can have the vocabulary on cards in front of them and test themselves at using as many of the words as they can.
High Attainers – Children can extend the game with larger numbers

Plenary

Ask children who can come up with the most words that apply to approximation and estimation. They could be tested for spelling accuracy and speed.

Lesson 4

Introduction

Write a list of numbers on the blackboard:
15 26 49 54 56 45
Ask questions such as *Find the number that is nearest to 50.*
Use vocabulary such as *49 is closer to 50 than 40.*
The nearest ten to 49 is 50.
Explain that this is rounding up to the nearest 10 and then introduce examples that can involve rounding down as well. Also explain that e.g. *35 is half way between 30 and 40*. We say that the nearest ten to 35 is 40 because we round up when the number is half way between the two tens.

Activities

Rounding to the nearest 10 (whole class/group)
a) Using a dartboard drawn on the blackboard and some card darts the darts can be 'thrown' and the scores rounded up to the nearest 10 or rounded down to the nearest 10 with one, two or three darts.
b) A 'hopscotch' shape can be drawn on card and a 'stone' thrown and the scores rounded up or down to the nearest 10.

(Individuals/pairs)
Using 0–100 number lines the children, working in pairs, can test themselves by choosing random numbers and rounding them up or down to the nearest 10.

Differentiation

Low Attainers – Use simple examples of numbers under 30 and round them up or down or both to the nearest 10.
High Attainers – Start to look at rounding numbers to the nearest 100.

Plenary

Recap the vocabulary used. Write down the rules for rounding numbers up and down and for those numbers that are half way between tens.

Lesson 5

Introduction

Collect together different sorts of scales with dials to show how much something weighs. Also collect together different containers for measuring liquids with scales along the side.
Ask the children to respond to questions:
What is the greatest weight in kg which can be shown on the dial?
What weight in grams does each small division represent?
What is the greatest volume of liquid that each container can hold?
What volume in litres/millilitres does each small division represent?

Activities

Reading scales and dials (whole class/group)
Collect together assorted objects to weigh in groups. First of all ask the children to decide which unit (g or kg) you would use to weigh each object. They must then estimate each object's weight before weighing the object and recording the result.
Using the containers for measuring liquids, each one can be filled with different amounts of water and the children can practise measuring each amount accurately.

(Individuals/pairs)
Use the weighing scales to find the weight of each child and their partner to the nearest $\frac{1}{2}$ kg. They can then find the difference between their weights.

Differentiation

Low Attainers – Write down three things in the classroom that you would weigh in kilograms. Write down three things in the classroom that you would weigh in grams.
High Attainers – Use electronic scales to measure small items very accurately.

Plenary

Discuss the results of the children weighing themselves. Recap on the units that have been used and stress the importance of being as accurate as possible. Go through Homework 11.

Theme 2 Mental addition

Objectives

- To add three then four single-digit numbers mentally
- To add three or four small numbers by putting the largest number first and/or finding pairs that total 10
- To be able to partition into 5 and a bit to add 6, 7 or 8

Vocabulary

calculate, counting on, pairs, partition, digits, plus, tens, units

Resources

Classroom clock, plastic money, timers, dominoes.
Copymasters 23 and 24. Homework 12.

Assessment

At the end of this theme is the pupil able to:

- Put the larger number first in order to count on;
- Add several numbers by using strategies such as looking for pairs;
- Add several numbers by partitioning and recombining?

Mental maths starter 2

Lesson 1

Introduction

Discuss where numbers appear in the classroom e.g. *How many chairs are there? How many windows are there? How many cupboards are there?* These totals can be recorded and then the number of chairs added to the number of cupboards added to the number of windows, mentally.

Activities

Adding single digit numbers mentally (whole class/group)

Using the classroom clock select three or four numbers and ask the children to add these mentally: *Add 4 o'clock, 3 o'clock and 2 o'clock (=9)*
Add together mentally the number of family members in each child's family.
Add together the number of letters in class members' names.
When these activities are over there can be a class discussion about strategies that the children have used to calculate the answers. Tell the children that the rest of the theme will deal with these and other strategies to increase their speed at mental calculation.

(Individuals/pairs)

The children work on Copymaster 23; and this activity can be timed and will be returned to at the end of the week.

Differentiation

Low Attainers – Use apparatus to add together single-digit numbers e.g. *using their number cards to make up their own calculations.*
High Attainers – Use addition squares for single-digit numbers. Turn them into speed tests. Can they beat their previous time?

Plenary

A further session of adding together 3 and 4 single-digit numbers at speed.
This could be made into a team game.

Lesson 2

Introduction

Tell the class that they are going to look at strategies for adding numbers together quickly.
If they are going to add two numbers together mentally then they should put the larger number first e.g. *7 + 20 should become 20 + 7 and then count on in ones from 20.* Go through a number of examples on the blackboard.

Activities

Put larger number first! (whole class/group)

Practise counting on in multiples of ten.
Introduce adding 10s together taking the larger number first e.g. *30 + 60 should become 60 + 30 and then count on in tens from 60.* The children could be used to represent each single ten always stressing that you start with the largest group first and add on from there.

(Individuals/pairs)

The children work in pairs taking it in turns to be the larger number while the other partner adds on the smaller number. Examples can be put on the blackboard.
Also in pairs the children can use the same strategy to add together amounts of money.
Again the time aspect is important so timers could be given out to each pair to test their speed against the clock. Is there a class champion?

Differentiation

Low Attainers – Further examples of adding small numbers together as a 'show me' activity using number cards and fan numbers.
High Attainers – Add longer lists of numbers together still using the larger numbers first e.g. *20 + 15 + 30 + 40 + 25 = ?*
Discussion about other strategies that can be used that might be useful later in the theme.

Plenary

Revise the strategy of putting the larger number first. Ask children to challenge the class to add together three/four-digit numbers in under 5 seconds. If the class fail the point is awarded to the questioner.

Lesson 3

Introduction

Revise strategy of adding numbers together starting with the largest number from Lesson 2. Use both single-digit and t. u. numbers. Can they improve on the class challenge from yesterday (add together 3 and 4-digit numbers in a set time)?

Activities

Pairs that make 10 (whole class/group)

The children act as digits (0–9).Line them up in front of the class and give the pupils a chance to add together pairs of numbers that total 10 *e.g.* $8 + 2, 7 + 3, 9 + 1$ *etc.*

Then produce examples of lists of 3 or 4 single-digit numbers and practise adding up the numbers that add up to 10 first – $2 + 7 + (4 + 6) = ?$

Ask the pupils to look for pairs of numbers that add up to 9 or 11, and add these to the total by adding 10 and then +1 or −1

e.g. $3 + 5 + (7 + 4) = 3 + 5 + (10 + 1) = ?$
$4 + 3 + (6 + 3) = 4 + 3 + (10 - 1) = ?$

(Individuals/pairs)

Each pair has group of dominoes. The dominoes are turned over and then they take it in turns to turn 3 or 4 back over and add the digits together as quickly as possible.

Differentiation

Low Attainers – Take single dominoes and add together the number of dots on each domino.

High Attainers – Give the pupils long lists of single-digit numbers (9 or 10) and timers to test their speed at adding them up.

Plenary

Recap on the strategies, looking for pairs that make 10, starting with the largest number and looking for pairs that make 9 and 11.

Lesson 4

Introduction

The children practise counting in fives: this can include looking at the 5× table and using their hands to count in groups of 5.

Remind the children that 10 is double 5 and 20 is 4 × 5 etc.

On squared paper the children can make their own pentominoes (shapes made out of 5 squares) to help them with their calculations.

Activities

Partition and recombine (whole class/group)

Explore how 6, 7, 8 and 9 can be broken down into 5 + 1, 5 + 2 etc.

Go through plenty of examples of adding 6, 7, 8 and 9 onto two-digit numbers

$12 + 6 = 12 + (5 + 1)$
$12 + 5 + 1$
$17 + 1$
18

$15 + 8 = 15 + (5 + 3)$
$15 + 5 + 3$
$20 + 3$
23

Using the pentominoes the class can look at larger numbers and how they can be grouped into lots of five with any remainders *e.g. 37 = 7 lots of 5 with 2 left over.*

(Individuals/pairs)

Using Copymaster 24 the children work in pairs with timers to improve their target time for completing the addition facts correctly.

Differentiation

Low Attainers – Add 5 and 6 onto single-digit numbers. The pentominoes will help with adding on 5. When adding on 6, stress that 6 is 5 and I more.

High Attainers – Using their knowledge of adding 6, 7, 8 and 9 to two-digit numbers, they can set each other five questions each and time each other to complete the answers correctly.

Plenary

Recap and continue to look at examples of breaking down 6, 7, 8 and 9 into '5 and a bit.' Is there a class champion for completing five facts based on the lesson in the quickest time?

Lesson 5

Introduction

Revise partitioning numbers between 10–100 into tens and units. Use the children to act as 'tens' and 'units' in front of the class. Make sure the class can record *e.g. 56 as 50 and 6 more.*

Activities

Tens and units (whole class/group)

Ask the children to copy these patterns and find the missing numbers.

$36 = 30 + 6$
$20 + 16$
$10 + ?$

$54 = 50 + 4$
$40 + 14$
$30 + ?$
$? + ?$
$? + ?$

Does the pattern still work with larger numbers?
Try 124, 159. What happens?

(Individuals/pairs)

Working in pairs the children partition equations into tens and units.

$26 + 33 = (20 + 6)$ plus $(30 + 3)$ or
$= (20 + 30) + (6 + 3)$
$= 50 + 9$

$26 + 33 = 26 + 30 + 3$
$= 59$
$= 56 + 3$
$= 59$

Differentiation

Low Attainers – More practice at breaking down numbers into tens and units and adding two-digit numbers together.

High Attainers – Look again at the whole class activity and the patterns that were made. Let the children make some more patterns of their own. Try them on their friends and see how fast they are!

Plenary

Give out Copymaster 23 and see if the children can improve on their time from the beginning of the week.
Go through Homework 12.

Theme 3 Money problems

Objectives

- To choose appropriate number operations and calculation methods to solve money or 'real life' word problems with one or more steps
- To explain and record the methods they use to solve the problems
- To be able to check their answer with an equivalent calculation

Vocabulary

problem, solve, solution, value, amount, price, cost, buy and sell

Resources

Copymasters 25 and 26, Homework 13.
Dice, coloured cubes, piles of books, calculators, plastic coins, old catalogues, old supermarket bills.

Assessment

At the end of this theme is the pupil able to:

- Solve simple word problems set in 'real life' contexts and explain how the problem was solved;
- Solve simple word problems involving money and explain how the problem was solved?

Mental maths starter 9

Lesson 1

Introduction

Give each pair of children three dice each.
Put the three dice together and you should be able to see two lines of dots *e.g.* $4 + 3 + 2$ *and* $5 + 6 + 4$.
Ask the children to decide which is the best method to use to total the number of dots in each line.
Choose from:

a) A straight mental method.
b) A mental method with jottings.
c) A pencil and paper method.

Ask the children to try out the best method on one or two examples.

Activities

Which method? (whole class/group)

Using the same dice:
What is the largest total you can make using three dice?
What is the smallest total?
How many totals can the children make?

Ask the pupils to use each one of the three methods used in the introduction. Try the same with four dice. Which is the quickest method?

(Individuals/pairs)

Using three dice and a shaker let the children make up their own sums using +, − and = *e.g.* $5 + 4 - 1 = 8$
Let the children use the three different methods to find the answers.

Differentiation

Low Attainers – Use two dice so that the children can make up more simple sums.
High Attainers – Explore the totals on the three dice and see if the group can make even totals and odd totals. Are all the totals on all the lines odd or even?

Plenary

Recap on the different methods that can be used for finding the totals of single-digit numbers. Start to introduce one or two simple problems using these numbers.

Lesson 2

Introduction

Put a box of the same coloured cubes/bricks (30) in front of the class.
Count the total number of cubes in the box. Ask these questions:
How many cubes are left if you take away 12 of them?
How many children can have 5 cubes each?
How many cubes would there be in three boxes of the same size?
How many boxes are needed to hold 60 cubes, 90 cubes?

Activities

One-step problems (whole class/group)

Look at three local examples within the children's experience.
e.g. *a) The number of children in the class.*
If all the Yr 3s left the room how many children would be left?
If all the girls with long hair left the room how many girls would be left?
b) The number of cars owned by parents.
Find out the colour of these cars and then ask for the number of cars left if all the red ones were sold.
c) If everyone in your group has two legs and two arms how many arms and legs are there altogether?

(Individuals/pairs)

Look at Copymaster 25 and ask the children to solve the problems on the sheet using mental maths, mental maths plus jottings and paper and pencil methods.

Differentiation

Low Attainers – Try problems such as *I think of a number and halve it. The answer is 9. What was my number?*
High Attainers – Make up their own problems based on ideas from home (*e.g. number of pets*).

Plenary

Ask the children for some examples they have tackled and go through them on the blackboard. Write a number sentence to show how the problem was solved.

Lesson 3

Introduction

Put two piles of books in front of the class. One pile has 15 books in it and the other pile has 17 books. Remove 20 of the books. How many are left?
Split the books into two different piles and ask the same questions. Then point out to the children that there are two operations to do in order to solve the problem. First of all you need to add two numbers together and then take away a third number.

Activities

Two-step problems (whole class/group)
Look at three local examples within the children's experience.
e.g. a) *There are 18 sheep, 21 cows and 19 goats in a farmyard. How many animals are there altogether?*
b) *There are 20 packed lunches on one shelf and 15 packed lunches on another shelf. 18 of the packed lunches are removed. How many packed lunches are left on the shelf?*
c) *There are 22 footballs in one bag and 15 footballs in another bag. 12 balls are used for practice. How many balls are not used?*

(Individuals/pairs)
Make sure that the children choose a suitable method to solve each problem. Where appropriate make sure they write a number sentence to show how the problem was solved.

Differentiation

Low Attainers – Practise simple two-step operations
e.g. $7 + 5 - 3 = 9$
High Attainers – Make up their own problems using the classroom for ideas. e.g. *Number of pencils in pots.*

Plenary

Ask the children for some examples they have tackled and go through them on the blackboard. Write a number sentence for each one and discuss the best method to solve each problem. Check each answer.

Lesson 4

Introduction

Check pupils understand decimal notation for money. Use poster on Copymaster 26 to illustrate that the decimal point separates the pounds from the pence. Decide whether to include use of the calculator and discuss entering amounts of money into the calculator.

Activities

Money problems 1 (whole class/group)
Using Copymaster 26 ask the children questions that involve calculating with money.
Discuss how the results are going to be recorded and, where appropriate, write a number sentence to show how the problem was solved.

(Individuals/pairs)
Working in pairs with or without calculators the pupils can work through Copymaster 26. Make sure the children have access to material (coins) in order to solve the problems.

Differentiation

Low Attainers – Revise writing down amounts of money properly. Using plenty of apparatus the group can add together small amounts of money and calculate the change from 20p, 50p and £1.
High Attainers – Looking at catalogues the group can use the cost of items to calculate the bill for 5–10 items. Change can be worked out from £5, £10, £20.

Plenary

Using old supermarket bills, projected on O.H.P. if possible, ask questions about the cost of multiple items and the difference in cost between items. Also calculate the change you would get from 20p, 50p, £1 etc.

Lesson 5

Introduction

The children need plenty of replica money in front of them. Revise how many 5ps make £1, how many 10ps make £1 etc. Then looking at all the coins ask the children to make up different amounts of money using 3 coins, 5 coins etc. Ask the class to record these groups of coins on paper and on the calculator.
e.g. 35p = 10p + 10p + 10p + 5p or 20p + 10p + 2p + 2p + 1p.
In how many different ways can the children make up the same amount of money?

Activities

Money problems 2 (whole class/group)
Collect together some sweet wrappers and the cost of the sweets or make a list on the blackboard of the prices of different chocolate bars etc.
Make a table to show which sweets' prices fall within each price range.
Use 1p to 50p, 51p to £1, £1.01 to £1.50.
Which price range has most sweets in it?
Which has the fewest?

(Individuals/pairs)
Working in pairs ask the class *If all the sweets went up by 20p, which price range would then have the most and which the least?*
Ask further questions about the coins you would use to buy a number of different combinations of sweets. Ask them to record their results in the most appropriate way (a number sentence or drawing round the coins making a pictorial display).

Differentiation

Low Attainers – Lots of practice at working in a shop situation and buying pretend items and giving change.
High Attainers – Answer questions such as *James offered two silver coins to pay for a 18p toy. Investigate how much change he got.*
Looking at the list of sweet prices, give the children an amount of money and ask them how many sweets they could buy for that amount and what change they might receive.

Plenary

Work through the first few examples on Homework sheet 13. Then ask the children if they have 'pocket money' each week and ask them to say what they spend it on. Note some prices/totals and discuss coins that can be used and change that can be given.

Theme 4 Shape

Objectives

- To make and describe shapes and patterns
- To relate solid shapes to pictures of them
- To read and begin to write the vocabulary of direction
- To make and use right-angled turns, and use the four compass points
- To solve shape problems or puzzles and explain reasoning and methods

Vocabulary

circular, triangular, rectangular, surface, pyramid, pentagon, hexagon, octagon, right angled, vertex, vertices, grow, column, map, plan, north, south, east, west, horizontal, vertical, diagonal, right angle

Resources

Plastic/wooden 2-D and 3-D shapes, geo-boards and elastic bands, a selection of grids on paper, old magazines to cut up. Copymasters 27 and 28. Homework 14.

Assessment

At the end of this theme is the pupil able to:

- Describe and classify common 3-D and 2-D shapes according to their properties;
- Make models, shapes and patterns with increasing accuracy, and describe their features;
- Describe positions and directions;
- Describe movements and understand angle as a measure of turn?

Mental maths starter 7

Lesson 1

Introduction

Using a collection of 2-D shapes let the children experiment with making a variety of patterns/pictures using as many of the different shapes as they can. They can then describe the picture or pattern and say which shapes have been used to make it. If they struggle with this activity suggest some pictures they can attempt first, *e.g. tree, house, school.* If there are enough shapes children could describe the one they have made and the class could copy it on their table or hold it up for the class to see.

Activities

2-D shapes (whole class/group)

Begin by discussing any four sided flat shape. Explain that it is called a quadrilateral. Ask questions such as *Are the sides all the same length? How many angles has the shape got Does it have any right angles?* Do the children know any special quadrilaterals and what they are called (squares and rectangles)? Then discuss what is special about a triangle. Talk about the name itself, *e.g. 'tri' means three, so it is a shape with three angles.* A circle is also a flat shape with no straight sides. Remind the children that a pentagon has five sides, a hexagon six sides and an octagon eight sides. Trace the shapes and use geo-boards to make different size rectangles, triangles etc.

(Individuals/pairs)

Use the Copymaster 27. Working in pairs or as individuals copy the patterns and work out how they are changing. Draw the next four shapes in each pattern.

Differentiation

Low Attainers – Use geo-boards again to produce flat shapes. Particularly look at pentagons, hexagons and octagons. Check the children know the number of sides each shape has.
High Attainers – Go back to the collection of 2-D shapes and use Venn and Carroll diagrams to sort them.

Plenary

Recap on the vocabulary used to describe each shape. Play 'Guess what shape'. Ask children to give their own description of a shape and the class have to guess what the shape is. The description can be split into three parts and points given for a quick answer.

Lesson 2

Introduction

Gather together a collection of solid shapes to include cones, triangular prisms, cubes, cylinders, spheres and cuboids (smartie tubes, cotton reels, matchboxes, dice can be useful)
Ask questions such as *Will the shape roll? Will the shape stack?* Pick out each different solid shape and label each one with its correct name.

Activities

3-D shapes (whole class/group)

Having labelled each solid shape during the introduction, record how many cones there are, how many cubes/cuboids etc. Look at one of the cubes. *How many faces has a cube? How many vertices has a cube? How many edges has a cube?* Repeat this for a cuboid. *What shape are the bases of the cones and triangular prisms?*

(Individual/pairs)

Give the children the nets for cubes and cuboids and ask them to stick them together and make the 3-D shape. Make sure that they ask themselves the same questions about each shape as in the whole class part of the lesson.

Differentiation

Low Attainers – Relate further 3-D shapes to pictures of them. Look for solid shapes being used around the classroom.
High Attainers – Give the group the chance to experiment with putting 3-D shapes together to make new shapes *e.g. Find all the different shapes that can be made by fitting four cubes together face to face.*

Plenary

Revise the labelling of 3-D shapes. Ask the pupils about the number of faces, vertices and edges that each shape has.

Lesson 3

Introduction

Using a compass make sure that the four main compass points are marked around the classroom. Plenty of practice at pointing at 'north,' 'south' etc. Place familiar 'landmarks' in each direction and talk about 'east' and 'west,' 'north' and 'south' being in opposite directions.

Activities

Direction (whole class/group)

Using a grid on the blackboard of twenty-five small squares labelled with numbers up the side and letters along the bottom, ask the children to find the position of a single square *e.g. B2*. The children can challenge themselves to produce all the positions of small squares on a new grid for *e.g. the initial letters of their names*. They can come out to the blackboard and one pupil can read out the references and another mark the squares.

(Individuals/pairs)

Working in pairs the children play noughts and crosses, telling the other player where to put a mark by using letters and numbers as references. (This activity can include a simple version of 'battleships'.)

Differentiation

Low Attainers – Working in pairs the children use a square grid and send each other on a pathway through the grid by using letters and numbers as references.

High Attainers – Make and use simple maps or plans on squared paper and describe the position of a landmark.

Plenary

Recap on the vocabulary of direction. Let the children direct themselves around the classroom by using compass directions. Can they get from one place to another without hitting anything?

Lesson 4

Introduction

Revise the compass directions from the previous lesson and give the class plenty of experience at deciding in which direction objects are in the classroom. Draw a grid on the blackboard and tell the children that it is a seating plan for a cinema. Ask them to put their friends in a seat by using direction markers (numbers and letters or N.S.E.W.).

Activities

Right-angled turns (Whole class/group)

Make a right angle from a circle of paper. Fold the paper into quarters. The children can use their right angles to check angles in the classroom. Try the doors, windows and tables. Do the walls make a right angle where they meet in the corner? Look in the playground. Are there right angles out there? Then point out to the children that the classroom clock can help with right-angled turns. Are the hands making a right angle? (3 o'clock, 9 o'clock etc.)? Can the children turn through one right angle? Can they follow the minute hand from o'clock to quarter past etc? *How many right angles do you pass through from o'clock to half past? How many right angles do you pass through from o'clock to quarter to? How many right angles do you pass through to come back to your starting point?*

(Individuals/pairs)

Working in pairs the children need a copy of Copymaster 28 and follow the route Bob takes. Do they notice something about the movement of Bob? He can only go forwards along the lines. If he wants to go in a different direction, he has to make a right-angled turn.

Differentiation

Low Attainers – Continue to practise right-angled turns in the playground. Can they describe the direction they face when they make the turn?

High Attainers – Draw some more routes for Bob. Write some directions for their friends. See if they can draw the route after reading the directions.

Plenary

Discuss with the children that after turning through half a turn, or two quarter turns in the same direction, you are facing the opposite direction.

Lesson 5

Introduction

Name a flat shape with exactly:
a) 3 straight edges
b) 5 straight edges
c) 6 straight edges
How many corners has:
a) a square
b) a pentagon
c) a circle?
Use your paper right angle to help you draw:
a) a shape with only 1 right angle
b) a shape with only 2 right angles.'

Shape puzzles (whole class/group)

With a rectangular grid of nine rectangles, each with a different 2-D shape in each space, the children play 'Shape Lotto.' The caller calls out shape names from a list. Players with that shape on their grid cover it. The first player with three markers in a row calls *Shape!* and becomes the next caller.

(Individuals/pairs)

The children make skeleton shapes with straws. Encourage them to test whether the shape is rigid or not. They can experiment by adding extra straws to make non-rigid structures rigid, for example diagonals to brace a cube.

Differentiation

Low Attainers – Take one 2-D shape and draw it on paper. They can then cut pictures from magazines and paste them onto the paper which resemble the shape chosen.

High Attainers – Draw around shapes to create pictures and patterns. Different effects may be created by overlapping the shapes, thus producing new shapes.

Plenary

Final questions about the properties of 2-D and 3-D shapes. *Can you draw the shape from this description?* Go through Homework sheet 14.

Theme 5 Measures

Objectives

- To read to 5 minutes on analogue and 12-hour digital clocks (9:40)
- To read and begin to write the vocabulary related to mass
- To measure and compare using kilograms and grams, and know the relationship between them
- To suggest suitable units and equipment to estimate or measure mass
- To read scales
- To record measurements using mixed units, or to the nearest whole/half unit *e.g. 3.5 kg*
- To choose appropriate number operations and calculation methods to solve measurement word problems with one or more steps. Explain and record method

Vocabulary

weight, weighs, heavy, light, balances, kilograms, half kilograms, units of 100 g, guess, estimate, roughly, nearly, about, approximately, minute, second

Resources

Different types of timers including stop clocks. Various weights from 10 g to 5 kg. Kitchen scales and spring balances. Shopping items of various weights.
Copymasters 29 and 30. Homework 15.

Assessment

At the end of this theme is the pupil able to :

- Understand and use the vocabulary related to mass;
- Suggest suitable units to estimate or measure mass;
- Suggest and use simple measuring equipment, reading and interpreting number scales with some accuracy;
- Understand and use the vocabulary related to time;
- Read the time on clocks;
- Solve simple problems involving measures?

Mental maths starter 5

Lesson 1

Introduction

Put a time line on the blackboard showing one week. Then children should enter what they have done on each day over the week. Remind the children that there are 60 minutes in one hour and that each analogue clock is divided into 5 minute blocks. (It might be worth revising counting in 5s up to 60.) Also discuss how a digital clock operates (no hands; just numbers).

Activities

Telling the time (whole class/group)

Using a clock on which you can move the hands easily, ask the children o'clock, quarter past, half past and quarter to times. The children should say what they are doing normally at those times. Relate those to a digital display – half past 5 means 5:30. Reminding the children where the 5 past and 10 past times are, repeat using the analogue clock to show random times. Match each analogue time to a digital display.

(Individuals/pairs)

Working in pairs use Copymaster 29 and let the children work through the times on the sheet. After finishing the sheet the children can look at a TV page from a newspaper and select programmes that begin at 5 past, 10 past the hour etc.

Differentiation

Low Attainers – Suggest a suitable unit of time to measure: to the end of the month, to boil an egg.
High Attainers – Estimate then check the greatest and least time taken to run 20 metres, how long you will be in school today etc.

Plenary

Discuss the programme times from the TV schedule and ask the children the length of certain programmes. What would these times be on an analogue clock?

Lesson 2

Introduction

Make a collection of supermarket items and examine their weight on the packet/tin or weigh the goods on scales. Stress that kilograms are used to measure the weight of heavy objects and are abbreviated to kg. Grams are used to measure the weight of light objects and are abbreviated to g. Talk about which unit is best for measuring the different items and show that 1 kg equals 1000 g.

Activities

Mass (whole class/group)

Children should have the opportunity to handle things that weigh one kilogram – a standard 1 kg weight or a bag of sugar or fruit – and use their hands as a balance to compare the kg weight with various items. The use of kitchen scales and spring balances calibrated in kg by the children extends the practical possibilities. Before weighing any items ask the children to make their best estimate.

(Individuals/pairs)

Ask the children to produce a chart to record things that weigh:

a) 1 kg 500 g b) 750 g
c) 1 kg 200 g d) 2 kg 800 g

Children work in teams of 2 to 4 members to find objects to fit the weights on the chart. Stop the children when the first team has completed the activity or set a time limit. Have the members from other teams take turns using the scales to check the weight of each object or set of objects used.

Differentiation

Low Attainers – Using floor scales the group can record their own weights and then put them in order, lowest weight first.
High Attainers – Using scales with grams, weigh smaller objects from around the classroom. Estimate the amount first.

Plenary

Discuss the relationship between grams and kilograms:
How many grams are in $\frac{1}{2}$ kilogram?
How many grams are in $\frac{1}{4}$ kilogram?

Lesson 3

Introduction

Examine this problem. Mum baked a cake. It weighed 1 kg. There were 10 people for tea. Mum cut the cake into 10 equal slices. How much did five slices weigh? What fraction of the whole cake was five slices? How much did half the cake weigh? How much did a quarter of the cake weigh?

Activities

Mixed units (whole class/group)

Make up some parcels. Find things to put in them. Make parcels weighing a) $1\frac{1}{2}$ kg or 1.5 kg b) 2 kg or 2.0 kg c) $2\frac{1}{2}$ kg or 2.5 kg d) 3 kg or 3.0 kg

Make a list of the things inside each parcel. Find things in the classroom that have a weight difference of about $\frac{1}{2}$ kg or $\frac{1}{4}$ kg.

(Individuals/pairs)

Each pair can look at a recipe

e.g. Syrup tart for 4

$\frac{1}{2}$ kg of pastry $\frac{1}{4}$ kg of syrup $\frac{1}{4}$ kg of breadcrumbs

Write the recipe for 8 people, 12 people etc.

Include recipes using grams.

Apple pie for 2

200g of pastry 50g of sugar 200g of apples

Write the recipe for 4 people, 6 people etc.

Differentiation

Low Attainers – Continue to estimate the weights of different objects and check by weighing.

High Attainers – Add and subtract weights in a practical situation. Put groups of objects into piles weighing kg/g/kg and g. Remove items in threes and add up their total weights. Subtract the total weights from each other.

Plenary

Further practice at converting from kilograms to grams, *e.g. 2.5 kg = 2500 grams*. More suggestions of objects that weigh less than 100 g/200 g/300 g etc.

Lesson 4

Introduction

Find three weights of 20 g, 50 g and 100 g. Ask questions such as *Which is the lightest weight?* and *Which is the heaviest weight?* Put the 20 g weight in one pan of some weighing scales and fill the other pan with peas until they balance. Ask the children to record the number of peas that balance 20 g. Now do the same with counters. Ask the children to calculate the number of peas and counters that balance 40 g, 60 g, 80 g and record as a number sentence.

(Group work)

In groups the children change the 20 g weight for the 50 g. Record how many marbles weigh 50 g, how many beads weigh 50 g and how many metal bottle tops weigh 50 g. Make an estimate and then calculate how many marbles/beads/metal bottle tops will balance 100 g. Check the calculation by using the scales. Make further estimation and calculations for 200 g, 500 g etc.

(Individuals/pairs)

Using Copymaster 30 the children work through the problems in pairs or as individuals. Encourage the children to record their calculations in a number of different ways. Some of the problems will need to be solved in two steps and the children will need to choose the appropriate number operation.

Differentiation

Low Attainers – Continue comparing different weights in grams and kilograms. 500 g = $\frac{1}{2}$ kilogram, 250 g = $\frac{1}{4}$ kilogram. Find items that weigh these amounts.

High Attainers – Use personal scales for the group to weigh themselves and produce a graph to show their results.

Plenary

Discuss with the children some of the problems that they have solved from Copymaster 30. Talk about the method they used and the way they recorded their results.

Lesson 5

Introduction

Using a stop watch ask the children to do common tasks in the classroom *e.g. stacking up cubes up to 100 or how fast they can say their tables*. Class champions can be organised and a chart put on the wall so that the times can be recorded and they can work out how many seconds faster one time is than another.

Activities

Time problems (whole class/group)

Working in small groups the children should investigate the variations in the time taken to complete a puzzle when the activity is carried out several times. For example, each child completes the puzzle four times and records the time taken in each case. The first and fourth times are compared. It is a good idea to start with an easy puzzle to give them confidence and progress from there. The more difficult the problem the longer it takes to solve it.

(Individuals/pairs)

Continue with timed activities:

a) the number of pulse beats in a minute.
b) The number of words written in a minute.
c) Starting at 0, counting in 2s, how many numbers can be written down in a minute?
d) Count how many times your heart beats in one minute.

Differentiation

Low Attainers – How many times can they bounce a ball in one minute? How many words can they read in $\frac{1}{2}$ minute

High Attainers – Make their own timers using sand and yoghurt pots and test them on timed activities: *How long does it take to clear up after an Art lesson?*

Plenary

Discuss the various results and congratulate the champions for each activity. Ask if they can estimate how much faster the activities can be done and make a note of these estimates for future reference. Go through the homework sheet **15.**

Theme 6 Number sequences

Objectives

- To count on in steps of 3 or 4 or 5 from any small number to at least 50 and back again
- To create and describe simple number sequences
- To investigate general statements about familiar numbers and give examples that match them
- To solve number puzzles and explain methods and reasoning orally and in writing

Vocabulary

multiple, count on, sequence, pattern, number grid

Resources

100 squares, a large ball, calculators, a stopwatch.
Copymasters 31 and 32. Homework 16.

Assessment

At the end of this theme is the pupil able to:

- Describe and extend number sequences;
- Count on or back in steps of any size;
- Recognise familiar numbers including multiples;
- Solve number puzzles and explain their methods and reasoning?

Mental maths starter 6

Lesson 1

Introduction

Use a 'human number line' in front of the blackboard, each child standing in front of numbers 1–20. Using a large ball the children practise passing the ball from one to another forwards and backwards. Ask questions: *How many passes/steps from 1–12, 10–5 etc?*

Activities

Counting on and back (whole class/group)

Use a hundred square on the blackboard and divide each square into four triangles. Colour in a triangle in each square taking steps of 3 and 4 (some squares will have two triangles coloured in *e.g. 12 and 24*). Stop at 50 and then ask the children to predict where the next steps will be as you move from 50–100. Mark the appropriate triangles.

(Individuals/pairs)

Working in pairs the children should have a copy of their own 100 square and enter the steps 3 and 4 up to 50. Continue by adding steps of 5 and 10. Ask the children to note the numbers that have more than one triangle coloured in. Can they predict where the next triangles will be coloured in up to 100? Make sure the children understand that the 100 square shows a pattern for the numbers 3, 4, 5 and 10.

Differentiation

Low Attainers – Go back to the number line and count out the steps for 3 and 4 again between 0 and 20, 0 and 30 etc.
High Attainers – Without using a 100 square let the group add to patterns illustrated *e.g. 3, 6, 9, —,—,*
4, 8, 12, —,—,

Plenary

Using their 100 squares the children count in 3s, 4s, 5s and 10s. *Can anyone count in these multiples without using the 100 square? How quickly can you count?*

Lesson 2

Introduction

Return to the 'human number line' and, starting at random numbers from 0–20, 'bounce on' in steps of 3, 4 and 5. Also start to 'bounce backwards' from the same numbers. Can the children predict where the 'bounces' will land?

Activities

Number patterns (whole class/group)

Using the calculator as a counting machine set up the 'constant function':

3 + + 3 = 0	4 + + 4 = 0
= 3	= 4
= 6	= 8

Record answers on paper from 0–50 and 0–100.

(Individuals/pairs)

Use subtraction to set up a constant to count backwards:
5 − − 5 = 0
Press starting number *e.g.* *50*
= 45
= 40 etc

Working in pairs, starting at random numbers between 0–50, let the children record the number pattern on paper or on number squares/lines.

Differentiation

Low Attainers – Recognise simple number patterns such as 3, 6, 9, —, —.
High Attainers – Use the constant function on the calculator and continue exploring patterns beyond 100.

Plenary

Ask the children to tell the class the most exciting pattern that they have found. *Can anyone set the class a pattern to complete?*

Lesson 3

Introduction

Start at 0 and add on in groups of 2 up to 20 either orally or on paper. Tell the children that these numbers are multiples of 2. Stress that multiples are just like times tables, so that the multiples of 2 are just the numbers in the 2 times table. Ask if anyone can say their 2× table: $-1 \times 2 = 2, 2 \times 2 = 4$. *Can anyone say the table any faster?*

Activities

Multiples 1 (whole class/group)

Some multiples are easier to spot than others. Examine the multiples of 10:

10, 20, 30, 40, 50, 60.

They all end in zero! It's nearly the same for 5:

5, 10, 15, 20, 25.

They all end in five or zero! And again for 2:

2, 4, 6, 8, 10.

They all end in 0, 2, 4, 6 or 8.

(Individuals/pairs)

Using the 100 squares from earlier in the week explore the multiples of 20. It ends in zero, so it's a multiple of 2, a multiple of 5 and a multiple of 10. 25 ends in five, so it's a multiple of 5. 14 ends in four so it's a multiple of 2.

Differentiation

Low Attainers – Using the constant function on the calculator, record the multiples of 2 up to 20, 5 up to 50.

High Attainers – Count in 50s to 1000, then back to zero. Write three different multiples of 50.

Plenary

Write a series of random numbers on the blackboard including 15, 25, 35, 20, 30 etc. Can the children point out which numbers are multiples of 2, which numbers are multiples of 5 etc?

Lesson 4

Introduction

Start with lines of multiples on the blackboard: 2, 4, 6, 8, 10 … 5, 10, 15, 20, 25 … 10, 20, 30, 40, 50 … Ask the following questions: *What is the 3rd multiple of 2? What is the 4th multiple of 5? What is the 6th multiple of 10?*

Activities

Multiples 2 (whole class/group)

To which set of multiples do these numbers belong:

a) 4, 8, 12, 16?
b) 5, 10, 15, 20?
c) 3, 6, 9, 12?

Sort these into two sets of multiples:

3 10 12 20
8 9 15

Say any six multiples of 5 greater than 25.

(Individual /pairs)

Use Copymaster 31 as a test of the children's knowledge of multiples to date. Pose questions such as *What is the multiple of five before 25? What is the multiple of 10 after 40? What is the next multiple of five after 55?*

Differentiation

Low Attainers – Write out the first 10 multiples of different small numbers.

High Attainers – What can they find out about the multiples of both 4 and 3, and the multiples of both 4 and 8 (some of them will be the same for both numbers)?

Plenary

Use the calculator to check their calculations of multiples and make sure the multiples are recorded to display in the classroom.

Lesson 5

Introduction

Start by explaining what a number puzzle is. Write one on the blackboard: *Joe burst into the classroom. 'Test my eyes,' he shouted. 'I have just seen 2 cars, each carried 4 magicians and each magician had 3 rabbits in his hat.*

'Calm down,' said Ann. 'There is a meeting of magicians in the town. Anyway how many rabbits did you see?'

Explain that there is often more than one step to solving the problem.

Activities

Number puzzles (whole class/group)

Answer questions such as:

a) 3 pop groups each have 5 musicians, each one with two guitars. How many guitars?
b) 3 boxes hold 20 apples each with 2 worms in each apple. How many worms?
d) 5 balloons, each carry 4 balloonists, each holding 3 bags with 3 buns in each bag. How many buns altogether?

Encourage the children to record their calculations showing the steps they have taken.

(Individuals/pairs)

Ask the children to work through the number puzzles on Copymaster 32. They may use calculators to check their answers and record the number operation they use on the sheet.

Differentiation

Low Attainers – Complete equations: $2 \times 3 \times ? = 12$
$3 \times 4 \times ? = 24$
$4 \times 2 \times ? = 24$

High Attainers – Make up their own stories/puzzles as in the 'whole class' part of the lesson

Plenary

Children who have made up their own stories/puzzles to ask the class to solve them orally or on paper.

Theme 7 Mental calculation

Objectives

- To add three two-digit numbers using apparatus or informal methods
- To partition numbers into tens and units and recombine
- To understand division as grouping or sharing, read and begin to write the related vocabulary
- To recognise that division is the inverse of multiplication
- To use doubling and halving, starting from known facts
- To be able to say or write a division statement corresponding to a multiplication statement

Vocabulary

more, add, sum, total, altogether, equals, sign, take away, subtract, how many are left, how much less is, how much more, minus, double, times, multiply, multiplied by, product, multiple of, share, halve, divide, divided by, left over, remainder

Resources

Number lines. *Snakes and Ladders*, *Ludo*, dice 1–6, dice 0–9, cubes, counters and dominoes.
Copymasters 33 and 34. Homework 17.

Assessment

At the end of this theme is the pupil able to:

- Continue to develop understanding of addition as counting on steps along a number line;
- Add mentally three or more two-digit numbers;
- Partition into tens and units and recombine;
- Understand division as grouping and sharing and the inverse of multiplication;
- Use knowledge of doubles and halves to multiply or divide?

Mental maths starters 1, 6

Lesson 1

Introduction

Using their own number lines practise adding on single-digit numbers to numbers from 0 to 50. This session could also involve using three dice to play Snakes and Ladders or Ludo.

Activities

Addition of numbers (whole class/group)

Let the children respond to oral questions such as $20 + 40 + 20 = ?$ Add the two 20s together to make 40 and then double the number; add together the tens as single digits $2 + 4 + 2 = 8$ and then times by 10; put the largest number first and then add the rest on. Apparatus can be used.

(Individual/pairs)

Explore in pairs partitioning into tens and units:

36 + 53 = (30 + 6) plus (50 + 3)
= (30 + 50) + (6 + 3)
= 80 + 9
= 89

Record onto paper after a mental estimation.

Differentiation

Low Attainers – Add several one-digit numbers by using strategies such as looking for pairs that make 10 and adding those first. Start with the largest number and look for pairs that make 9 or 11 and adjust by 1.
High Attainers – Add four two-digit numbers together using any of the strategies that they have learned.

Plenary

Ask how many different ways children can add together three 2-digit numbers, explaining their methods each time. Is there a best way?

Lesson 2

Introduction

Write $8 \div 2 =$ on the board. Discuss the sign and what it means, *i.e. 8 shared between 2 or How many two's in 8?* Take 8 cubes and say that you want to share these equally between 2 children. Choose 2 children and give them the cubes alternately, saying, 'One for you, one for you,' etc. Ask the children how many they have each, *i.e. 4*. Ask if they have equal amounts. Say *There are 4 twos in 8.*

Activities

Understanding division (whole class/group)

Show the children a rod of 8 cubes. Break it up into 4 groups of 2 and say *There are 4 groups of 2 in 8.* Illustrate further using a number line, counting in leaps of 2 from 0 to 8, i.e. 4 leaps. Write the answer on the board. Repeat with different divisions.

(Individuals/pairs)

Tell the children to work in pairs with cubes. Write some multiples of 2 on the board and tell the children that you want them to share them by 2 or find how many twos in each number. They each write down the appropriate division and the answer.

Differentiation

Low Attainers – Keep using the cubes and divide by 2 and 3 only.
High Attainers – Repeat activities dividing by 3 and 4 etc.

Plenary

Link doubling of known multiplication facts to division, *e.g.*
12 divided by 2 = 6
24 divided by 2 must be double 6 = 12 because 24 is double 12.

Lesson 3

Introduction

Write $10 \times 5 =$ on the board. Ask the children to find the product, i.e. 50, and write it on the board. Write $5 \times 5 =$ on the board. Ask the children to find the product, i.e. 25, and write it on the board. Ask what they notice about the two answers, i.e. 25 is half of 50. Explain that 5 is half of 10 so the answer must be half of 50, i.e. 25. Repeat with different multiplications that children are already familiar with.

Activities

Multiplication/division (whole class/group)

Write on the board $50 \div 5 =$. Ask the children what the question is asking them to do: *How many fives in 50 or 50 shared by 5?* Display 50 cubes in a rectangle 5×10. Split this rectangle into strips of 5 cubes and ask the children, *How many fives in 50?* i.e. 10. Say *There are 10 fives in 50* Using the 50 cubes, choose 5 children to come out and share the cubes equally, giving the children cubes alternately. The children tell the class how many cubes they have each i.e. 10. Say *50 shared between 5 equals 10* Write the answer on the board.

(Individuals/pairs)

$50 \div 5 = 10$

Ask the children how they could check if their answer was correct. Write on the board and refer to the introduction:

$5 \times 10 = 50$ or $10 \times 5 = 50$

Write some multiples of 2, 5 or 10 on the board and ask the children to divide by 2, 5 or 10 respectively. Children can work in pairs. One child writes down the division and the other child checks by writing the multiplication to go with it. Rotate roles and repeat.

Differentiation

Low Attainers – Continue practising dividing by small numbers with plenty of apparatus.

High Attainers – Continue by dividing by any numbers.

Plenary

Starting with the example from the introduction ($10 \times 5 = 50$) ask the children how they could check that their multiplications are correct by using division:

$10 \times 5 = 50$

$50 \div 5 = 10$ or $50 \div 10 = 5$

Lesson 4

Introduction

Children work in pairs and use dominoes for their apparatus. They spread out the dominoes face down. They take it in turns to turn over a domino and multiply the two numbers together and write down the multiplication and the product. The partner then shakes a dice to determine the number of times the multiplication has to be doubled, e.g.: *2 and 5 on the domino and 3 on the dice First child would write* $2 \times 5 = 10$. *Other child doubles three times:* $4 \times 5 = 20$ $8 \times 5 = 40$ $16 \times 5 = 80$. Multiplications may get complicated, so calculators can be used where appropriate. Repeat but halving this time starting with $16 \times 5 = 80$.

Activities

Division/multiplication statements (whole class/group)

Ask the children what they are doing to a number when they are multipying by 2, i.e. doubling. Write down a double on the board e.g. $4 \times 2 = 8$. Ask the children how they would check if this was correct, ie by using division because it is the inverse of multiplication. Ask the class what the inverse of $\times 2$ is i.e. divide by 2 or halving. *Write 8 divided by 2 = 4 or 8 divided by 4 = 2.*

(Individuals/pairs)

Children work in pairs. One child shakes a dice (0–9) and multiplies the number by 2, saying the multiplication aloud and the product. The other child says the division (halving) that goes with it. They write down corresponding multiplication and division statements each time. Repeat.

Differentiation

Low Attainers – Children just use a 1–6 dice when making the statements.

High Attainers – Children use two 0–9 dice and make a 2-digit number to multiply by 2, and do the corresponding division.

Plenary

Show the children that if they double repeatedly and halve repeatedly they get back to what they started with, because $\times$ is the inverse of division and therefore doubling is the inverse of halving:

$2 \times 5 = 10$	*40 divided by 5 = 8*
$4 \times 5 = 20$	*20 divided by 5 = 4*
$8 \times 5 = 40$	*10 divided by 5 = 2*

Point out the doubles and halves.

Lesson 5

Introduction

Use doubling, working mentally, and explaining the reasoning. Work out the $4\times$ tables facts by doubling the $2\times$ table facts *e.g.* $2 \times 2 = 4$ *doubled is* $2 \times 4 = 8$

Put on the board $1 \times 25 = 25$ and deduce by doubling that

$2 \times 25 = 50$ $4 \times 25 = 100$ $8 \times 25 = 200$ etc

Activities

Mental calculations/multiplication and division (whole class/group)

Explain to the children how to find quarters of numbers by finding a half and then halving again. Work out mentally: *One quarter of 20 is 5 because one half of 20 is 10 and then halve the answer again to get 5.* Ask the children to work through Copymaster 33 in their groups.

(Individuals/pairs)

Ask the children in pairs to use the numbers 2, 5 and 10 and say or write four different multiplication or division statements relating to the numbers. Ask the children to work through Copymaster 34 to consolidate this concept.

Differentiation

Low Attainers – Make another $\times$ statement out of $4 \times 3 = 12$ and $5 \times 4 = 20$ etc. Extend to making one division statement as well.

High Attainers – Without apparatus answer oral questions like *You know that* $4 \times 6 = 24$. *What is* 6×4, *or 24 divided by 6 or 24 divided by 4?*

Plenary

Reminder to check subtraction with addition, check halving with doubling, check division with multiplication. Explain Homework 17 on adding three or more 2-digit numbers.

Theme 8 Solving problems

Objectives

- To choose appropriate number operations and calculation methods to solve money or 'real-life' word problems with two steps
- To be able to explain and record the methods they use
- To be able to check results e.g. *check division by multiplication, halving by doubling*

Vocabulary

double, halve, calculation, operation, solve, solution, answer

Resources

Copymasters 35 and 36. Homework 18.

Assessment

At the end of this theme is the pupil able to:

- Solve simple word problems set in real-life contexts and explain how the problem was solved;
- Make decisions about solving the word problems and check their results?

Mental maths starters 1, 9

Lesson 1

Introduction

Write on the board *There is a box of socks that holds 18 pairs. How many pairs are there in 3 boxes?* Encourage the children to think of various methods to solve the problem. Write the methods on the board, e.g.

$18 + 18 + 18 =$		$18 \times 3 =$
$20 + 20 + 20 - 6 =$	or	$(10 \times 3) + (8 \times 3) =$
$66 - 6 = 54$		$30 + 24 = 54$

Activities

Solving problems 1 (whole class/group)

Write on the board *Carmen was having a party and she had 2 plates of sandwiches with 12 sandwiches on each plate. At the end of the party there were 3 sandwiches left. How many were eaten altogether?* Tell the children that the problem is in two parts. Encourage them to find various ways of checking their calculations with equivalent calculations

e.g. *Double 12 = 24*
24 – 3 = 21 sandwiches eaten CHECK:
12 + 12 =
10 + 10 + 2 + 2 = 24
21 + 3 = 24

(Individuals/pairs)

Work through Copymaster 35 in pairs. Encourage the children to read through the questions slowly and carefully and record exactly how they tackle each problem.

Differentiation

Low Attainers – Use numbers within 20.
High Attainers – Use larger numbers.

Plenary

Use some of the problems that the children have written to solve as a class. Encourage the children to record exactly how they tackle each problem.

Lesson 2

Introduction

Write on the board *I think of a number, then subtract 10. The answer is 25. What was my number?* Make sure the question is read out to the children slowly. Underline the main parts of the question after discussion with the children:
'a number' 'subtract 10' 'answer is 25' 'What was my number?'
Ask the children to write down the operation they think is needed, and try to solve the problem.

Activities

Solving problems 2 (whole class/group)

Discuss the methods used to solve the problem in the introduction. Ask the children to use a box for the unknown number:

$\square - 10 = 25$

Use inverse operations to help with the calculation.

$25 + 10 = 35$

Check by replacing $\square$ with 35:

$35 - 10 = 25$

(Individuals/pairs)

Work in pairs and change the digits and the operations in the last example so that the children practise all four rules:
I think of a number, then multiply it by 4. The answer is 24. What was my number?
I think of a number, then divide it by 3. The answer is 15. What was my number?

Differentiation

Low Attainers – Use smaller, familiar numbers e.g. $5 + \square = 10$
High Attainers – After using larger numbers, give the children a set of operations. They write their own word problem around them.

Plenary

Use the word problems that the children have composed to solve with the rest of the class. Encourage the children to record how they tackle each problem.

Lesson 3

Introduction

Write this problem on the board: *An octopus has 8 tentacles. How many tentacles do 5 octopuses have? Now work out how many tentacles 6 octopuses have.* Underline the important parts of the problem: *8 /How many/ 5 octopuses/ how many/6 octopuses*

Write down the facts that they know:

1 octopus = 8 tentacles.

Activities

Solving problems 3 (whole class/group)

Discuss with the children what operations they think they need to do to solve the problem posed in the introduction. Write down the methods on the board:

1 oct = 8 *2 oct = 16*
3 oct = 24 *4 oct = 32*
5 oct = 40 or $5 \times 8 = 40$

Discuss the final part ($5 \times 8 = 40$) and advise the children to use what they know from doing the first part, *i.e. 5 octopuses have 40 tentacles, 6 octopuses have 8 more:*

$40 + 8 = 48$ or $6 \times 8 = 48$

Say 5 octopuses have 40 tentacles and 6 octopuses have 48 tentacles.

(Individuals/pairs)

Working in pairs repeat the same type of question as in the whole class activity, but change the numbers. Children write down how they solved the problem and discuss. Check with inverse operations i.e. division or repeated subtraction.

Differentiation

Low Attainers – Use small numbers and numbers they are familiar with, *e.g. 2, 3, 4, 5, 10.*

High Attainers – Use larger numbers *e.g. hundreds and thousands.*

Plenary

Go over more problems *e.g. A lorry has 6 wheels. How many wheels altogether in a pair of lorries. An egg box has 4 eggs in it. How many eggs will there be in 7 boxes. There is a five-a-side tournament. How many players will take part if there are 8 teams?*

Lesson 4

Introduction

Write on the board *There are 19 computer games on the top shelf and 32 computer games on the bottom shelf. 24 of the computer games are removed. How many computer games are left on the shelf?* Underline the important parts of the problem after discussion with the children: *19/32/24/ removed/ How many computer games are left on the shelf?* Encourage the pupils to draw a picture where relevant. Draw a picture on the board showing the problem. Tell the children that they need to use two operations in order to be able to solve the problem. Children try to solve the problem.

Activities

Solving problems 4 (whole class/group)

Discuss the operations used in the example in the introduction:

$19 + 32 = 51$ *computer games altogether.*

$51 - 24 = 27$ *computer games left on the shelves.*

Remind the children that this answer can be checked with + (inverse operation) *i.e.* $24 + 27 = 51$

Repeat this problem with different numbers.

(Individuals/pairs)

Working in pairs the children can work through Copymaster 36. Remind the children to check their results, *e.g. check division by multiplication, halving by doubling etc.*

Differentiation

Low Attainers – Use number bonds to 10 and 20 and small numbers for subtraction.

High Attainers – After using larger numbers, give the children a set of operations. They can then write their own word problem around them.

Plenary

Use the computer games on the shelf problem and extend the numbers used to multiples of 5, and 100 computer games on the shelves altogether.

Lesson 5

Introduction

Write on the board: *There are 18 red cubes, 21 blue cubes and 19 green cubes in a box. How many cubes are there altogether?* Let the children try to solve this problem and discuss their methods. Tell them that two steps are needed. Go through the methods on the board i.e. $21 + 19 = 40$, $40 + 18 = 58$ *cubes altogether.* Point out that $21 + 19$ was calculated first because looking at the units, they add up to ten, making the addition easier. Add on an extra part to the question: *If 14 more cubes were taken away how many were left altogether?*

Activities

Solving problems 5 (whole class/group)

Say, *I think of a number, double it, then add 5. The answer is 35. What is my number?* Write this on the board as you are saying it. Ask the children to try to work out this problem. Tell them they need two steps. Discuss the children's methods. Demonstrate the method of using inverses:

$(\square \times 2) + 5 = 35$

Work back from the number at the end doing the inverse operations to that number:

$35 - 5 = 30$ Subtraction the inverse of addition.

30 divided by 2 $= 15$ Division the inverse of multiplication.

15 is the first number.

(Individuals/pairs)

Ask the children to look at the last example. How could they check if 15 was the right answer? Put the number in the original problem to see if you get 35: $15 \times 2 = 30$, $30 + 5 = 35$.

Repeat this problem (beginning with a different number!) to practise all four number operations.

Differentiation

Low Attainers – Children solve problems where only addition and subtraction is required.

High Attainers – Ask the pupils to try to write their own 'I think of a number …' problems to get as many numbers as they can, starting from 1 *I think of a number, double it, take away 1 and my answer is 1. What is my number? Answer = 1.*

Plenary

Solve some of the high attainers' problems as a whole class. Explain Homework 18.

Theme 9 Equivalent fractions

Objectives

- To begin to recognise simple equivalent fractions

Vocabulary

part, fraction, one whole, one half, one quarter, three quarters, one third, two thirds, one tenth

Resources

Centimetre squared paper. Scissors. Scrap paper. Paper circles. Fraction dominoes.
Copymasters 37 and 38. Homework 19.

Assessment

At the end of this theme is the pupil able to:

- Recognise and find simple fractions;
- Recognise the equivalence between these fractions;
- Compare two simple fractions in practical contexts?

Mental maths starters 5, 7

Lesson 1

Introduction

Draw a circle on the board and colour half of it in. Tell the children that $\frac{1}{2}$ of the shape is coloured and $\frac{1}{2}$ is not coloured in. Make sure the children understand how the fraction is written, that the circle has been divided into 2 *equal parts* and that 1 equal part has been coloured and 1 equal part has not been coloured.
Repeat for other shapes using quarters, thirds and tenths.

Activities

Fractions of shapes (whole class/group)

Draw three shapes on the board:

a) a square
b) a rectangle
c) a parallelogram
Tell the children that each picture is a quarter of a whole shape and ask them to draw the whole shape.

Using squared paper and scissors ask the children to cut out strips and colour them to show $\frac{1}{2}, \frac{3}{4}, \frac{2}{3}, \frac{3}{10}$.

(Individuals/pairs)

Give the children a piece of 6×6 cm squared paper each and ask them to show as many different fractions as they can by colouring.
Also, working in pairs, give the children a paper square divided into quarters with one quarter coloured in. Ask them to find other ways of colouring in a quarter of a square.

Differentiation

Low Attainers – Give the group plenty of opportunity at folding and cutting out simple fractions from scrap paper.
High Attainers – Choose other 2-D shapes and show as many different fractions as they can.

Plenary

Revise the writing down of the fractions used during the lesson. Stress the importance of remembering that a fraction divides a shape into *equal parts*.

Lesson 2

Introduction

Draw four cakes/pies on the board:

1) divide into 2 equal parts
2) divide into 3 equal parts
3) divide into 4 equal parts
4) divide into 10 equal parts.

Pie one will serve 2 people and each will receive $\frac{1}{2}$.
Pie two will serve 3 people and each will receive $\frac{1}{3}$ etc.

Activities

Fractions comparison (whole class/group)

Looking at the pies from the introduction ask questions such as *Which is larger, a third or a half? Which is smaller, a tenth or a quarter?*
Give the children a paper circle each and ask them to fold it into four equal parts. Remind them that the circle represents *a whole one* and each equal part is a quarter. Write on the board $1 = \frac{4}{4}$. Fold another circle into eight equal parts and write about it. Fold another circle into two equal parts and write about it. *What happens to the size of a part when you make more of them?* (It gets smaller.)

(Individuals/pairs)

1 whole one $= \frac{2}{2}$
1 whole one $= \frac{4}{4}$
1 whole one $= \frac{8}{8}$

Cut up the folded parts of the children's paper circles and make sure each part is labelled with its fraction name. By matching up the different parts write statements:

$\frac{1}{2} = \frac{2}{4}$
$\frac{1}{4} = \frac{2}{8}$
$\frac{1}{2} = \frac{4}{8}$ etc

Differentiation

Low Attainers – Fold and cut further shapes into halves and quarters and compare them to each other.
High Attainers – Extend the folding and cutting to thirds and tenths. *How many thirds make one whole one? How many tenths make one whole one? How many tenths make one quarter?*

Plenary

Revise all the statements that the children have written down during the lesson.

Lesson 3

Introduction

Draw a 'Fraction Wall' on the board representing halves, quarters and eighths.

ONE WHOLE ONE							
$\frac{1}{2}$				$\frac{1}{2}$			
$\frac{1}{4}$		$\frac{1}{4}$		$\frac{1}{4}$		$\frac{1}{4}$	
$\frac{1}{8}$	$\frac{1}{8}$	$\frac{1}{8}$	$\frac{1}{8}$	$\frac{1}{8}$	$\frac{1}{8}$	$\frac{1}{8}$	$\frac{1}{8}$

Ask questions about the wall: *How many quarters make half? How many eighths make a quarter?*

Activities

Equivalent fractions 1 (whole class/group)

Using a 'Fraction Wall' showing fifths and tenths, ask the children the following questions.

How many tenths make one whole one?
How many tenths make one half?
How many tenths make one fifth?

(Individuals/pairs)

Working in pairs the children can play 'Fraction Dominoes'. These are dominoes with halves, quarters, thirds, fifths and tenths marked on them (made out of card with lots of the same fraction used):

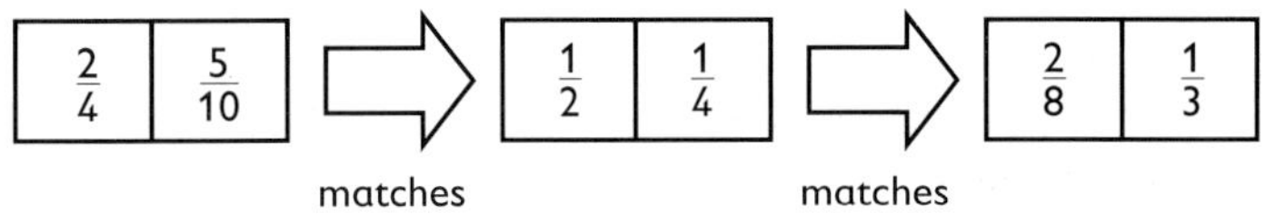

The children only match the fractions that are equivalent.

Differentiation

Low Attainers – Let the group use strips of card already divided into quarters and eighths and ask them to colour in an equivalent fraction.
High Attainers – Repeat but use card marked in fifths, sixths, thirds, tenths etc.

Plenary

Tell the children to ask their own questions to the class about the Fraction Walls.

Lesson 4

Introduction

Draw a rectangle of 10 small squares on the board. *What fraction does each small square represent? How many tenths make one whole one?* Shade 5 of the squares in. Ask *How many squares are shaded in? How many tenths are shaded in? Is there an equivalent fraction to $\frac{5}{10}$'s?* Repeat with rectangles of 8 squares and 16 squares.

Equivalent fractions 2 (whole class/group)

Fractions are the same if you can divide the *top* and *bottom* of one fraction by a number to end up with the other fraction *e.g. $\frac{3}{6}$ is the same as $\frac{1}{2}$ because you can divide the 3 of $\frac{3}{6}$ by 3 and the 6 of $\frac{3}{6}$ by 3 and finish with $\frac{1}{2}$.*

Write these examples on the board.

$\frac{5}{10}$ and $\frac{1}{2}$ $\frac{5}{10}$ and $\frac{1}{3}$
$\frac{2}{3}$ and $\frac{8}{12}$ (divide by 4) $\frac{4}{10}$ and $\frac{2}{5}$
$\frac{8}{10}$ and $\frac{4}{5}$

Which of these are equivalent?

(Individuals/pairs)

Use Copymaster 37. This will require the children to pick out equivalent fractions from the illustrations on the sheet. They can work in pairs or as individuals.

Differentiation

Low Attainers – Continue to work with halves, quarters and eighths. Fraction Dominoes game.
High Attainers – Draw 4 lines each 18 cm long. Colour this fraction of each line:
$\frac{1}{3}, \frac{3}{9}, \frac{2}{6}, \frac{6}{18}$.
What do the pupils notice?

Plenary

More practice at checking equivalent fractions by dividing by the same number as covered by the whole class part of the lesson.

Lesson 5

Introduction

Introduce lots of practical material that can be easily cut/broken into equal parts, *e.g. a chocolate bar.* Ask the children if they would like $\frac{2}{4}$ or $\frac{1}{2}$ of the whole bar to eat or if they would like $\frac{1}{3}$ or $\frac{2}{6}$ of a chocolate cake. Extend this to money and ask if $\frac{2}{8}$ of a pound will give you more money than $\frac{1}{4}$ of the same amount Go through the examples and make sure the children know that the two amounts are always the same.

Activities

They are the same! (whole class/group)

Put these questions on the board:

Find $\frac{2}{8}$ of £2, find $\frac{1}{4}$ of £2
Find $\frac{1}{3}$ of £3, find $\frac{2}{6}$ of £3
Find $\frac{2}{10}$ of £1, find $\frac{1}{5}$ of £1

Discuss the fact with the children that these amounts are equal and that $\frac{2}{8} = \frac{1}{4}, \frac{1}{3} = \frac{2}{6}$ etc.

Ask *How many eighths make up $\frac{1}{2}$? How many tenths make $\frac{1}{5}$.*

(Individuals/pairs)

Work in pairs or as individuals on Copymaster 38 in order to emphasise the equivalence of halves, quartwers, fifths, tenths etc.

Differentiation

Low Attainers – Draw their own fraction wall for halves, quarters and eighths.
High Attainers – Draw their own fraction wall for thirds, sixths and eighteenths.

Plenary

Which fraction is bigger: $\frac{2}{8}$ or $\frac{2}{4}$? Which fraction is the same as $\frac{1}{3}$?
The children can make up their own questions to ask the class.
Explain Homework 19.

Theme 10 Bar charts

Objectives

- To solve a given problem by organising and interpreting data in bar charts
- To understand the intervals that the bar charts are marked in

Vocabulary

sort, set, represent, graph, chart, pictogram, diagram, table, list, count, tally, axis, label, title, most/least common or popular

Resources

Tubes of Smarties, large squared paper, writing materials, dice, assorted library books.
Copymasters 39 and 40. Homework 20.

Assessment

At the end of this theme is the pupil able to:

- Solve a given problem by collecting, sorting and organising information in the form of a simple bar chart?

Mental maths starters 4, 7, 8

Lesson 1

Introduction

The children need to understand that handling data decisions have to be made about how best to collect, process and interpret the data given and this can be discussed. Tell the children that this work is best done using situations that they can relate to. e.g. *Using a tube of Smarties ask the children to count the number of different coloured sweets and record the information by drawing the Smarties in columns with headings yellow/red/green etc.*

Activities

Recording information (whole class/group)

Extending the work done in the introduction ask the children to explore other tubes of Smarties and see if the results are the same. Using large squared paper collect and record the birthday months of everybody in the class.
Are there months when nobody was born? Do you think this record would be the same for all the other classes in the school?

(Individuals/pairs)

Working in pairs spread a handful of Smarties on the table. Estimate how many and record it. Count them and record it. How close was your estimate? Spread another handful of Smarties on the table and repeat the process. Does your estimating improve? Compare with other pairs.

Differentiation

Low Attainers – Repeat counting exercises with counters/bricks etc. Make sure they choose a sensible way of recording the information.
High Attainers – Make a collection of data about animals/Olympic records/facts from the *Guinness Book of Records*.

Plenary

Discuss the different ways people have recorded their information. What questions can be asked about the data?

Lesson 2

Introduction

Make a list on the board of the children's favourite toys. Then tell the children that they have to vote for their favourite from the list. Record on the board in the form of a tally chart.
Ask questions such as *How many voted for each one of the toys?* record *Which toy is most popular? Which toy is least popular? Which toy had more than 10 votes? Which toy had fewer than 8 votes?*

Activities

Tally charts (whole class/group)

In front of the class arrange a variety of writing materials from around the classroom e.g. *chalk/pencils/coloured pencils/felt tip pens/ink pens.* Draw a tally chart on the board to show how many there are of each type. Ask the same questions as were asked in the introduction to the lesson.

(Individuals/pairs)

a) Using a variety of plastic or real fruit make a tally chart to show how many of each fruit there are.
b) Ask the children in the class their favourite colours and record on a tally chart.

Differentiation

Low Attainers – Throw a dice 30 times. Draw a tally chart to show how many times you throw each number.
High Attainers – As for Low Attainers but extend using two dice or a ten-sided dice.

Plenary

Ask the children who have used the dice to produce tally charts to present their work to the class.

Lesson 3

Introduction

Draw a frequency table on the board and ask the children to vote for their favourite sport:

Ask *Which sport had the most votes? Which sport had the second most votes?* etc.

Activities

Bar charts 1 (whole class/group)

Use Copymaster 39 to show the children a bar chart and how it is drawn. Talk about how squares are coloured in to match the number of votes cast. Emphasise that each square on the vertical axis matches *one vote*. Ask the class to add up the votes for each sport by adding up the number of squares (one square = one vote).
Answer the questions on the copymaster.

(Individuals/pairs)

The class have to gather information using frequency tables or tally charts and produce their own bar chart. Topics could include:

a) Find 20 different books. Write the last name of each author. Record the number of letters in each last name.
b) Gather together a collection of coins and record how many there are of each coin. Draw a bar chart to show the results.

Differentiation

Low Attainers – Use a prepared tally chart to produce a bar chart.
High Attainers – By asking their classmates find out their feelings about a class outing. Plan the outing.

Plenary

Ask for feedback about the class outing and find out how the group used the information they gathered.

Lesson 4

Introduction

Use a computer with a simple graphing program to enter and display data. Discuss how quickly the computer can do it and which chart, graph or table shows the information best.

Activities

Bar charts 2 (Whole class/group)

Working in pairs talk about what you do in one day:
How many hours are you awake?
How many hours are you at school?
How many hours do you spend, eating? playing? watching TV ?
Produce a bar chart for each pair.

(Individuals/pairs)

Use Copymaster 40 and note that the vertical axis is different from charts that they have looked at so far. Each square now stands for two items and not just one. Make sure the children understand that $\frac{1}{2}$ a square stands for one vote.

Differentiation

Low Attainers – What time do people arrive at school in the morning? How can I find out? Can you make a bar chart to show your results?
High Attainers – Choose 4 books from the library. Draw a bar chart to show the number of pages in each of the 4 books.

Plenary

Look at more bar charts with a vertical axis marked in one square = 2 items. Can the children compose their own questions?

Lesson 5

Introduction

Having introduced the idea of scale in graphs, children should be encouraged to use it for all graphing activities. They should also explore the possibility of using a scale of 1 square representing 5 or 10 items when large samples are encountered. Discuss with the class how such a square can be divided to represent numbers which do not fit exactly.

Activities

Computerised bar charts

Use a television page from a magazine or newspaper and enter information into the computer data-base about the length of five popular TV programmes. When the computer has produced the bar chart answer these questions: *How much longer was one programme than another? How long will it take to watch 2 or 3 programmes one after the other?* Make sure the children check the axis first so that their numbers are correct.

(Individuals/pairs)

Working in pairs find information from the class about what pets they would like to own. Draw a bar chart to show the results.

Differentiation

Low Attainers – Enter information into the computer about a topic of their choice.
High Attainers – Collect information from more detailed sources and adapt this information to produce various bar charts.

Plenary

Before looking at the graphs that the children have produced ask them to test a hypothesis such as *I think that most children would like a rabbit for a pet* then go on to look at their charts. Go through Homework 20.

Theme 1 Comparing, ordering and rounding

Objectives

- To compare two three-digit numbers and say which is more or less and give a number that lies between them
- To round any three-digit number to the nearest 100
- To order a set of whole numbers to 1000 and position them on a number line
- To identify unlabelled divisions on a number line or measuring scale

Vocabulary

place value, compare, between, half-way between, more than, less than, rounding up/down, nearest 100, order, position, number line, scale, divisions, larger, smaller than

Resources

Number lines, dice, spinners 0–9.
Copymasters 41 and 42. Homework 21.

Assessment

At the end of this theme is the pupil able to;

- Make and order 3-digit numbers on a number line, then say the numbers that come in between;
- Say a 3-digit number and round it to the nearest 100;
- Order numbers on a number line;
- Recognise unlabelled divisions on a number line?

Mental maths starter 1

Lesson 1

Introduction

Make two 3-digit numbers with the place value cards and put them on the board. Ask the children which number is the largest and which number is the smallest. Repeat this with other 3-digit numbers. Make sure that the children understand the place value of each number.

Activities

3-digit numbers (whole class/group)

Draw a line on the board and ask the children to put one of the smallest numbers at the beginning of the line, and one of the largest at the other end. Then add the numbers that can be found in between. Use a hundred square and repeat the activity. Make sure the children understand the place value of each number.

(Individuals/pairs)

Children work in twos with a piece of string and a set of place value cards, placed face down in sets of hundreds, tens and units. They each turn a card over from each pile to make a 3-digit number. The smallest number is placed at one end of the string and the largest at the other. The children then write down a number that is found in between them. Repeat. Make sure that the string is not too long and that the 3-digit numbers are formed correctly, using the place value cards.

Differentiation

Low Attainers – Use tens and units cards only. Continue with simple sequence work (2, 7 , 12, 17, —, —).
High Attainers – Use thousands cards as well. Continue with sequence work (150, 300, 450, 600, —, —).

Plenary

Say two 3-digit numbers for the children to make and order on a number line. Then they say numbers that come in between.

Lesson 2

Introduction

Prepare a selection of cards between 0 and 1000. Some should be easy to round to the nearest 100, others more difficult. These can be sorted into boxes (each number to the nearest 100). Remind the children about '50' (half way) and rounding up to the next 100.
Mark the board:

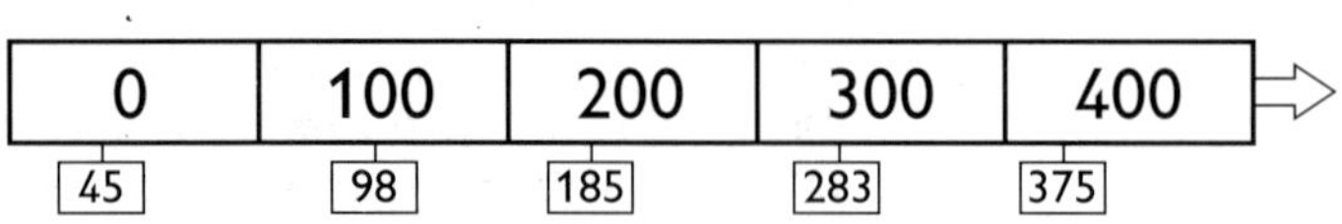

Activities

Rounding (whole class/group)

Draw a number line split into 10 divisions, then write '300' at one end and '400' at the other. Get the number card 320 and ask the children to place this number in the correct place on the number line. Ask them which multiple of hundred it is closest to, ie. 300. Tell the children that if they were rounding to the nearest 100, they would round 320 to 300. Repeat with 360, 310 and 350 (telling them the rule that half way or more goes to the next 100).

(Individuals/pairs)

Repeat the process, changing the hundreds numbers at either end of the number line, and moving the children on to 3-digit numbers that are not multiples of 10, so that they need to estimate the position on the number line before rounding. Give similar examples for children to do.

Differentiation

Low Attainers – Revise rounding to the nearest ten.
High Attainers – Extend to rounding to the nearest 1000.

Plenary

Without using a number line say a 3-digit number and ask the children to round it to the nearest 100. Ask them to explain why it was rounded in that way.

Lesson 3

Introduction

Investigate how many possible combinations of 3 numbers are available to make car number plates. Children will need to decide whether to start at 000 or 100. This is also a good investigation for getting organised, and listing numbers so that none are missed or repeated. Within the list of numbers, children can look at how often a particular digit arises.

Activities

Numbers to 1000 (whole class/group)

Write the numbers 385 to 395 in random order on the board. Ask the children to order them from smallest to largest and write them on the board in order. Ask *What is the middle number? What is the smallest number? What is the largest number? What is the difference between the smallest and largest number?* Write the numbers 426 to 436 in random order on the board. Draw a blank number line with divisions marked on for the numbers. Ask the children to write various numbers in turn in the correct places.

(Individuals/pairs)

Working in pairs repeat the whole class activity with other numbers, but using a number line with no divisions marked on it.

Differentiation

Low Attainers – Order 1- or 2-digit numbers on a number line with divisions.
High Attainers – Order 5/6-digit numbers on blank number lines.

Plenary

Repeat ordering numbers on a number line. Write the even numbers 2 to 20 in random order on the board. Tell the children to order them on a number line.

Lesson 4

Introduction

Working in pairs, take three dice. One represents hundreds, one represents tens and one stands for ones/units. Roll the three dice at the same time and record the number on a calculator. One of the dice is then used again, and the number is altered accordingly. Ask the children which column has changed. Is it greater or less than before and by how much?

Activities

'Big numbers' (whole class/group)

Each child has 3 squares marked on paper in which to write a three-digit number. A spinner with numbers 0–9 is used and each child places the number made (hundreds, tens and units) in one of the squares. Once a number has been written in a square it cannot be removed. The spinner is spun again, and the process repeated twice more. The winner is the child, or children, with the greatest three-digit number.

(Individuals/pairs)

Working in pairs ask the children to work through Copymaster 41 to compare and order numbers up to 1000.

Differentiation

Low Attainers – Work with a dice with 4, 5, 6 covered to reduce the size of the three-digit numbers that are made.
High Attainers – Order random numbers 500–1000, 1000–1500.

Plenary

Revise place value aspect of any of the numbers made. Ask questions such as *How many tens altogether in 250?* Answer 25 (20 tens make 200!).

Lesson 5

Introduction

Each child has 2 sets of 3 squares connected by an inequality sign (< or >). A spinner is used 6 times, one square being filled in after each throw. The object is to finish with two numbers that make the inequality statement true.

Activities

High and low (whole class/group)

Working in groups a player takes 3 single-digit cards from a pack of cards with 0–9 on. They form a three-digit number, but do not show the others. Each player then nominates his or her number as highest, lowest or middle (for three players). They compare numbers and score a point if they were correct. Note that players may choose, given their three digits, to go for a high or low number. Point out that 0 could be used in the hundred space to give a much lower number.

(Individuals/ pairs)

Ask the children to work through Copymaster 42. Can they find a number with 3 stages, 4 stages or more than 5 stages?

Differentiation

Low Attainers – Return to numbers below 300 and compare them, recording them as being more or less than each other.
High Attainers – Look at 'Kaprekars Constant' and calculate using pencil and paper only (no calculators).

Plenary

Question the class with random pairs of numbers and ask them *Which is larger? Which is smaller? How many tens are there altogether? How many ones are there altogether?* Explain Homework 21.

Theme 2 Mental addition and subtraction

Objectives

- To extend understanding of addition and subtraction
- To add several small numbers
- To add or subtract a near multiple of 10 to a two-digit number, by adding or subtracting the nearest multiple of 10, and adjusting
- To be able to use patterns of similar calculations

Vocabulary

addition, pairs, total, larger, first, add, subtract, multiple

Resources

Assorted dice, number cards 1–20, counters, dominoes. Copymasters 43 and 44. Homework 22.

Assessment

At the end of this theme is the pupil able to:

- Understand the operation of addition and the related vocabulary, and recognise that addition can be done in any order;
- Understand that more than two numbers can be added together;
- Understand the operation of subtraction and the related vocabulary;
- Add or subtract 9, 19, 29 or 11, 21, 31 by adding or subtracting 10, 20, 30 and adjusting by 1;
- Use known number facts and place value to add or subtract a pair of numbers mentally?

Mental maths starter 2

Lesson 1

Introduction

Tell the children that they need to make 10. The teacher says a digit and the children say the digit that goes with it to make 10 *e.g.*

Teacher	*Class*
2	*8*
6	*4*

Write *18 + 3 + 5 + 7 =* on the board.
Ask the children to do the calculation mentally using their knowledge of pairs to make ten.

Activities

Addition and subtraction 1 (whole class/group)

Following on: choose a child to explain the process for

18 + 3 + 5 + 7 =	18 + (3 + 7) + 5 =	(18 + 10) + 5 =
28 + 5 =	(28 + 2) + 3 =	30 + 3 = 33

Identify all of the pairs that make 10 in the calculation.
Repeat with similar calculations.

(Individuals/pairs)

Children work in threes with a set of number cards 10–20 in a pile face down, and a dice 0–9. One child turns over a card; another child then adds them up using the 'pairs to make ten' method. That child gets a counter for every pair to make ten identified in the calculation. Swap roles and repeat.

Differentiation

Low Attainers – The children shake the dice three times and add three 1-digit numbers together, grouping the pairs to make ten.
High Attainers – The children turn 2 numbers cards over and shake the dice 3 times, so that they are then adding 2 two-digit numbers to 3 one-digit numbers.

Plenary

The children explain some of their calculations and identify the pairs that make ten.

Lesson 2

Introduction

Tell the children they are going to make totals of 9. Shake a dice and say the number. The children say the number to go with it to make 9:

Teacher	*children*
3	*6*

Write the pairs on the board. Continue until all of the pairs are found. Repeat for pairs to make 11. Write *13 + 6 + 2 + 9 =* on the board and ask the children to use their knowledge of pairs to make 9, 10 and 11.

Activities

Addition and subtraction 2 (whole class/group)

Following on: choose a child to explain the methods used:

13 + 6 + 2 + 9 =
10 + (3 + 6) + (2 + 9) =
10 + (9 + 11) =
10 + 20 =
30

Repeat for similar calculations.

(Individuals/pairs)

Children work in threes with a set of number cards in a pile face down and a dice 0–9. One child turns over a card, another child throws the dice 3 times and the third child writes down the four numbers. Then the third child adds them up using the 'pairs to make 9,10 or 11' method. That child gets a counter for every pair to make 9, 10 or 11 identified in the calculation. Swap roles and repeat.

Differentiation

Low Attainers – Children throw the dice 3 times and add 3 one-digit numbers together, finding pairs that total 9, 10 or 11.
High Attainers – Children turn over 2 number cards and shake the dice 3 times.

Plenary

Children write some of their problems on the board, and the class calculate the answers, identifying the number pairs to make 9, 10 or 11. Different number pairs may be identified by different children.

Lesson 3

Introduction

Write on the board $2 + 5 + 8 + 19 =$. Do the above calculation mentally and discuss the method they use. Encourage the children to use mathematical vocabulary when explaining methods and to put the larger number first when adding several small numbers.

e.g. $19 + 2 + 5 + 8$ *(putting the larger number first)*

$19 + (2 + 8) + 5$

$(19 + 10) + 5$ *(pairs to make 10)*

$29 + 5 =$

$25 + 4 + 5 =$

$(25 + 5) + 4 =$

$30 + 4 =$ *(pairs to make 10)*

34

Activities

Adding small numbers (whole class/group)

The children work in pairs with a 1–100 square chart, a dice and a counter each. Both start with their counters on 1. The children take it in turns to shake the dice, move their counter accordingly, and write down the number they land on. When 4 numbers have been written down, they are added, and the child with the highest total gets a cube. The children then place their counters back on 1, and the process is repeated. The winner is the child with most cubes at the end.

(Individuals/pairs)

Children work in threes or fours with a set of dominoes spread out face down on the table. The children take it in turns to turn over 2 dominoes and add the four numbers, one from each side of each of the dominoes. The other children check the answer. If it is correct, they keep their dominoes, if not they have to replace them. The winner is the child with the most dominoes at the end.

Differentiation

Low Attainers – Children turn over one domino and add the numbers from each end.

High Attainers – The group turn over 1 domino and treat it as a 2-digit number, *e.g.*

3	1

The number could be 31 or 13. They turn over another domino and add on the 2 numbers from each end.

Plenary

The children explain some additions using the methods covered in the lesson.

Lesson 4

Introduction

Write $19 + 26 =$ on the board. Ask the children to round 19 to the nearest 10, reminding them to look at the units digit, and decide which ten it is nearest. (NB If the number is half way or above, round up.) Add the 20 to the $26 = 46$. Remind them that they rounded up by 1, so now they need to take the 1 away again to make 45. Repeat with other calculations.

Activities

Adding multiples of 10 (Whole class/group)

Write $37 - 28$ on the board. Ask the children to round 28 to the nearest 10, i.e. 30. Subtract the 30 from $37 = 7$. Remind the children that they rounded up by 2, so they need to add 2 on to 7 to make 9. Repeat with other calculations.

(Individuals/pairs)

Work through Copymaster 43. Remind the children how many they have rounded up or down by each time, so that they know the number to subtract or add at the end.

Differentiation

Low Attainers – Use 2-digit numbers added to 1-digit numbers where the 1-digit number needs rounding.

High Attainers – Use 3-digit numbers.

Plenary

Give the children more addition calculations, to reinforce this method of addition. Repeat with subtraction examples.

Lesson 5

Introduction

Children work in pairs with different coloured counters, a 1–100 square chart and one of each type of dice. They both place their counters on 1 and take it in turns to shake the dice. The 0–9 dice represents the tens digit, and the other dice represents the units. When they are both shaken, a 2-digit number is made. This number is added to the number on which the counter is currently placed, and the total is where the counter is moved to.

e.g. A counter is placed on 1 and the dice are shaken, making the number 28. $1 + 28 = 29$

Ask the children what is the nearest multiple of 10 to 29 (30). The counter is then moved to 30. The above method is used for each turn. The winner is the first to pass 100.

Activities

Multiples of 10 (whole class/group)

Repeat the methods used in the introduction for subtraction, where the children start with their counters on 100 and subtract the 2-digit numbers shaken. Encourage the children to write down their calculations each time.

(Individuals/pairs)

Work through Copymaster 44 which involves similar examples to the above and will consolidate what they have learnt.

Differentiation

Low Attainers – When doing the addition, children shake a 0–9 dice and add a 1-digit number each time. The winner is the first to pass 50. When doing the subtraction, they start at 50.

High Attainers – Children set a time limit to reach the end, *e.g. 5 minutes*. Change the time limits where appropriate.

Plenary

Discuss some of the calculations from the game and the addition and subtraction method used each time.

Theme 3 Solving problems

Objectives

- To choose appropriate number operations and calculation methods to solve money or 'real-life' word problems with one or two steps
- To explain and record the method used and check the results
- To use informal pencil and paper methods to support, record or explain TU + TU, HTU + TU and HTU + HTU

Vocabulary

operation, sign, symbol, number sentence, equation

Resources

Assorted coins, calculators, menus, Base 10 apparatus, number cards 0–9
Copymasters 45 and 46. Homework 23.

Assessment

At the end of this theme is the pupil able to:

- Solve simple word problems set in 'real-life' contexts and explain how the problem was solved;
- Choose and use appropriate number operations and ways of calculating to solve problems;
- Develop pencil and paper methods for additions that cannot, at this stage be done mentally?

Mental maths starter 9

Lesson 1

Introduction

'Guess my number' – The teacher asks riddle-type questions such as *I am thinking of a number; it has 100 in it. It has three units in it. I'm not going to tell you how many tens. Can you guess what it is?* The children can ask their own questions to help with the answer.

Activities

Using numbers over 100 (whole class/group)

You will need money that includes 1p, 10p, £1 coins. Make the links between units, tens and hundreds with money
e.g. 10 × 1p = 10p, 10 × 10p = 100p, 100p = £1
Give the opportunity of lots of sorting/counting experience with the coins. A record of each amount of coins can be written on the board and recorded on a graph divided into areas labelled 1p, 10p and pounds.

(Individuals/pairs)

Point out to the children that a problem can often be solved in several different ways, so there is rarely only one correct method. The first stage is to decide what the problem is asking you to do. *How much will 6 books cost, at £1.99 each?* Ask the children if they are going to add, subtract, multiply or divide. Then tell them to estimate the answer. £1.99 can be rounded up to £2.00 which will help the calculation. Then ask the children to work through Copymaster 45.

Differentiation

Low Attainers – Decide which operation to use to solve various money problems and if they should use pencil and paper or a mental method.
High Attainers – Children should set problems for each other and specify which method should be used.

Plenary

Discuss that some problems are easily worked out in the head, whereas pencil and paper may be useful for others. Using a calculator might be quicker at other times.

Lesson 2

Introduction

Explain to the children that an *operation* is just one of +, −, ×, or ÷. Write on the board *10* ☐ *12* = 22 and ask if anyone can put the right sign in the space. Try other examples and tell the children that if the answer is bigger than the other two numbers in the sum, the operation must be + or ×. If the answer is smaller than the other numbers, the operation must be − or ÷.

Activities

Making decisions (whole class/group)

For these activities the hardest part is turning the words into a sum. That means choosing the right operation and putting the numbers in the right places. *5 sharks eat 10 fish each. How many do they eat altogether? 5 × 10 = 50 It's 5 lots of 10 fish, so we multiply them.*
Carmen gave 2 of her 17 cheese sandwiches to Hannah. How many sandwiches does Carmen have left? (17 ? 2 = ?)
Hannah puts these 2 with her other 46 sandwiches. How many does she have in her collection now? (46 ? 2 = ?)
Hannah accidentally loses half her sandwiches. How many sandwiches does she have left? (48 ? 2 = ?)

(Individuals/pairs)

When you add up a list of numbers, it really doesn't matter which ones you add up first. That means you can always add the numbers a different way to check your answer. 2 + 3 is the same as 3 + 2: they both add up to 5. So 2 + 3 = 3 + 2 and the same is true whatever the numbers are. Working in pairs, ask the children to work through Copymaster 46.

Differentiation

Low Attainers – More practice at single-digit additions and subtractions and deciding which sign/operation to put in the sum.
High Attainers – TU + TU examples and checking their answers by adding the numbers the other way round.

Plenary

Ask the children to talk about some of their calculations and how they checked their answers.

Lesson 3

Introduction

Collect together a series of menus or make up some of your own. Take some of the smaller prices and add those together mentally. Remind children of how they should record amounts of money and when to use a £ sign and when only to use p for pence (£0.45 = 45p).

Activities

Money problems (whole class/group)

Put this menu on the board

CHIPS £1.00, £1.20
BURGER £2.50
VEGGIE BURGER £2.50
FIZZY DRINK 80p, 90p, £1.00

Work out the cost of these meals in your head: burger and large chips; small chips and fizzy drink. I have £3.50 in my pocket. If I buy a veggie burger what else can I afford? Choose a meal for: £4.50, £4.70, £3.30.

(Individuals/pairs)

Make up your own 'Specials Board' with various unusual items and their prices. Then working in pairs the children can work out their own menus given different amounts of money to spend. The calculations can be done mentally or using pencil and paper to make notes.

Differentiation

Low Attainers – Keep the prices to small amounts that they can add mentally. They could make their own 'Classroom Shop' to help.

High Attainers – Using catalogues this group can use pencil and paper methods to add up 5 or 6 items.

Plenary

Discuss with the children when they should use mental strategies and when they should use pencil and paper to work out their totals.

Lesson 4

Introduction

People in real life use a variety of methods to add large numbers, depending on how large the numbers are, and how many of them there are. Ask children how they solve additions. Suggest they try out each other's methods. Modelling the process being described by their friend will help them to see the possible variety of steps and stages.

Activities

Pencil and paper procedures (whole class/group)

Using Base 10 apparatus the class can model sums on their tables:

27 + 42 = 69
= 2 tens and 7 ones add 4 tens and 2 ones = 6 tens and 9 ones

Sums can be presented horizontally so that children need to organise them using their understanding of place value, first with the apparatus and then with the numbers. In examples where there is no carrying figure, they may begin adding with the 100s. Similar methods may be used if children are happier using counters or an abacus, rather than Base 10 apparatus.

(Individuals/pairs)

Working in pairs using a pack of 27 numeral cards containing 3 of each of the numbers 0–9 the children can build numbers written on the board. Then break them down into hundreds, tens and ones. These can then be added and the results recombined into the final form.

Differentiation

Low Attainers – Practise with adding TU to TU using Base 10 apparatus.

High Attainers – Practise with adding HTU to HTU using numeral cards and recording the process by writing notes using pencil and paper.

Plenary

Discuss alternative methods of recording their additions linking apparatus to pictorial recording and the use of numbers.

Lesson 5

Introduction

Look at counting on in multiples of 100, 10 or 1

e.g. *74 + 45 = 74 + 40 + 5 = 114 + 5 = 119*

	+40		+5	
74		114		119

225 + 126 = 225 + (100 + 20 + 6)
= 325 + 20 + 6
= 345 + 6
= 351

	+100		+20		+5		+1	
225		325		345		350		351

Activities

Additions (whole class/group)

Begin to record calculations in preparation for an efficient standard method. Emphasise that units line up under units, tens under tens and so on. The children can be labelled into 100s 10s and 1s; they can then group themselves together by 'finding' someone who is labelled in the same way. Then by using groups of children 'sums' can be modelled on the board. *Is there an efficient way of lining the digits up to make it easy to add together?* The children can then be put into lines and the addition worked out.

(Individuals/pairs)

Working in pairs using apparatus as required the children can use paper and pencil to work out sums modelled on the board.

Differentiation

Low Attainers – Use apparatus to make up their own sums and then work out each other's examples.

High Attainers – Add two- and three-digit numbers with a carrying figure.

Plenary

Discuss when to use mental strategies and when to use paper and pencil methods to work out TU + TU, HTU + TU, HTU + HTU. Go through Homework 23.

Theme 4 Measuring capacity

Objectives

- To read and begin to write the vocabulary related to capacity
- To measure and compare using litres and millilitres, and know the relationship between them
- To be able to suggest suitable units and equipment to estimate or measure capacity
- To be able to read scales and record measurements using mixed units
- To choose appropriate number operations and calculation methods to solve measurement problems

Vocabulary

full, empty, holds, roughly, nearly, about, approximately, litres, millilitres

Resources

Measuring jugs and cylinders. Assorted containers and bottles. Fish tank. Egg cup. Bottle tops. Small bowls. Jelly cubes. Ball. Copymasters 47 and 48. Homework 24.

Assessment

At the end of this theme is the pupil able to:

- Begin to make decisions about the appropriate units for measuring capacity;
- Develop an understanding of the usefulness of estimation;
- Select and use suitable measuring equipment;
- Read scales, labelled and unlabelled, to the nearest division;
- Solve problems relating to measurement?

Mental maths starters 5, 7

Lesson 1

Introduction

Remind the children about the units they have used for measuring length and mass. In this lesson they will be measuring capacity, which is measuring how much a container holds. They will be finding out about the capacity of different things. Write on the board *1000 millilitres = 1 litre* and discuss this. Let them handle measuring jugs and cylinders with different scales and say which would be best for measuring certain amounts.

Activities

What's in it? (whole class/group)

The class will use different methods to find the capacity of different containers. Show them how to fill a container, pour the contents into a measure and read the amount. They are to write how many millilitres they use each time. Stress the need to be as accurate as possible.

(Individuals/pairs)

Working in pairs give the children a collection of bottles in assorted shapes and sizes. Tell them their task is to find out the capacity of each one but first they must decide which holds the least and which holds the most. Allow time for discussion as the containers are ordered, especially if there are some unusual shapes. Ask for suggestions about the best way to test the capacity of each. You could make available only 100 ml graduated jugs or cylinders, depending on the children's ability. After measuring the bottles ask if there are any surprises. Why did some bottles seem to hold more than others?

Differentiation

Low Attainers – Use 1 litre bottles fill with different amounts of water and make musical notes with them.
High Attainers – Try using bigger than 1 litre containers and fill with 1 litre of water to discover if they produce a range of sounds.

Plenary

Remind the children that they have been measuring capacity, or what a container will hold, and they need to remember that the units they have used are litres and millilitres.

Lesson 2

Introduction

With large bottles and plastic cups on view ask the children to determine the best way of finding the capacity of one of the bottles. By finding the capacity of the cup is it possible to find the capacity of the larger container?

Activities

Measures (whole class/group)

Using a large container such as fish tank, ask the children to estimate its capacity. Make it a competition, with the child who comes closest to the correct answer being the winner. Check the estimates by filling or emptying the tank.
A consumer survey can be organised and begun to be carried out amongst parents and staff. Ask children to think of suitable questions to ask e.g. *What size washing-up liquid do you buy? What products do you buy that are measured in litres?*

(Individuals/pairs)

Working in pairs they will need some large bottles with a strip of paper glued down the side, a funnel and a 100 ml measure. The aim is to write a scale up the side of the bottle in 100 ml. Ask them to find the total capacity of the bottles.

Differentiation

Low Attainers – Give the children 10 ml measures such as spoons and droppers. Ask them to estimate how many measures it will take to fill a container. Check by filling.
High Attainers – Children should each calibrate their own container in 10 ml, then estimate the capacity of other containers of less than 1 litre. Check by filling.

Plenary

Discuss why containers of different widths fill to different levels with the same amount of liquid (conservation)?

Lesson 3

Introduction

Children should estimate the capacity of an egg cup and bottle top, then fill them with a medicine spoon. They should repeat this with a 'dropper,' record the results in a table and discuss them. *Which holds more, the egg cup or the bottle top?* Discuss the need for a standard small unit.

Activities

Investigation (whole class/group)

Make a jelly with the children. Before making the jelly, discuss with the children how many small bowls can be filled from 1 litre of water. Check some of their estimates. Use enough jelly cubes for 1 litre of hot water and repeat the process for the liquid jelly. Discuss the results asking questions such as *Why is there more liquid jelly than there is water? When the jelly is set is there more than when it was liquid? What would happen if more jelly cubes were added? What would happen if fewer cubes were used?*

(Individuals/pairs)

Ask the children if the same thing happens with anything else you mix with water. How about squash? How much concentrated squash should be added to 1 litre of water to make a drinkable mixture? Conversely, how much water should be added to a litre of squash to make a mixture that is pleasant to drink? If the children work in groups to use the squash some of them can check out foods that thicken during the cooking process as well *e.g. custard.*

Differentiation

Low Attainers – Use their own graduated containers to measure the capacity of ice-cream boxes.

High Attainers – Prepare a sheet to take home to record the amount of liquids used in the kitchen using standard and non-standard measures.

Plenary

Look at recipe books and discuss making savoury sauces or gravy.

Lesson 4

Introduction

Children should devise a capacity party, where the choice of food is restricted to those that are measured in litres or millilitres, either in the preparation, the cooking or in the serving: milkshakes, colas, ice-cream, jellies, pancakes.

Activities

Party time (whole class/group)

Continuing the party theme using an assortment of containers the children can answer questions such as *How many scoops of ice-cream can be served from 1 litre? How many children would get a drink from 1 litre of juice or milk?* A birthday party being planned at home is a natural extension, and offers opportunities for home/school links, as well as a means of introducing the differing requirements for large and small parties. This can be planned during this part of the lesson.

(Individuals/pairs)

Working in pairs use Copymaster 47. Encourage the children to be accurate to the nearest whole or half unit. Also use some mixed units to measure with.

Differentiation

Low Attainers – Break down various litre and $\frac{1}{2}$ litre amounts into millilitres.

High Attainers – Work out a recipe for 8 people or 2 people by doubling or halving quantities in a simple recipe for 4 people.

Plenary

Using a 2 litre container discuss how it can be filled with 500 ml and 200 ml measures:

2 litres = 500 ml + 500 ml + 200 ml + 200 ml + 200 ml + 200 ml + 200 ml.

Lesson 5

Introduction

Children used to have to solve problems about filling and emptying baths, which involved questions on capacity and time. *The hot tap fills the bath with 1 litre of water every 5 seconds. The cold tap fills the bath with 1 litre of water every 10 seconds. How long does it take to fill the bath with 50 litres of hot water? How long does it take to fill the bath with 50 litres of cold water? When the plug is pulled out, the water drains away at 1 litre every 6 seconds. How long does it take to drain 40 litres?*

Activities

Measurement problems (whole class/group)

Emphasise that you can add and subtract measurements just like normal numbers. Model a number of questions e.g. *Yesterday, Penny drank 300 ml of cola, 450 ml of orange juice and 800 ml of water. How much liquid did she drink altogether? Sammy Snail weighs 3 kg. His shell weighs 6 kg. His friend Sid Snail weighs 20 kg. How much do they weigh altogether? A ball rolled 55 cm across the floor and stopped. It then rolled a further 35 cm. How far did it roll altogether?*

Remind the children to record their calculations and not to forget to put the correct units with the answer.

(Individuals/pairs)

Ask the children to work through Copymaster 48. Before they start remind the children about the vocabulary of measurement and the different units that are used (litres, millilitres, grams, kilograms, centimetres and metres). Facts such as 100 cm = 1 metre, 1000 grams = 1 kilogram and 1000 millilitres = 1 litre could be on display.

Differentiation

Low Attainers – Use an assortment of scales to compare the weights of different everyday objects.

High Attainers – Use spring balances for weighing collections *e.g. Find the heaviest potato in this bag.*

Plenary

Discuss how you might find the mass, length or capacity of a single item. Use a spring balance to find the mass of a tennis ball; calculate the mass of ten balls and check with the balance. Go through Homework 24.

Theme 5 Symmetry and angles

Objectives
- To identify and sketch lines of symmetry and recognise shapes with no lines of symmetry
- To sketch the reflection of a simple shape in a mirror
- To read and begin to write the vocabulary of position, direction and movement
- To be able to recognise that a straight line is two right angles
- To be able to compare angles with a right angle, saying whether they are more or less
- To investigate general statements about shapes, and suggest examples to match them. Explain reasoning

Vocabulary
fold, match, mirror line, reflection, symmetrical, grid, row, column, map, plan, compass point, horizontal, vertical, diagonal, descend, ascend, angle, is a greater/smaller angle than

Resources
Card and plastic shapes. Mirrors. Pictures of flags. Pinboards. Clocks.
Copymasters 49 and 50. Homework 25

Asssessment
At the end of this theme is the pupil able to:
- Recognise line symmetry in simple cases;
- Describe positions and directions;
- Describe movements;
- Investigate general statements about shapes?

Mental maths starter 7

Lesson 1

Introduction
Fold a piece of paper in half in front of the children. The fold is a line of symmetry. Ask them to predict what will happen if you cut a shape in the paper around the fold. When you have cut and opened the paper, the two halves can be compared.

Activities
Line symmetry 1 (whole class/group)
Give the children a collection of regular paper shapes and ask them to find any lines of symmetry that they show. Explain that, as with the folding and cutting activity, if they have found the line of symmetry, the two halves should be exactly the same. They should be able to predict where the line should be and test their predictions by folding the shapes. How many lines of symmetry can they find? This will involve much trial and error.

(Individuals/pairs)
Use Copymaster 49 and ask the children if they can say where the lines of symmetry should be for each shape. The lines can be drawn to check their predictions. Mirrors can also be used with this page to test children's theories. If a mirror is placed where they think the line should be, children will be able to see if the two halves are the same.

Differentiation
Low Attainers – More folding activities to explore lines of symmetry.
High Attainers – Sort regular and irregular shapes into those with and those without symmetry.

Plenary
Ask the children to demonstrate the shapes they have found which show line symmetry.

Lesson 2

Introduction
Write a number of words in capital letters on the board:

——BED—— ——CASE—— ——ARM——

Demonstrate that one of the words (bed) has a line of symmetry by using a mirror placed on the lines vertically and horizontally. Remember it is only symmetrical when one side of the line is an exact reflection of the other.

Activities
Line symmetry 2 (whole class/group)
Tell the children that they are going to design three flags. (A poster of flags would be very useful to illustrate the fact that many flags have simple designs; triangles, rectangles etc.) The first flag must show a vertical line of symmetry, the second flag a horizontal line of symmetry and the final flag no lines of symmetry at all. Use a mirror to check the designs. Also let the class explore shapes that have more than 1 or 2 lines of symmetry. Particular attention should be paid to the square (4 lines of symmetry).

(Individuals/pairs)

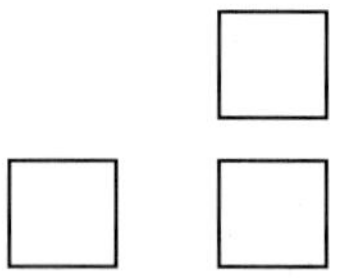

Working in pairs, investigate the above shapes by using one side of a mirror. Ask the children to place the mirror so that you can see only one square. Then move it to see 2, 3, 4, 5 and 6 squares.

Differentiation
Low Attainers – Look at the poster of maps and decide which flags show line symmetry and which do not.
High Attainers – Make up more words that have line symmetry.

Plenary
Look at and discuss the flags they have designed and decide if the symmetry is correct.

Lesson 3

Introduction

Draw a small grid on the board with a vertical axis of numbers up to 4 and a horizontal axis of letters from A to E. Shade in one of the squares on the grid and ask the children to descibe where it is to the class. Encourage the use of the letters and numbers as reference points i.e. B2 or A3 etc.

Activities

Movement (whole class/group)

Choose or make a shape to draw around on the board. Use it to make a turning pattern.

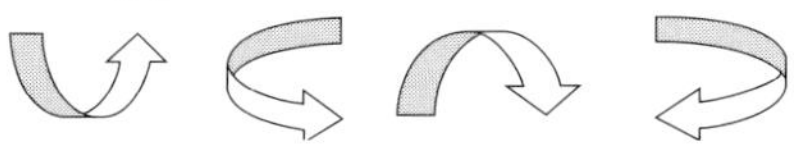

A sliding pattern

A 'flip over' pattern

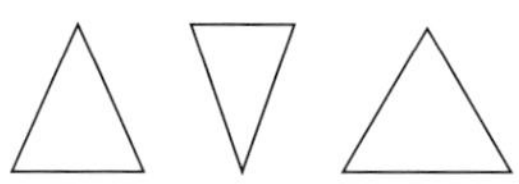

How are the patterns the same? How are they different?

(Individuals/pairs)

Working in fours each child makes the same shape on four pinboards or squared dotty paper:

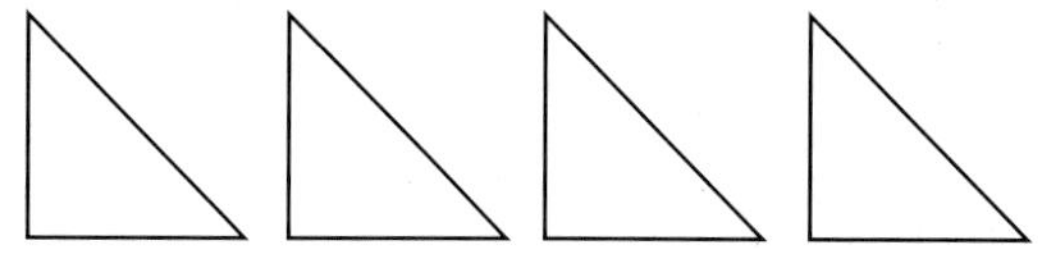

Make different patterns by fitting the 4 boards/designs together in a square.

Differentiation

Low Attainers – Design a book of prints and patterns with some friends.

High Attainers – Collect 'moving' words *e.g. twist, bend, stretch, slide, turn.*

Plenary

Talk about how the patterns are the same and how they are different. Use the right vocabulary.

Lesson 4

Introduction

The angle between two lines is how much you have to turn one of the lines so that it matches up with the other one. Use a clock with hands to show that the big hand has to turn exactly quarter of the way round to touch the small hand. Emphasise to the children that a $\frac{1}{4}$ turn is called a right angle.

Activities

Right angles (whole class/group)

Get each child to fold an A4 piece of paper into a fan ready to hold up. By folding the fan half way the class can show that they have made a right angle. Then open out the fan fully and show that by making two right angles they have made a straight angle or straight line. Continue to use the fan to show angles that are less than a right angle and more than a right angle.

(Individuals/pairs)

Working in pairs use two geo-strips to make and draw half and quarter turns from the same starting position. Use the geo-strip 'right angle' to measure random angles around the classroom. Are they greater than one? Are they less than one? Are they between one and two right angles? List the different angles that are measured in three columns.

Differentiation

Low Attainers – Use the clocks with hands to make different angles and ask their partner if these angles are larger or smaller than one right angle.

High Attainers – Explore right angles in regular shapes. How many right angles are in a square?

Plenary

Ask the children to model angles with their fans and ask the class if these angles are smaller or larger than a right angle.

Lesson 5

Introduction

Shapes have different names. They are named after their number of sides. Show the class a selection of triangles. 'Tri' at the start of a word means three. Show the children a collection of four sided shapes and explain that these are called quadrilaterals. 'Quad' at the beginning of a word means four.

Activities

Plane shapes (whole class/group)

Display a selection of triangles and quadrilaterals of different sizes (plastic/card shapes). Choose any two shapes. The shapes can be the same or different. Put them together to make a four-sided shape. How many different four-sided shapes can the children make in front of the class? Each one has to be made from 2 shapes. Ask them to draw the results onto squared paper. Make general statements about some of the shapes *e.g. A square always has four equal sides and four right-angled corners.*

(Individuals/pairs)

Use Copymaster 50 and put together halves and quarters of different shapes to make the whole shape. The children can try and make 4, 5 and 6-sided shapes in as many different ways as possible (plastic/card shapes can be used to help).

Differentiation

Low Attainers – Select some of the shapes and put these together in repeating patterns.

High Attainers – Use a ruler to draw their own shapes. Count the sides and name the shapes.

Plenary

Ask the children to model statements about any of the shapes they have looked at so that the class can guess the name of the shape. The class could be split into teams and the questions made into a quiz.

Theme 6 Properties of number

Objectives

- To recognise two-digit and three-digit multiples of 2, 5, and 10 and three-digit multiples of 50 and 100
- To solve number puzzles and explain methods and reasoning orally and in writing

Vocabulary

odd, even, multiples, smallest, largest

Resources

Number cards 1–20, 0–99 number square, number line 0–100, Snakes and Ladders game.
Copymasters 51 and 52. Homework 26.

Assessment

At the end of this theme is the pupil able to:

- Describe and extend number sequences to recognise two-digit and three-digit multiples of 50 and 100;
- Recognise familiar multiples;
- Solve mathematical problems or puzzles and explain the reasoning behind the solution?

Mental maths starters 4, 8

Lesson 1

Introduction

Discuss odd and even numbers with the children. Ask the children to come and circle some even numbers on a number line. *Why are these numbers even?* Can they recognise even numbers with two or more digits? *How do you know this?* Ask the children about the odd numbers. *How would you recognise a multiple of 5 or 10?* Some might be able to say how they would know the multiples of 100.

Activities

Multiples (whole class/group)

Ensure everyone has a set of cards with 0, 2, 5, 10 written on them. Explain that you will write a number on the board and if they think it is a multiple of 2 they hold up the 2 card when you say GO! Some of the numbers will be multiples of all three, in which case they hold up 2, 5 and 10, but if the numbers you write are not multiples of these hold up 0. Give all the children a 0–99 square and have an OHP grid on the board for the children to refer to. Ask them to circle all the multiples of 10. Then draw a square round all the multiples of 5. *What can you say about the numbers with a square and circle?*

(Individuals/pairs)

Continue with the same 0–99 square with the squares and circles on it. Next put a triangle round the multiples of 2. *Which would be the next number after 100 to have a square, circle and triangle? How many more between 0 and 100; between 0 and 200?* and so on. (Can they predict these outcomes and test them on number squares?)

Differentiation

Low Attainers – On a 0–30 number line ask the children to count in 2s starting with 0 and ask what they notice about the units digit.

High Attainers – On a 0–100 number line ask the children to count in 2s starting with 0 and ask what they notice about the units digit.

Plenary

Time children at counting on in 2s, 5s and 10s up to random numbers. *How far can you get in 1 minute, 2 minutes etc? Can anyone get to 100 counting in 2s or 5s?*

Lesson 2

Introduction

Write a simple number pattern on the board, such as 2, 4, 6, 8. Ask the children to talk about the pattern and predict how this would continue. Add more patterns including 0, 5, 10, 15 etc and 0, 10, 20, 30 etc. The children can continue their predictions. Write up some of the children's comments about each pattern.

Activities

Patterns (whole class/group)

Look at a 0–100 number line and mark out the line in multiples of 10. Count in 10s from random numbers on the line. Can the children say what they notice about each multiple of 10 (each answer has a nought on the end) and explain their reasoning? On the same number line mark off divisions of 5 and count on from random numbers in multiples of 5. Can the children comment on their answers (answers which end in 0 and 5) and explain their reasoning? The children can then predict what a number line would look like showing multiples of 100.

(Individuals/pairs)

Working in pairs, use two number lines marked in divisions of 2s and 5s up to 100. Each child covers up single numbers on the lines and asks a partner what the missing number is. They could keep a record of their scores (1 point for each successful guess) and there could be a 'class champion'.

Differentiation

Low Attainers – Give the children some cut-out sections from a blank number square, with some numbers filled in. Can the children fill in the missing numbers?

High Attainers – Draw a 6 × 6 number square on 2 cm squared paper. Working in pairs, one child covers up some of the numbers and the other has to say which numbers are covered.

Plenary

Ask questions:

If I count in 2s from zero will I reach 29?
If I count in 5s from zero will I reach 34?
If I count in 10s from zero will I reach 90?

Lesson 3

Introduction

Can anyone give me 2 odd numbers that total 28?
Write an odd and an even number that total 25?
What are the multiples of 5 up to 60 and what are the multiples of 10 up to 200? Discuss with the class what they could use to help them if they do not know the answer (number lines, number grids, calculators).

Activities

Number puzzles (whole class/group)
Using calculators the children are only allowed to use the digits 2, 6 and 9 and × and + once each.
Make: The largest odd number you can. The largest even number you can. The smallest odd number you can. The smallest even number you can. A number which is a multiple of 10. A number between 50 and 60.

(Individuals/pairs)
Use calculators and + and × once each. Choose three digits which will give you the smallest odd number possible. All the digits must be different. Choose three more which cannot give you an odd number. Display any double digit number less than 50. Use any signs, as often as you wish. Choose two single digit numbers up to 10. Use them to make the double digit number a multiple of 10. How many steps did you need?

Differentiation

Low Attainers – Use the numbers 2 and 5 and the signs +, × and = and make as many different answers between 10 and 100 as possible.
High Attainers – Use a computer program to develop a strategy for rearranging the order of objects.

Plenary

Check the answers to their work in pairs. Who took the fewest number of steps?

Lesson 4

Introduction

Numbers which follow each other are called consecutive numbers. 1 and 2 are consecutive numbers; so are 5, 6 and 7.
Some totals can be made by adding two consecutive numbers
e.g. $3 + 4 = 7$ $5 + 6 = 11$
Find other totals under 20 which can be made by adding two consecutive numbers, three consecutive numbers or even four consecutive numbers.

Activities

Make a hundred (whole class/group)
Ask the class to choose any number from these:
8, 4, 9, 6, 5, 3, 2, 1, 7, 10
Tell the children that the number they choose will be changed to 100. Write the number down. Double it. Add the number you first chose. Add 6. Divide by 3. Take away the number you first chose. Multiply by 5. Multiply by 5. Double it 100! Choose another number to see if it works again.

(Individuals/pairs)
Using calculators and working in pairs:

a) Make up to 100. Enter a number less than 100. With one addition the partner has to make it up to 100. Take turns.
b) Reduce to 100. Enter any three-digit number. With one subtraction your partner has to reduce it to 100. Take turns.
c) Reverse a number. Enter any two digit-number. By adding or subtracting your partner has to reverse the digits. If it is done in one step, score 3 points. If it is done in two steps, score 1 point.

Differentiation

Low Attainers – Play 'Snakes and Ladders' and count how many spaces are missed if you go down a snake or up a ladder.
High Attainers – Make up their own number machines:
IN——25 OUT—— 50
What has the machine done?

Plenary

Try out some more numbers in the Make a hundred game and complete Copymaster 51.

Lesson 5

Introduction

Use number cards 0 to 20. Write on the board the numbers 7 and 5 and state that they have a difference of 2. How many other pairs can you find? They must all have a difference of 2. Can you use all the cards? Choose another difference. Find as many pairs as you can. Can you use all the cards?

Activities

What a difference (whole class/group)
Using calculators ask the children to put the number 24 on the display. The rule is you are only allowed to subtract and you must get to the answer 4. How many different ways can the children find?
$24 - 12 = 12$ $12 - 8 = 4$
Make sure that the calculations are recorded. As the children get used to the calculations harder numbers can be used.

(Individuals/pairs)
Work in pairs with a peg board and pegs per pair. Arrange eleven pegs on the board in two columns: 6 in the first column and 5 in the second column. The columns have a difference of one peg. Rearrange the pegs to make other differences. Record all the differences you can make. Which differences below 10 are impossible to make? Why is this? Now use 12 pegs and repeat. Without using the pegboard, what differences are possible if you have 14 pegs? Follow up with Copymaster 52.

Differentiation

Low Attainers – Write all the numbers you can make on an HTU abacus with only three beads.
High Attainers – Write all the numbers you can make on an HTU abacus using five beads.

Plenary

Discuss the use of more difficult numbers in the whole class session and the amout of numbers made from the HTU abacus. Explain Homework 26.

Theme 7 Mental calculations

Objectives

- To begin to find remainders after division
- To round up or down after division
- To use known facts and place value to multiply and divide mentally
- To choose appropriate number operations and calculation methods to solve money or 'real-life' word problems with one or two steps
- To explain and record methods and check results

Vocabulary

double, times, multiply, share, half, divide, left over, remainder, operation, sign, symbol, number sentence

Resources

Place value material, cubes and counters, multiplication squares and 0–100 number lines.
Copymasters 53 and 54. Homework 27.

Assessment

At the end of this theme is the pupil able to:

- Understand the operation of multiplication;
- Understand the operation of division;
- Understand the idea of a remainder;
- Use their knowledge of number facts and place value to multiply or divide mentally;
- Solve simple word problems?

Mental maths starters 3, 5, 10

Lesson 1

Introduction

Explain that this lesson is about multiplication and when we might use it in everyday life. Remind the children that we use multiplication when equal numbers of things are needed. *For example, 6 children each need to bring 10 coloured pencils to school this is the same as $10 + 10 + 10 + 10 + 10 + 10$ we can write this as 10×6 or 6×10 we say '6 lots of 10' or '6 times 10.'*
Show this as counting the same size of step on the number line.

Activities

How many (whole class/group)
The children can suggest some other times when they might need to use multiplication.
Most of you will be working on money problems because we often buy several small items that are the same, such as packets of crisps. Display a list of small items they might buy or have some pictures with prices under them. Ask questions about buying multiples of different items for the children to solve mentally. Remind them that doubling is the same as multiplying by 2.

(Individuals/pairs)
Work in groups on multiples of 10 and the effect of multiplying any number by 10. Initially work on 10 sets of a number, such as 10 sets of 2, showing how this can be recorded on a place value mat. Start with numbers less than 10 but ask the children to predict what the answers might be if they multiplied larger numbers by 10. Can they model some of the larger numbers using cubes? This is a good time to use a calculator so that they can see the pattern of multiplying larger numbers by 10.

Differentiation

Low Attainers – Write some everyday problems together involving multiplication by 10, such as 10 toffee apples and 10 packets of crisps.
High Attainers – Write some everyday problems involving multiplication by 10.

Plenary

Children can demonstrate what they have been learning about multiplication by 10.

Lesson 2

Introduction

Draw an array on the board and ask the children to work in pairs and write some statements describing it. Write the statements on the board adding any they might have missed out. Use the vocabulary of 'sets of' and 'lots of' as well as
$3 + 3 + 3 + 3 = 12, 4 + 4 + 4 = 12, 3(4) = 12$ and $4(3) = 12$

Activities

Finding products (whole class/group)
Ask one of the children to come to the board, throw a large dice and make a 'stick' that length from cubes, *e.g. 5 cubes long if 5 was thrown.* Ask a second child to throw the dice and make that many 'sticks' the same length as the 5, *e.g. 2 'sticks' of 5 if 2 is thrown.* Draw the array and write the number statements using multiplication. On a large blank 100 square show how this array could be drawn and coloured. Repeat the dice throws and use a different colour to show these new numbers as an array on the 100 square.

(Individuals/pairs)
Prepare some multiplication squares large enough for the children, working in pairs, to work out the answers and write them in the squares.

	1	2	3	4	5
1	*	**	***	****	*****
2	**	****	******	********	**********
3					

As they are working discuss the shapes the children are making. Why do they think all the models make rectangles and squares?

Differentiation

Low Attainers – Ask them to take a handful of cubes and make them into a square or rectangle.
High Attainers – As above but then draw the shape and write about it using words and numbers.

Plenary

Discuss the chart that was produced earlier in the lesson and show the links with division. *$3 \times 4 = 12$, $4 \times 3 = 12$ so 12 divided by $3 = 4$ and 12 divided $4 = 3$.*

Lesson 3

Introduction

You will need a large area to introduce this lesson. Ask the children to divide into pairs with any left over coming to stand by you. Discuss the number of groups of 2 that can be made with everyone in the class and how many left (make sure there is an odd number to start with). Get the children to regroup in 3s and again see if any are left. Continue with an increasing number of children to a group. Explain that sometimes when they are dividing a number of objects into equal sets there might be some left over and that these are called the remainder. Show them how this is written as a number sentence.

Activities

Leftovers (whole class/group)

Working in groups of four they should each take some cubes using one hand. If the cubes can be grouped in 2s with none left over, they can score 2. If the cubes can be grouped in 3s with none left over, they score 3 and so on. Do this up to 9s. What number of cubes, including, but not bigger than 20, would they most like to take? Help the children to record some of their findings.

(Individuals/pairs)

Working in groups, give each group some collections of small numbers of counting items in bags. Ask them to find out if these can be put into equal sets of 2 and to draw pictures of what they have done and write number sentences, using the division symbol. Then put them into groups of 3 to draw and write.

Differentiation

Low Attainers – Ask this group to find out which numbers between 1 and 20 will divide exactly by 2 and which have a remainder.
High Attainers – Tell this group to imagine they have 24 biscuits; they must find out how these could be shared equally between different numbers of children.

Plenary

Pose some mental division problems, both with and without remainders.

Lesson 4

Introduction

Explain that when doing division we sometimes have to decide whether to round up or to round down. Use the tables in the classroom as an example. These often seat either 6 or 4 depending on their shape. Relate the activity to your own class. *e.g. There are 28 children in the class and they can sit 6 to a table. How many tables will be needed?* Explain that the number of tables has to be rounded up so that everone has a place. Give an example of rounding down. *A child has 55p to spend on stickers. How many packs costing 10p each could be bought?* Explain why the remainder is rounded down in this instance.

Activities

The leftover bit (whole class/group)

Keep as a whole class. Give more examples of each situation mentioned in the introduction, asking the children to explain whether the answer has to be rounded up or down and why this is the case. Use a collection of containers such as different sized egg boxes. Tell the children that they have, for example, 20 eggs that need to be packed in boxes of 6 and you want them to find out how many boxes will be needed for that many eggs. How might they record what they have done both in pictures and in numbers? *What if the same number of eggs are to be packed with 12 in a box?* Continue by working with different numbers and size of grouping. Explain that for most of this work they are rounding the numbers up because all the eggs need to be put into containers. Give them an example where rounding down is more appropriate *e.g. I have 50p. How many sweets costing 15p can I buy?*

(Individuals/pairs)

Work through Copymaster 53. This worksheet requires the children to make decisions about rounding numbers up or down depending on the situation. For some of the questions it might help if the children use money or practical equipment to help them make decisions about the remainders.

Differentiation

Low Attainers – Explore division with remainders on a calculator, *e.g. enter the number 24 and subtract 5. How many times can 5 be subtracted? What number is left in the calculator?*
High Attainers – Find out some of the times they use division at home, *e.g. sharing out the cutlery to lay the table or dividing a packet of biscuits between members of the family.*

Plenary

Think of times when we use division in our everyday lives.

Lesson 5

Introduction

Write some 2-digits numbers on the board. Remind the children about doubling and halving numbers and give them some examples to calculate quickly. Can they make the link with multiplying and dividing by 2? Point to one of the numbers on the board and ask them to show you its double. Can they show you the answer if it is doubled again? Write the number with the two doubles on the board. Can children suggest another way of doing this? What if the number is halved and halved again?

Activities

Number lines and squares (whole class/group)

Challenge them to decide how to find the answer to 21×8 by using doubling. Ask them to work in pairs and then share their method with the class. Did anyone else do it the same way? Display a large 0–100 number line and 100 square. Record some hops forward as *$2 + 2 + 2 + 2 + 2 + 2 = 12$; 6 lots of 2 steps makes 12.* Then show them how division 'undoes' that. Record *$12 - 2 - 2 - 2 - 2 - 2 - 2 = 0$* and write it on the board as *12 divided by 2 = 6*

(Individuals/pairs)

Ask the children to use multiplication squares to show the answer to 5×4. After trying several examples, ask if they think the square can be used for division by starting with the answer to a multiplication problem. Try some examples. Use Copymaster 54 to give the children some multiplication square problems and discuss how they might find the missing numbers.

Differentiation

Low Attainers – Do some practical sharing activities in the classroom, *e.g. I have 6 pieces of paper. How many pieces can 3 children have?*
High Attainers – Numbers are doubled twice and then they have to find the number to divide by to get back to the original number *e.g. $3 \times 2 - 6 \times 2 - 12$ divided by ? – 3.*

Plenary

What did you find easy today? Have you learned something new today? Go through Homework 27.

Theme 8 Fractions

Objectives

- To compare two familiar fractions
- To know that $\frac{1}{2}$ lies between $\frac{1}{4}$ and $\frac{3}{4}$
- To estimate a simple fraction of a shape

Vocabulary

part, fraction, one whole, one half, one quarter, three quarters, one third, two thirds, one tenth

Resources

String and pegs, 0–20 number cards, paper rectangles, chocolate sweets, buttons and cubes.
Copymasters 55 and 56. Homework 28.

Assessment

At the end of this theme is the pupil able to:

- Recognise and find simple fractions;
- Recognise the equivalence between them;
- Compare two simple fractions in practical contexts?

Mental maths starter 1

Lesson 1

Introduction

Prepare a long 'washing line.' Ask the children to put cards numbered 1–10 on it in the correct place, with wide spaces between. Ask the class questions involving fractions: *What comes half way between 2 and 3? Write the number half way between $10\frac{1}{2}$ and 11.* They can write their answers on blank cards and hang them in place on the line. Continue until all the halves and quarters between 0–10 have been written.

Activities

Number line fractions (whole class/group)

Practise counting along the prepared number line using the whole numbers and the halves. Can the children continue counting beyond the numbers on the line? Now count along the number line using all the fractions. *What comes next on the number line?* Explain that they will be making their own number lines beginning with a fraction number line to 10 that includes the halves and quarters. Ask them to find half of some of the numbers and also a quarter of the same number. Explain that finding a half of a half is the same as finding a quarter. Ask if they can find a quarter of all the numbers up to 10. Start with 1.

(Individuals/pairs)

Give each child a long strip of paper. Ask them to draw a long line, mark where 0 comes and then write all the numbers out up to 5, equally spaced out. Next they write in all the halves. Using only their 0–5 cards they turn over two cards and find the number that comes half way.

Differentiation

Low Attainers – Give the children activities that involve working with halves and quarters.
High Attainers – Extend the number line to 0–20 and cards 0–20, including halves.

Plenary

Count in halves from 0 to 10. Count in quarters from 0 to 10.

Lesson 2

Introduction

Each child needs a paper rectangle. Ask them to fold the rectangle into half to make another rectangle. Discuss how they know what a half is and remind them that both halves need to be the same or equal. Ask them to fold the shape again and open it out. How many pieces are there now? Are they all the same size? Show them how to write the word a **quarter** and get them to write it on each piece. Fold the paper again into quarters and fold again. Again count the pieces and ask what these might be called and how an **eighth** might be written. Ask them to write the word on the back of each fraction of paper.

Activities

Who has most? (whole class/group)

Play 'Show me the fraction.'
Show me half. Fold the paper so that you can see the fraction.
Show me two-eighths.
Ask for the equivalent in quarters and how many eighths are left.
Show me two quarters. How many halves is that? How many eighths is that?
Fold a square in half. Does everyone have the same shape?
How many ways can the square be folded in half? (A rectangle and a triangle.)

(Individuals/pairs)

Continue with folding paper to help the children identify equivalent fractions using halves, quarters and eighths, then to record either with gummed paper shapes or by drawing. This will help them to show practically that $\frac{2}{4}$ is the same as $\frac{1}{2}$ and so on.

Differentiation

Low Attainers – Draw shapes and colour in halves and quarters.
High Attainers – They should start to identify fractions of a shape that are coloured and fractions that are not coloured.

Plenary

Can you have a bigger half of anything?
Stress that each fraction of a whole is the same size and write the equivalent fractions on the board:
$1 = \frac{2}{2} = \frac{4}{4}$ etc.

Lesson 3

Introduction

Draw a number of rectangles on the board. Divide the rectangles into grids of 12 small squares. Ask the children for suggestions as to how they could colour in $\frac{1}{2}$ of one of the grids (one way would be to count up the number of small squares and divide by two). *If $\frac{1}{2}$ of the grid is coloured in what fraction is not coloured in?* Repeat the exercise for $\frac{1}{4}$ being coloured in and $\frac{3}{4}$ not coloured. Are there different ways of colouring the fractions/squares in?

Activities

Fractions of shapes (whole class/group)

If you divided a bar of chocolate (some bars are divided into cubes and are very useful for this exercise) into 4 equal pieces and kept 3 of the pieces you would be very 'greedy' and only leave 1 piece for anyone else. If you divided another bar of chocolate into 8 equal parts and took 6 of the parts for yourself would you be just as greedy? *Is $\frac{3}{4}$ the same as $\frac{6}{8}$? What other fractions are equivalent to each other?* Take 20 cubes (5 green, 5 blue, 5 yellow, 5 red). Make a shape using half the cubes. Make a shape using quarter of the cubes.

(Individuals/pairs)

Ask the children to work through Copymaster 55, which will involve colouring in different parts of various shapes. They can work in pairs and use plenty of apparatus.

Differentiation

Low Attainers – Ask this group to divide strips of paper into various fractions. *If you divide this into 3 equal bits you get thirds. If you divide this into 10 equal bits you get tenths.*
High Attainers – *What is a third of 12 melons?* 12 divided by 3 = 4
What is a third of 18 melons? 18 divided by 3 = 6

Plenary

Start to talk about finding fractions of different amounts:
$\frac{3}{4}$ of 12 = 12 divided by 4 then times by 3 i.e. 12 divided into 4 equal parts and taking 3 of the parts.

Lesson 4

Introduction

Gather together plenty of everyday objects and tell the children that they are going to find fractions of the different amounts. To do that the children have to count each group of items first. Then the children have to be clear that they are going to divide each group into *equal* amounts depending on which fraction is involved.

Activities

Fractions of? (whole class/group)

Collect together a number of cubes, buttons or sweets and count them in front of the class e.g. *There are a total of 16 cubes.* Then explain that you are going to find $\frac{1}{4}$ of the cubes. In order to do that the 16 cubes will need to be divided into 4 groups (the denominator tells us that it is 4.) Use 4 children to represent each group and share the cubes out until there are none left. *How many cubes has each child got?* Each child has a $\frac{1}{4}$ of the cubes. Therefore $\frac{1}{4}$ = 4 cubes. How many cubes make $\frac{3}{4}$? ($3 \times 4 = 12$ cubes.)

(Individuals/pairs)

Working in pairs ask the children to work through Copymaster 56. This will involve finding fractions of an assortment of everyday objects and stating what is left when the fraction is taken away.

Differentiation

Low Attainers – Keep to halves and quarters of the objects on display e.g. *How many sweets will I have if I take $\frac{1}{2}$?*
High Attainers – Find $\frac{1}{2}$ of all the numbers up to 30.

Plenary

Help the children to recognise that finding $\frac{1}{2}$ of a group of objects is the same as finding $\frac{2}{4}$ or $\frac{4}{8}$.

Lesson 5

Introduction

Fill different sized containers with varying amounts of water or coloured liquid. Then ask:
Is this container about $\frac{1}{2}$ full?
Is this container about $\frac{1}{4}$ full?
What fraction of this container is full? Is it $\frac{1}{2}$ or $\frac{3}{4}$ or $\frac{2}{8}$?

Activity

Approximate fractions (whole class/group)

Arrange some of the children in front of the class. *What fraction of the children are standing in front of you?* Give the children a choice of answers if they find it difficult. Also ask *If $\frac{1}{4}$ is in front of you how many are still sitting in their places?* Extend this into assembly time and ask what fraction of the whole school is one particular class. Model questions such as *If one class goes swimming what fraction of the school will be left?*

(Individuals/pairs)

Put a series of spelling/tables test scores on the board (they can be made up if necessary) and ask each pair to tally how many people got 10 out of 10, 9 out of 10 etc. Then calculate the fraction of the class that got full marks etc.

Differentiation

Low Attainers – Only work with a few scores i.e. 5 or 10 out of 10, 4, 9 out of 10, 1or 8 out of 10. Say what fraction achieved 10 out of 10.
High Attainers – Explore their own tables and spelling results and work out the fraction of their scores that were 5 out of 10 etc.

Plenary

Who would like $\frac{1}{2}$ of these sweets and who would like $\frac{2}{4}$?
Who would like $\frac{1}{3}$ of these sweets and who would like $\frac{1}{4}$?
(12 sweets is an easy number to work with.)

Theme 9 Addition, subtraction and time

Objectives

- To add using pencil and paper procedures
- To use known number facts and place value to add/subtract mentally
- To use informal pencil and paper methods to support, record or explain TU-TU and HTU-TU
- To be able to use a calendar and solve time word problems

Vocabulary

more, add, total, altogether, equals, minus, subtract, difference between, century, calendar, date

Resources

Assorted clocks, a calendar, 0–9 numeral cards, number snap, dartboard shape, dice, Base 10 apparatus.
Copymasters 57 and 58. Homework 29.

Assessment

At the end of this theme is the pupil able to:

- Understand the operation of subtraction and the related vocabulary;
- Use known number facts and place value to add or subtract a pair of numbers mentally;
- Use pencil and paper methods for additions that cannot be done mentally;
- Use a calendar;
- Solve problems involving time?

Mental maths starters 2, 6, 9

Lesson 1

Introduction

Revise adding pairs of numbers on the board and ask the children what they think will be a good way to add them. Can they show the others their method on the board? Are the answers different if they are done in a different order?

Activities

Addition (whole class/group)

Today we will be using what we know about numbers that add up to 10 or 20 and so on to help us add several numbers together. Work with some examples: $46 + 14 + 13$ and $4 + 51 + 6 + 9$. Repeat the calculations by writing the numbers in a different order. Use some examples where three numbers total 10, *e.g.* $1 + 12 + 6 + 3 + 8$.

(Individuals/pairs)

On some large sheets of paper write about four or five 2-digit numbers that can be added to make multiples of 10, *e.g.* $34 + 45 + 15 + 16$. Ask the children to work in pairs and decide how they are going to add the numbers, using the method used in the whole class activity. They can then write the numbers in a different order and try a different method. Talk with them about the ways of adding the numbers and discuss which method is the most helpful.

Differentiation

Low Attainers – Play 'Snap'. The numbers to be 'snapped' must add up to 10.
High Attainers – Do some 'dartboard' activities. What totals can be made with three (or more) 'throws'?

Plenary

Does it matter which order the numbers are written in?
Ask the children to suggest what happens.
What happens if the smaller number is put first?

Lesson 2

Introduction

Write the calculation $14 + 58 =$ on the board. Use the 100 square to show the children how this can be done by starting on the 14, counting 50 down in 10s and then counting on 8 more (or alternatively, 6 more to get to 70 and then counting on the remaining 2). This example shows that by starting with 14, the 58 had to be partitioned into 5 tens plus a 6 to bring 64 up to 70 and the remaining 2 had to be added.

Activities

Mental calculations (whole class/group)

Ask if the example that has just been looked at could have been done in any other way. Could the 58 have been partitioned differently? $20 + 20 + 10 + 6 + 2$. If no one suggests putting the larger number first, ask if this could be done and then invite one of the children to show on the number square how much easier this would be. Try a different example, again putting a smaller number first, such as $7 + 64$.

(Individuals/pairs)

Working in pairs start by asking the children to turn over two of their 0–9 cards to make a 2-digit number. One more card is turned over and added mentally to the 2-digit number. Ask for any strategies the children have used. Continue by making 3-digit numbers and adding first a 1-digit, progressing to 2-digit numbers.

Differentiation

Low Attainers – Give these children two 1, 1, 2, 2, 3, 3 dice. Explain that they are to throw the dice to make a 2-digit number. They then repeat this to make a second 2-digit number, then add the two numbers putting the larger one first.
High Attainers – Using 1–9 cards make 3-digit numbers and add a multiple of 10.

Plenary

Play game of 'Back to Back' where two children stand back to back and are given an addition calculation, such as $6 + 184$. The first to answer chooses another child to stand back to back and another calculation is given.

Lesson 3

Introduction

It is important when discussing how to find the difference between two two-digit numbers to find out how the children would attempt to do it. Encourage any ideas which use methods they are familiar with, like number lines, Base 10 apparatus, the abacus and the calculator.

Activities

Subtraction (whole class/group)

Put this calculation method on the board 76 – 25

tens	*ones*	*tens*	*ones*	
*******	******	7	6	76
				– 25
**	*****	–2	5	____
pictorial recording		*recording sheet*		*symbolic form*

These three methods can be recorded in the children's books and repeated with other examples.

(Individuals/pairs)

Working in pairs the children work on alternative methods of subtraction. They use a number line and count up from the lower number to the higher in steps they can cope with easily.

127 – 35   35 = jump 5 to 40 then jump 60 to 100; jump 20 to 120 and then 7 to 127 = 92.

Differentiation

Low Attainers – Children can generate problems for themselves using dice or number cards.

High Attainers – Use formal methods of calculation to work on *HTU – TU* *e.g.*

```
  157
 – 46
 ____
```

Plenary

Discuss the calculation methods used and how successful they have been. Model some questions and ask the children which method is the most appropriate.

Lesson 4

Introduction

Begin by putting this rhyme on display:

Thirty days hath September, April, June and November;
All the rest have thirty-one,
Except February alone, which has twenty-eight days clear,
And twenty-nine in each leap year.

Discuss with the children how many days make each month and encourage them to learn the rhyme.

Activities

The calendar (whole class/group)

Ask the children to calculate the number of days in months put together e.g. *June and April, March and July.*

They will also need a copy of a calendar month ready to answer questions: *How many Tuesdays are there in May? What day is the 2nd of September?* They could also make a month clock with numbers 1–12 around the edge to match with the months of the year. Then they could use this to help with writing the date in numerals *e.g. 21st July 1992 = 21.7.92*

(Individuals/pairs)

Working on their own, children can write six dates which are important to them and say why they have chosen them. Then work through Copymaster 57 in pairs to consolidate what they have done.

Differentiation

Low Attainers – Write the names and dates of birth of some of the people in the class. Put them in order and make up questions about them.

High Attainers – Make up some questions for a friend about the year calendar. Check their answers.

Plenary

Write some of the class register on the board including dates of birth. Which child is the oldest? Which child is the youngest? Whose birthday is in June?

Lesson 5

Introduction

Remind the children that *analogue* clocks are the ones with hands and *digital* clocks just have numbers. *The big hand tells you the minutes past. The little hand tells you the hour.* Go through plenty of examples of telling the time with both clocks.

Activities

Time problems (whole class/group)

What sort of places do we visit and things do we do that require us to know the time? Look at a bus or train timetable (if they are too complicated, then make one up) and locate a train/bus that you could use to go from A to B. *How long does it take for the journey? How long do other journeys take? Which is the shortest journey and which is the longest? How long is the school day? How long do you have for PE every week?*

(Individuals/pairs)

Working in pairs use :, 5 and 0 as many times as you wish. Make different digital times and write them in order. Then work through Copymaster 58.

Differentiation

Low Attainers – Make a 'time line' for a school day for you or your class.

High Attainers – Think of times when it would be amusing if a.m. and p.m. times were changed.

Plenary

Plan a school trip. Draw the things you would do and see. Write times for each one. Explain Homework 29.

Theme 10 Venn and Carroll diagrams

Objectives
- To solve a given problem by organising and interpreting data in Venn and Carroll diagrams

Vocabulary
sort, set, represent, graph, chart, pictogram, diagram, table, list, count, tally, axis, label, title

Resources
Solid shapes of various colours,other collections of items suggested by the children.
Copymasters 59 and 60. Homework 30.

Assessment
At the end of this theme is the pupil able to:
- Solve a given problem by collecting, sorting and organising information in simple ways?

Mental maths starters 4, 5, 6, 8

Lesson 1

Introduction
Discuss the different ways of representing data. Revise the graphs that they have used already (bar charts). Revise how the information can be collected (tally charts/frequency tables). Also talk about topics that the children would like to investigate.

Activities
Carroll diagrams 1 (whole class/group)
Explain to the children that a **Carroll diagram** is a way of sorting things into groups, or sets.

	cube	not cube
red	1	2
not red	3	4

Draw the above example on the board and explain that in a box of shapes some shapes are red, some shapes are cubes and some are neither red nor cubes. You can use a Carroll diagram to sort these shapes into four sets. In box 1 go cubes that are red. In box 2 go cubes that are not red. In box 3 there are shapes that are red but are not cubes. In box 4 there are shapes that are not red and not cubes.

(Individuals/pairs)
Working in pairs ask the children to copy the diagram from the board with the cubes in their correct boxes. Then ask the group where they would place a red cylinder, a yellow sphere and a blue cube. They can then test each other with the placement of other shapes in the Carroll diagram.

Differentiation
Low Attainers – Collect their own data on a topic of their own choosing *e.g. even and odd numbers.*
High Attainers – Draw their own Carroll diagram on a topic of their choosing.

Plenary
Ask the children to explain what is in each box and why. Include one or two other solid shapes in the diagram.

Lesson 2

Introduction
Write down the multiples of 5 up to 50. Write down as many 2-D shapes as possible. Write down a list of books from the library. Explain to the class that they are going to use this information, sort it out and enter it into a Carroll diagram.

Activities
Carroll diagram 2 (whole class/group)
Choose one of the sets of information or look at
Jack wants to file his collection of numbers. Put the numbers 5, 14, 33, 42 and 55 in the right box in his filing system.

	under 30	not under 30
even numbers		
not even numbers		

Look at a completed Carroll diagram

	with pics	without pics
animals	John Sarah Andrew	Bill
no animals	Peter Rachel	Kim

Ask the following questions. *How many children are reading picture books about animals? Which girl is reading a picture book not about animals? What is Bill reading? Which children are not reading picture books?*

(Individuals/pairs)
Working in pairs take one of the Carroll diagrams that have been produced and write some questions for the chart that a partner can answer.

Differentiation
Low Attainers – Use just part of a Carroll diagram and compose their own questions.
High Attainers – Respond to questions such as *What information should we collect, and how? How shall we organise it?*

Plenary
Discuss some of the questions that have been posed. Comment on possible improvements.

Lesson 3

Introduction

Return to talking about the different ways of representing data. A **Venn diagram** is a drawing to show how different things can be sorted into groups. The groups are known as sets. In some places the sets in a Venn diagram overlap or intersect. Things that belong to two or more different sets at once are placed in those intersections.

Activities

Venn diagrams (whole class/group)

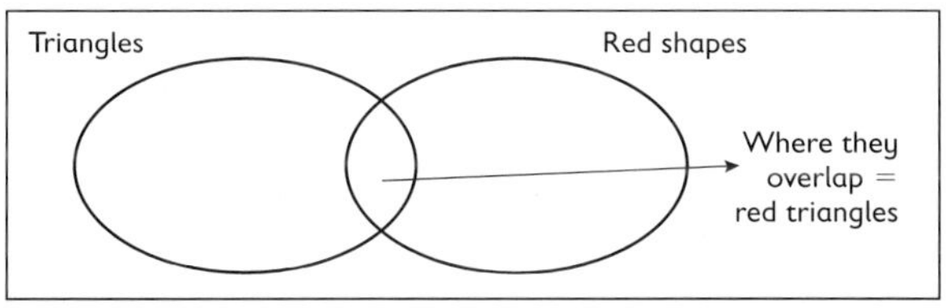

Collect together a box of solid shapes of different colours and tell the class they are going to sort out the shapes using the diagram as above *i.e.*

TRIANGLES will fit in the diagram
RED SHAPES will fit in the diagram
RED TRIANGLES will fit in the diagram
The rest of the shapes will remain outside.

(Individuals/pairs)

Using Copymaster 59 and working in pairs, sort information into each of the Venn diagrams.

Differentiation

Low Attainers – Sort objects/information into one 'oval' only (what doesn't fit remains outside).
High Attainers – Compose questions about the demonstration Venn diagram.

Plenary

Is using a Venn diagram a quicker way of sorting information than a Carroll diagram? What advantages does it have?

Lesson 4

Introduction

Tell the children that they are going to gather information about odd and even numbers under these headings:
Even numbers
Numbers with a 3 in
Even numbers with a 3 in
Numbers that are not even and do not have a 3 in

Activities

How to sort it? (whole class/group)

Using the information gathered label and complete the following Venn diagram:

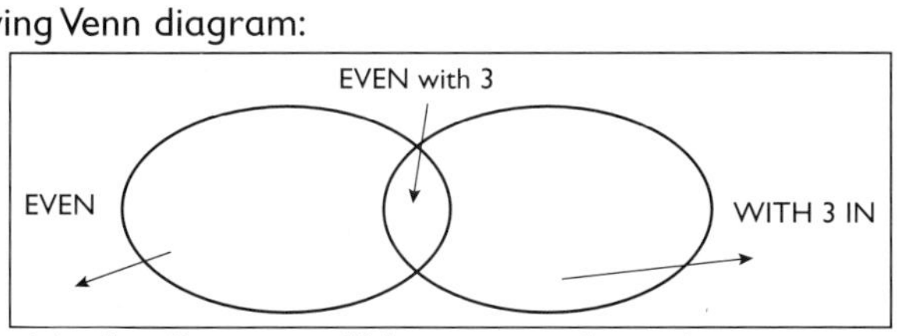

** Outside the diagram will be any numbers that are not even and do not have 3 in them.

(Individuals/pairs)

Ask the class to look at the following labelled Venn diagram and fill it in.

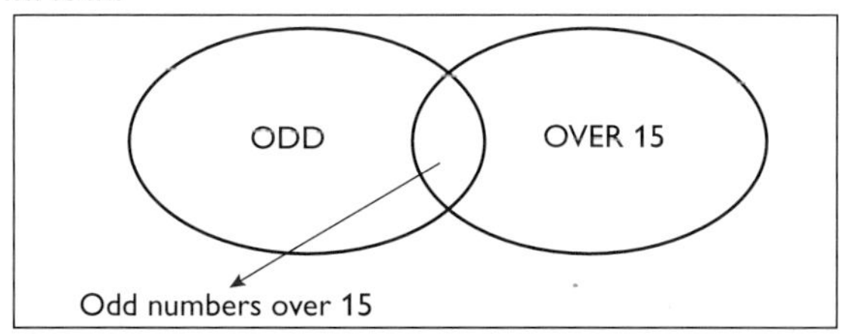

Differentiation

Low Attainers – Produce a Venn diagram for the girls and boys in the class who have blonde hair.
High Attainers – Produce a Venn diagram for the male and female teachers who wear glasses.
(These ideas can be changed to fit the situation in your class or school.)

Plenary

Discuss the language of using Venn diagrams and how to explain what they show.

Lesson 5

Introduction

Make a list of numbers from 1 to 20.
Write out the 2× table on the board.
Ask the children what numbers in both lists are under 10.

Activities

Grouping things (whole class/group)

Refer to the information above and put ***4, 5, 6, 3, 16, 13, 26, 56* etc** onto the Venn diagram.

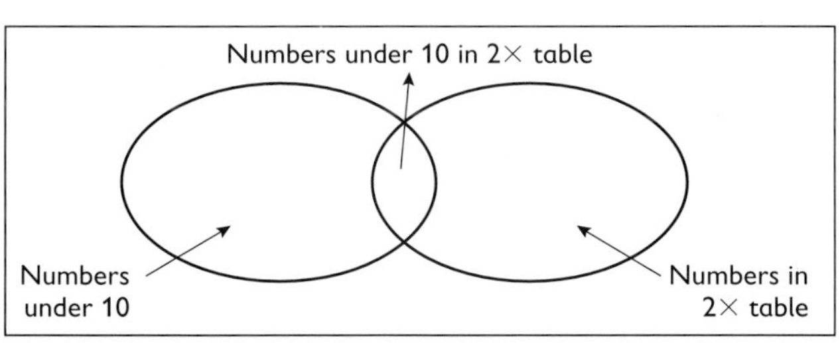

numbers that are not in the 2× table or under 10 are outside the two ovals.

(Individuals/pairs)

Working in pairs use the information on Copymaster 60 to make up and label a suitable diagram for each piece of information.

Differentiation

Low Attainers – Repeat the diagram from the main part of the lesson with different numbers.
High Attainers – Repeat the diagram from the main part of the lesson and fill in for the 5× table.

Plenary

Discuss all the different ways the children have gathered and represented their information, including bar charts and block graphs, during the year.

Addition vocabulary

9 add 3 = 12
10 add 5 = 15
6 plus 4 = 10

The total of 3, 5 and 2 equals 10

Total · Plus · Add · All mean +

Fill in the missing words in these statements:

4 ________ 7 = 11

3 ________ 8 equals 11

6 ________ 9 ________ 15

The ________ of 4, 6 and 2 equals 12

Fill in the missing symbols in these sentences:

4 ☐ 9 = 13

5 ☐ 12 = 17

6 + 20 ☐ 26

4 ☐ 12 ☐ 16

Subtraction vocabulary

12 take away 6 = 6
20 subtract 10 equals 10
15 minus 7 = 8

Take away Subtract Minus All mean —

Fill in the missing words in these statements:

9 ________ 6 = 3

12 ________ 5 ________ 7

20 ________ 2 ________ 18

12 ________ 2 ________ 10

Fill in the missing symbols in these sentences:

12 ☐ 9 = 3

15 ☐ 7 = 8

20 − 2 ☐ 18

15 ☐ 7 = 8

Shopping 1

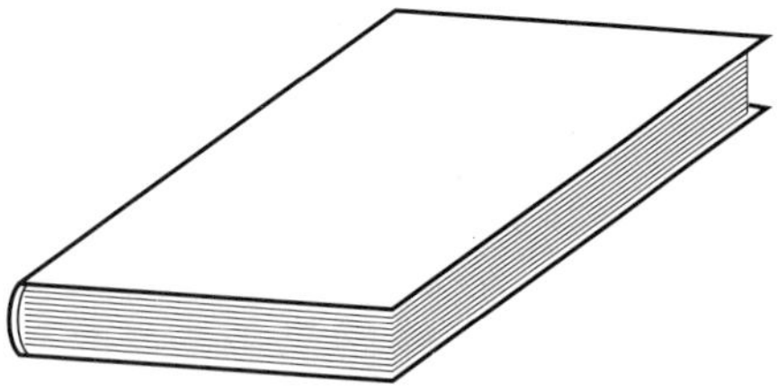

Book 35p

Pen 25p

Notepad 40p

Chocolate 30p

Doll 45p

Ball 50p

Choose 2 items from those above.

Which is the cheapest? Put a ring around it.

How much do they cost added together?

Eg Book = 35p (Pen = 25p) 60p

Cheapest

		Cost		Cost	Total
1.		= ___		= ___	________
2.		= ___		= ___	________
3.		= ___		= ___	________
4.		= ___		= ___	________
5.		= ___		= ___	________

Shopping 2

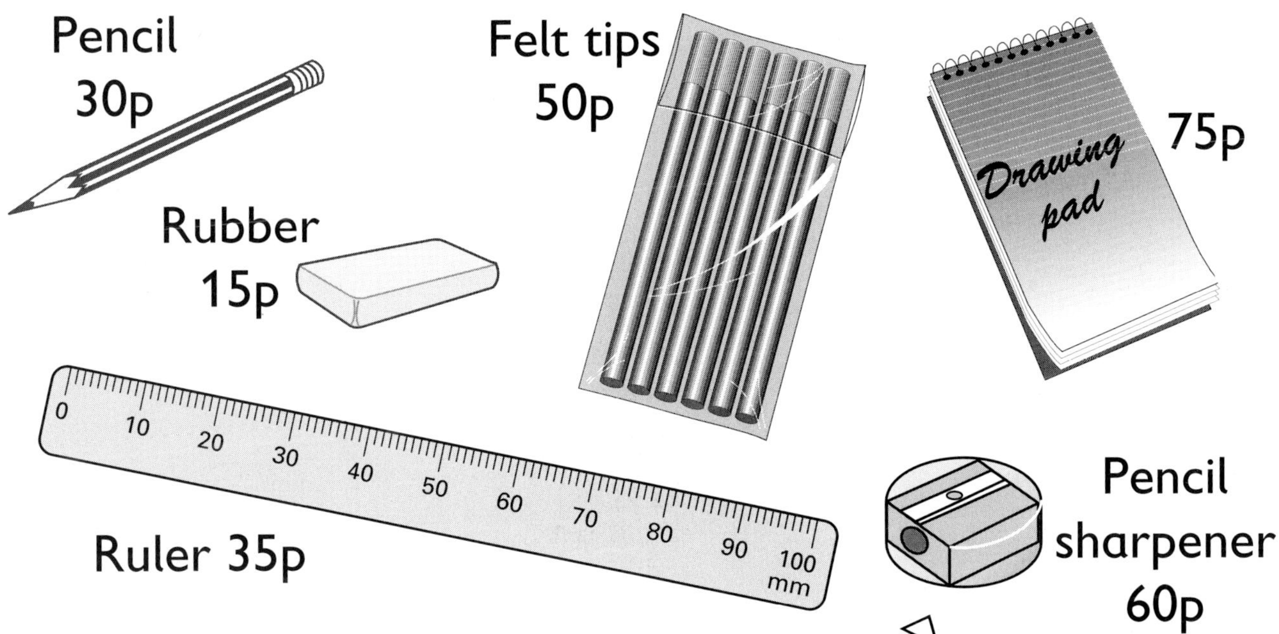

Choose 2 items from those above.

1) Which is the most expensive? Put a circle around it.

2) What is the difference between the two prices?

Eg (Pencil = 30p) Rubber = 15p 15p

Most expensive

		Cost		Cost	Difference
1.		= ___		= ___	___________
2.		= ___		= ___	___________
3.		= ___		= ___	___________
4.		= ___		= ___	___________
5.		= ___		= ___	___________

Clock faces

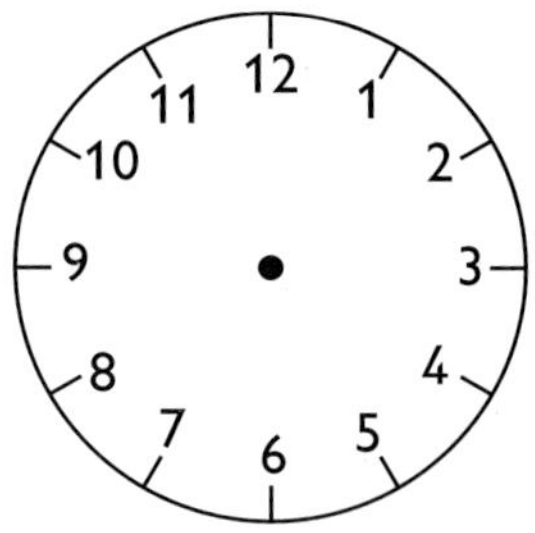

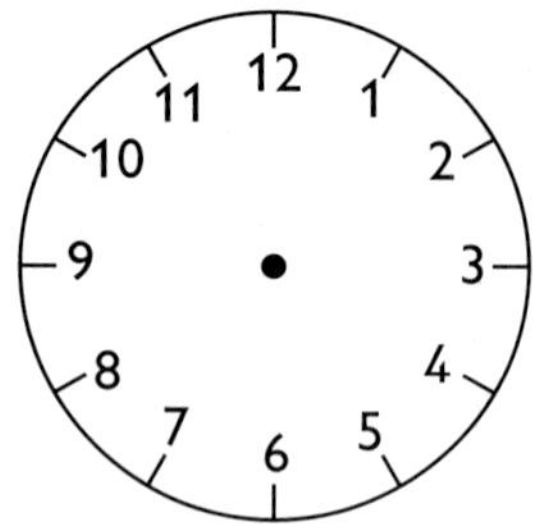

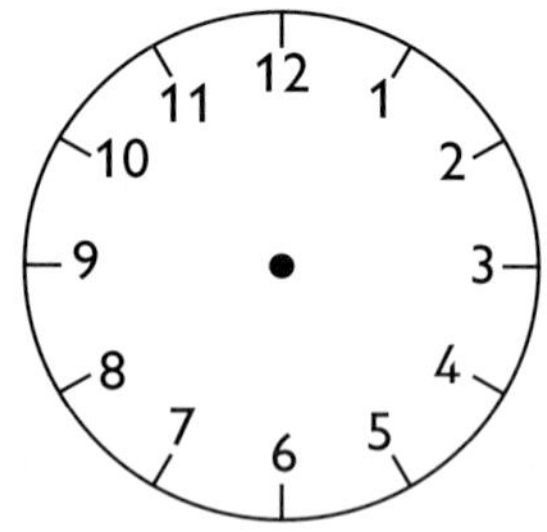

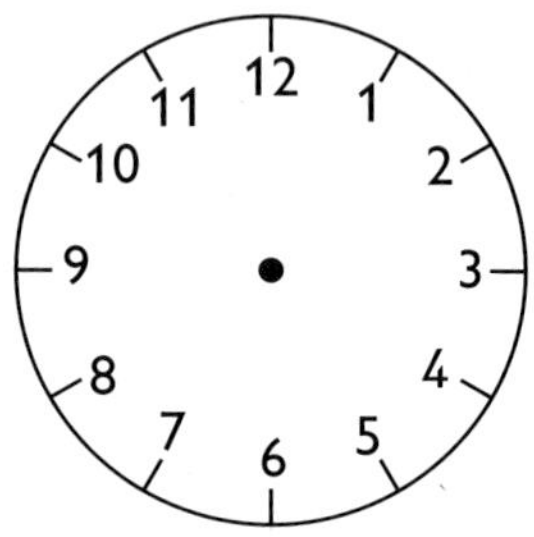

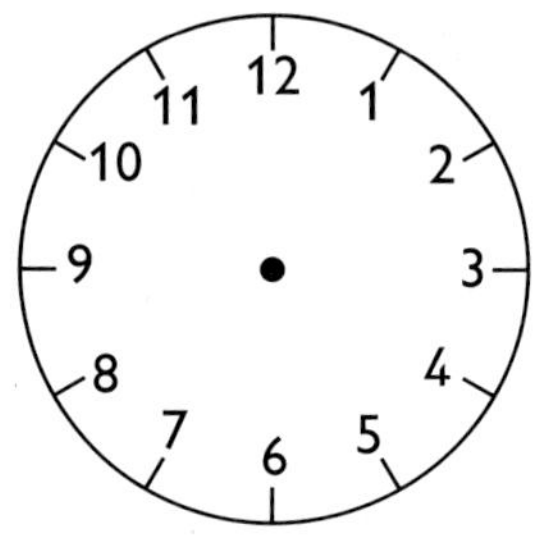

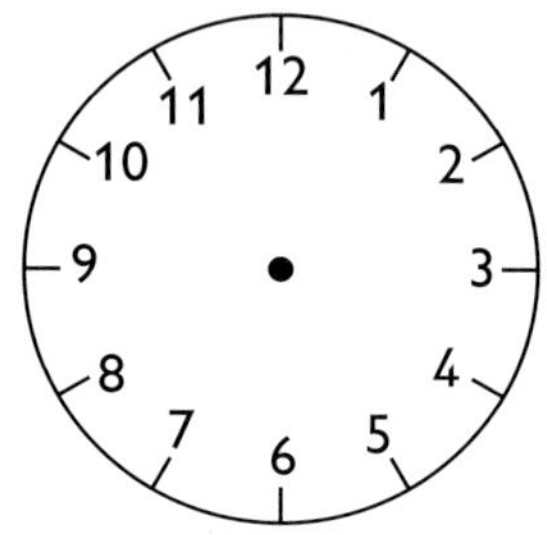

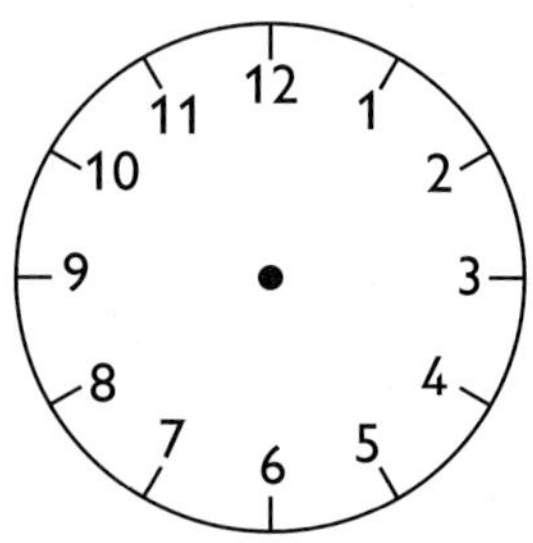

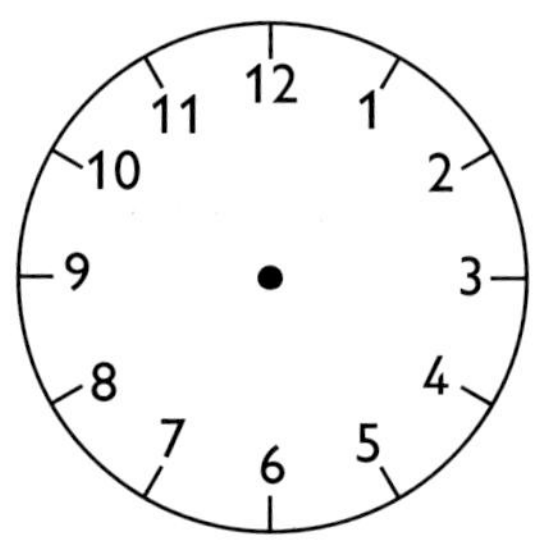

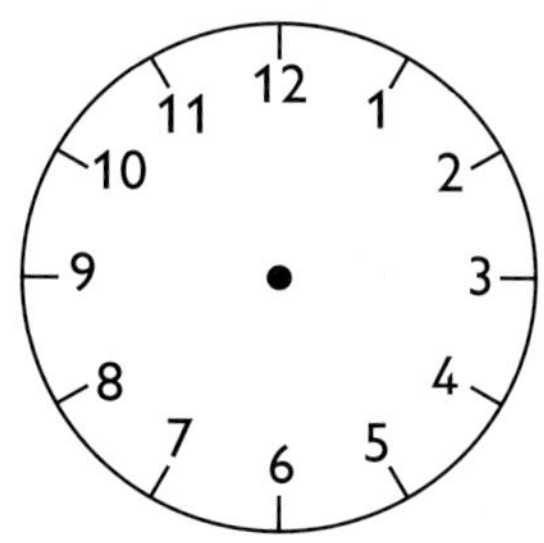

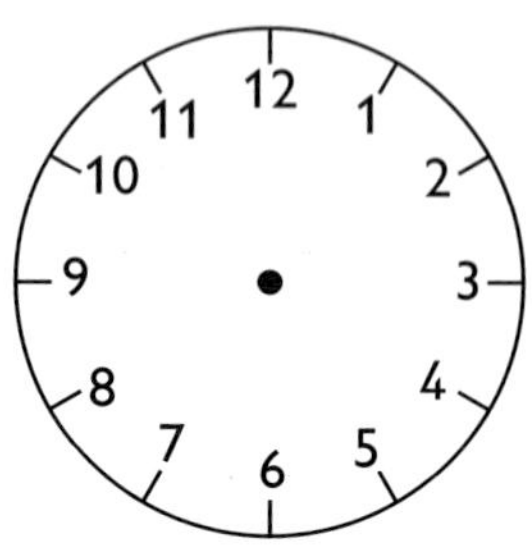

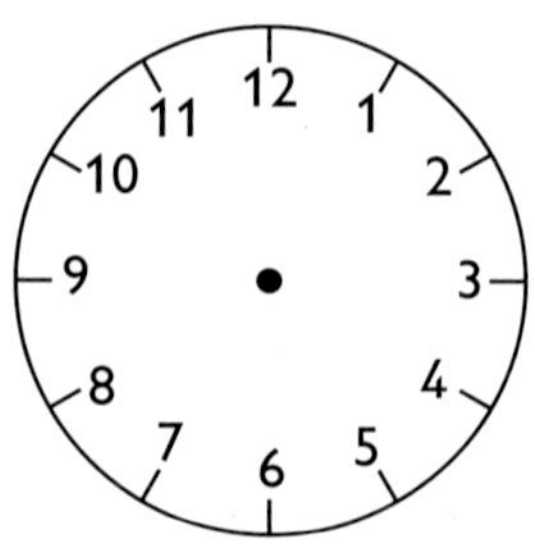

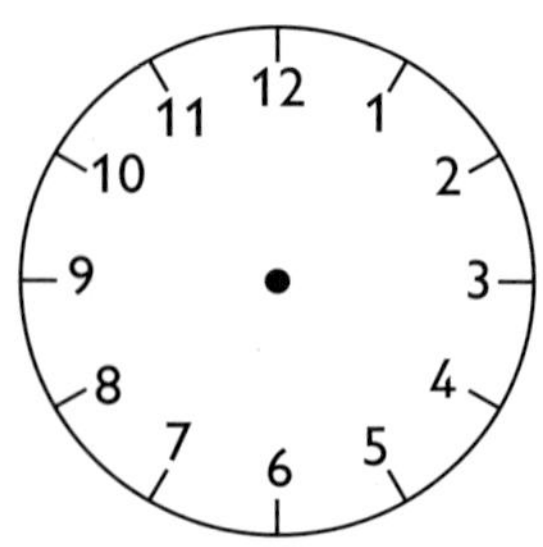

Clock faces

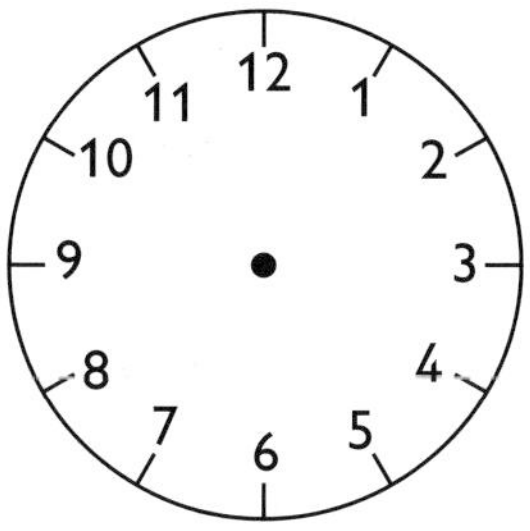
12 1 2 3 4 5 6 7 8 9 10 11

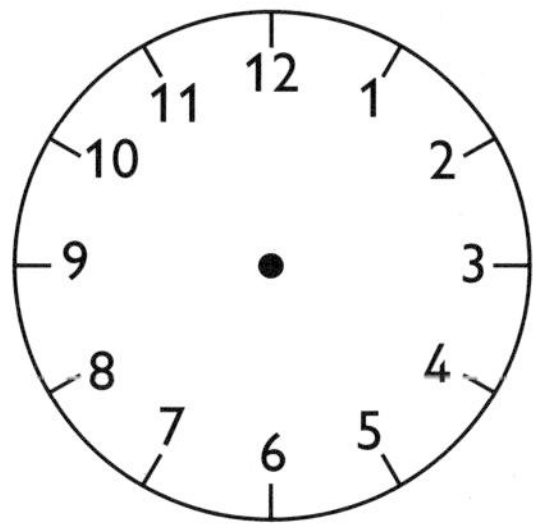
12 1 2 3 4 5 6 7 8 9 10 11

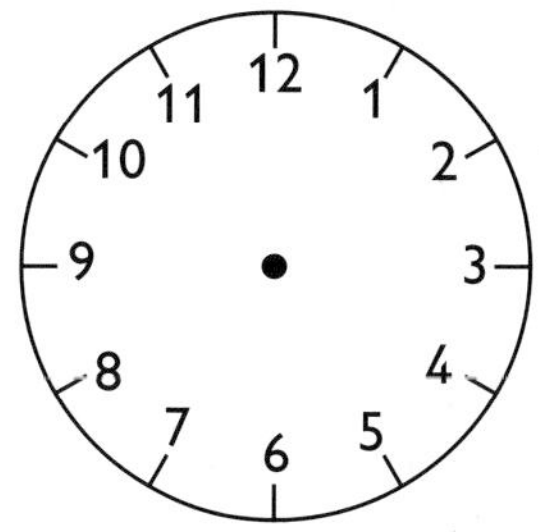
12 1 2 3 4 5 6 7 8 9 10 11

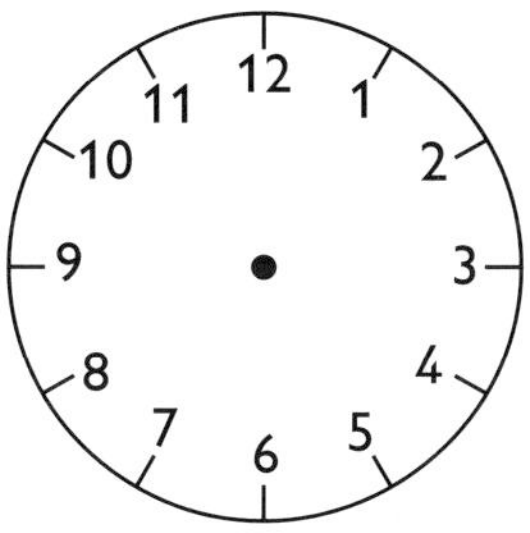
12 1 2 3 4 5 6 7 8 9 10 11

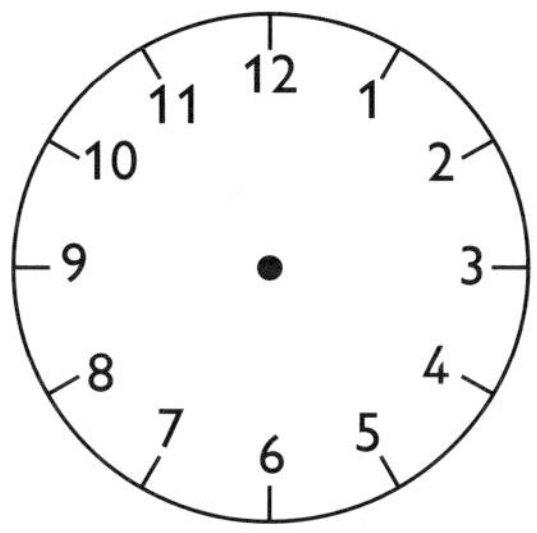
12 1 2 3 4 5 6 7 8 9 10 11

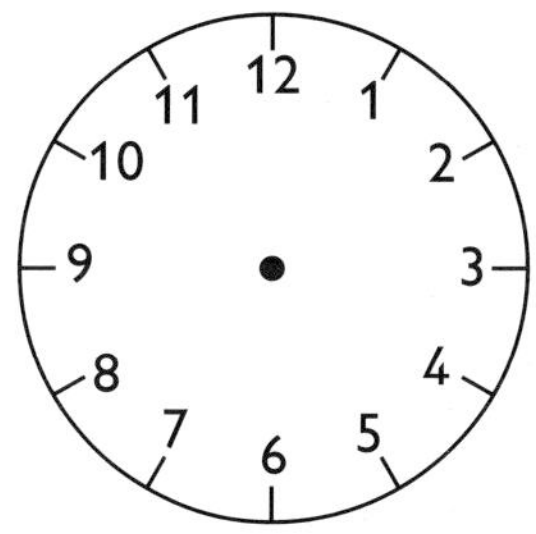
12 1 2 3 4 5 6 7 8 9 10 11

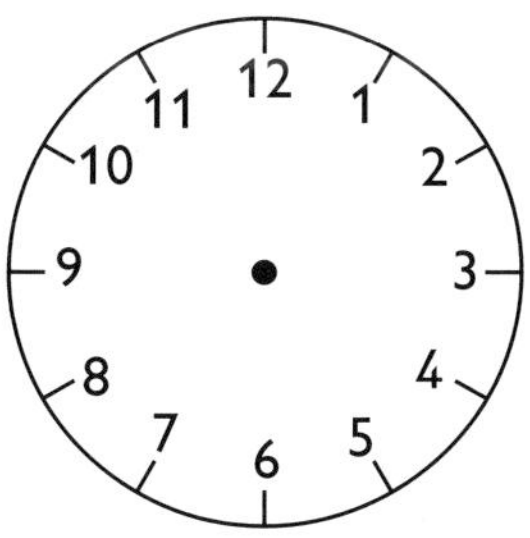
12 1 2 3 4 5 6 7 8 9 10 11

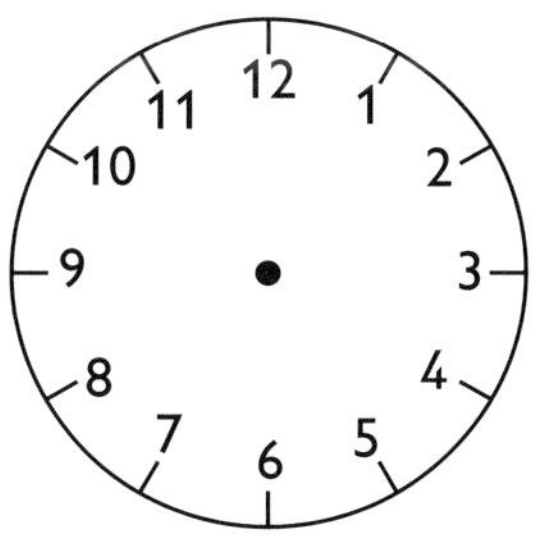
12 1 2 3 4 5 6 7 8 9 10 11

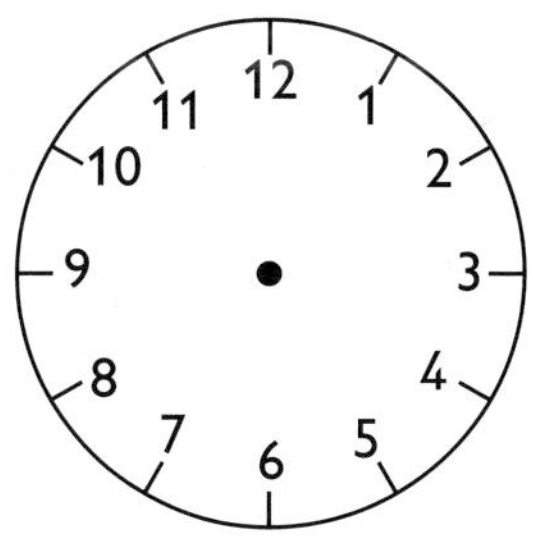
12 1 2 3 4 5 6 7 8 9 10 11

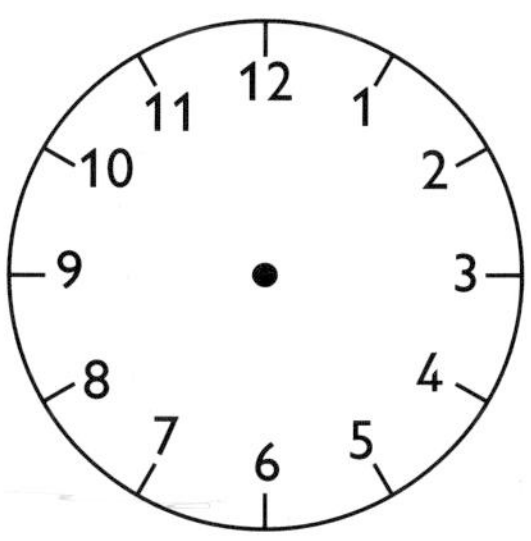
12 1 2 3 4 5 6 7 8 9 10 11

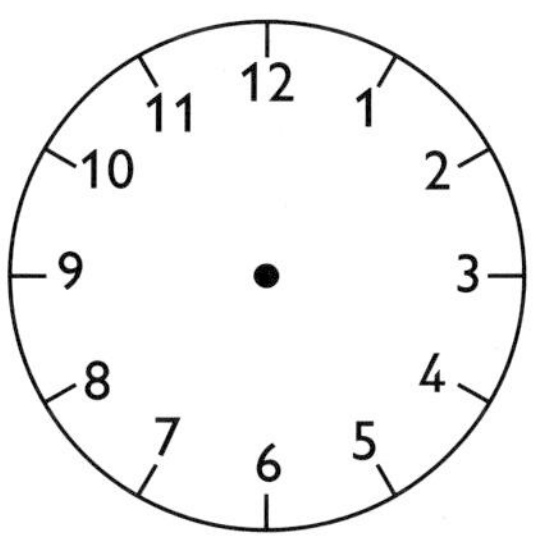
12 1 2 3 4 5 6 7 8 9 10 11

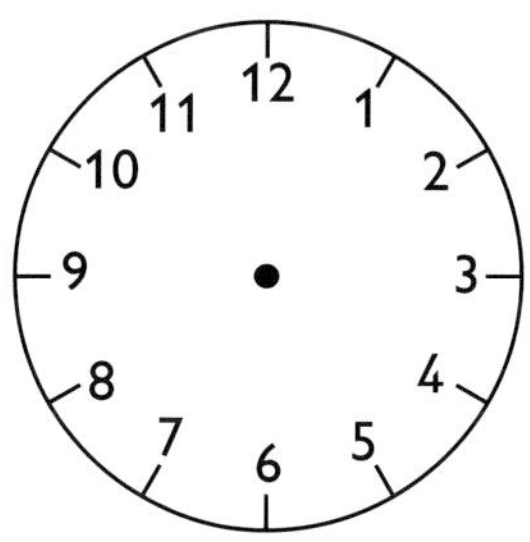
12 1 2 3 4 5 6 7 8 9 10 11

Measuring lengths

Look for the things listed in this table.
Estimate and measure them to the nearest half metre.

Classroom object	*Estimate*	*Measurement to the nearest $\frac{1}{2}$ metre*
The height of my chair		
The height of my friend's chair		
The width of the door		
The height of the door		
The width of the window		
The width of the board		
The height of my friend		
The width of the cupboard		
The height of the cupboard		
The height of my teacher		
The height of the teacher's table		
The width of the computer table		
The length of the classroom		
The width of the classroom		

Measuring to nearest centimetre

Make sure the ruler is placed carefully alongside the object.

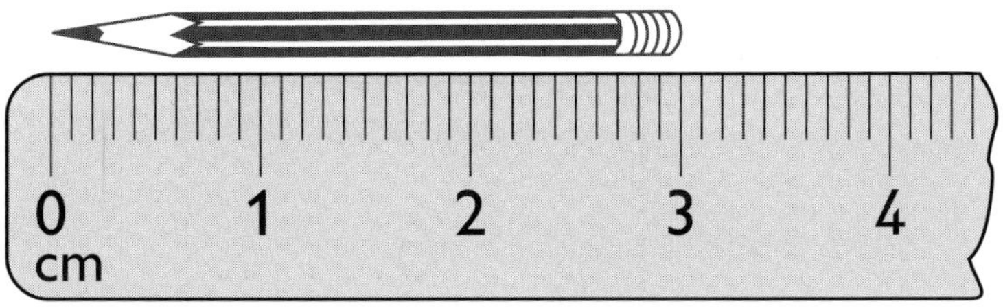

START AT 0!!

This pencil measures 3 centimetres.

Measure these objects.

	Estimate	Measurement to nearest cm
Pen		
Pencil		
Rubber		
Exercise book		

	Estimate	Measurement to nearest cm
P. E. bench		
Height of door		
Length of noticeboard		
Piano		

	Estimate	Measurement to nearest metre
Length of playground		
Width of hall		
Length of hall		
Length of corridor		
Length of football pitch		

Properties of 2-D shapes

Complete the table.

name of shape	sketch	number of sides	vertices
hexagon		6	
	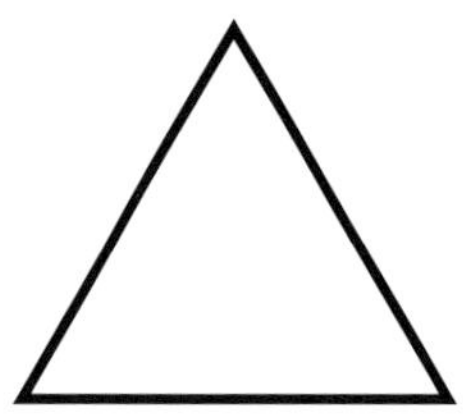		3
square		4	
			4
	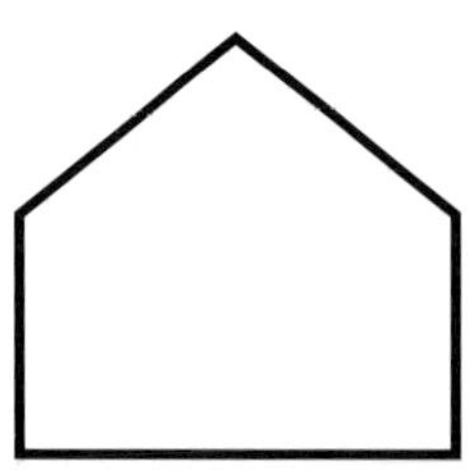		
	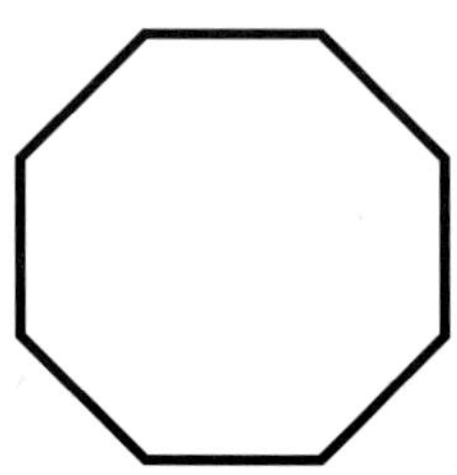	8	

Right angles

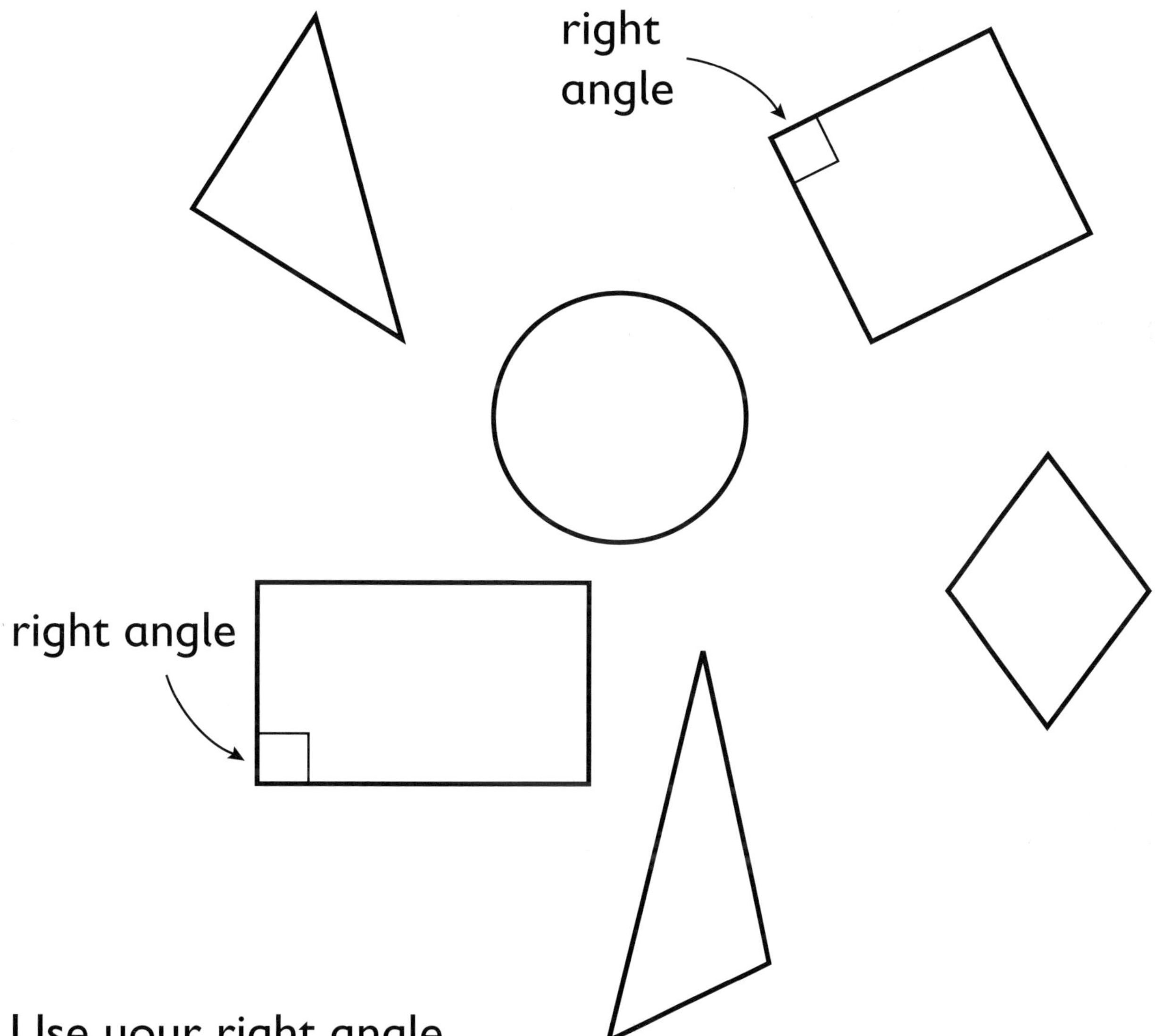

Use your right angle measurer to mark the right angles on these 2-D shapes.

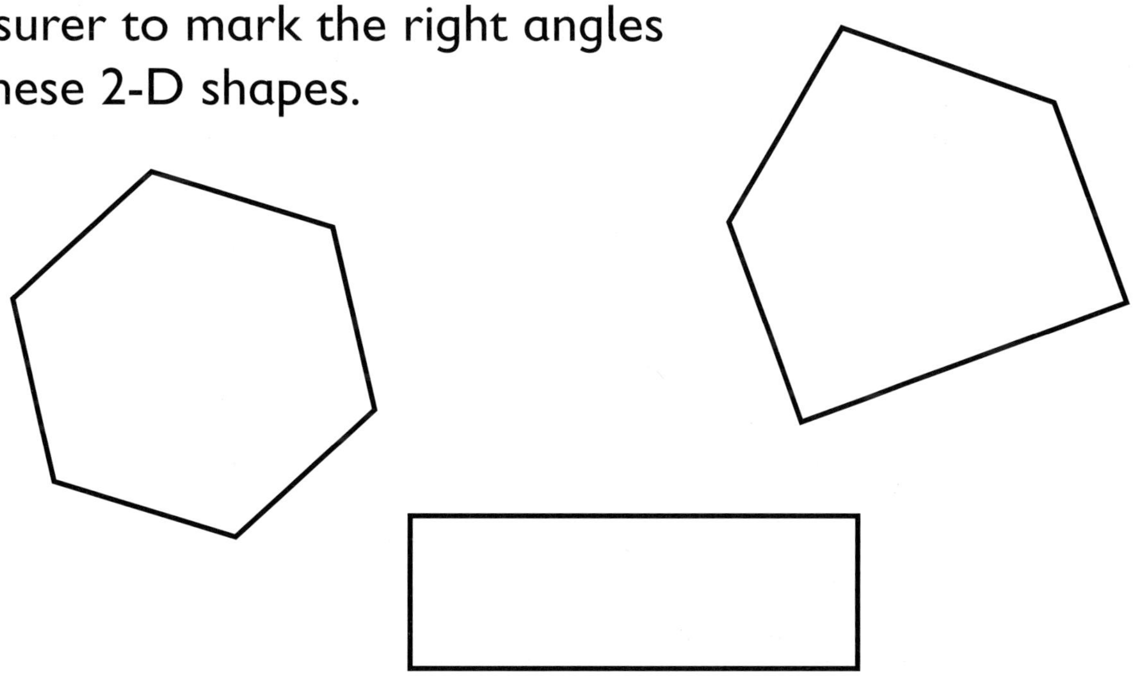

Counting on in 2s

Count in 2s from:

8 __ __ __ __ __ __ __ __ __ __ __ __ __ __ __ 40

12 __ __ __ __ __ __ __ __ 30

42 __ __ __ __ __ __ __ __ 60

Count back in 2s from:

26 __ __ __ __ __ __ __ __ __ __ __ 2

54 __ __ __ __ __ __ __ __ __ __ __ __ __ 26

60 __ __ __ __ __ __ __ __ __ __ __ __ 34

Fill in the missing spaces:

4	6			12		16

10	12	14				22

20	18	16	14			8

40	38	36			30

Patterns and puzzles

Complete the times tables below.

$1 \times 2 = \bigcirc$ → $2 \times 2 = \bigcirc$ → $3 \times 2 = \bigcirc$ → $4 \times 2 = \bigcirc$

$5 \times 2 = \bigcirc$ → $6 \times 2 = \bigcirc$ → $7 \times 2 = \bigcirc$ → $8 \times 2 = \bigcirc$

$9 \times 2 = \bigcirc$ → $10 \times 2 = \bigcirc$

18	+ 2	=	☐
16	− 2	=	☐
14	− 2	=	☐
12	+ 2	=	☐
10	− 2	=	☐
8	+ 2	=	☐
6	− 2	=	☐
4	+ 2	=	☐
2	− 2	=	☐
0	+ 2	=	☐

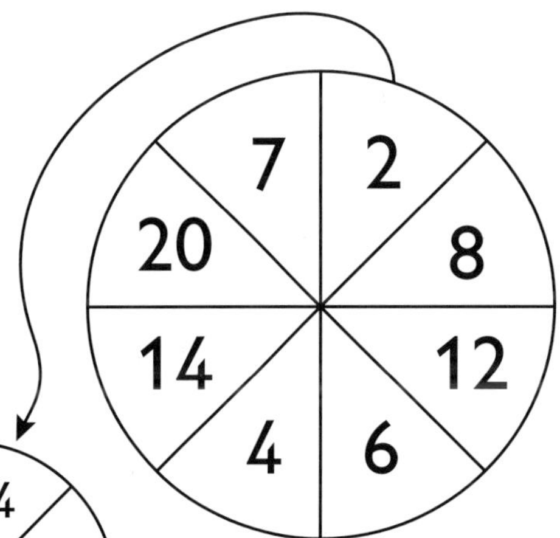

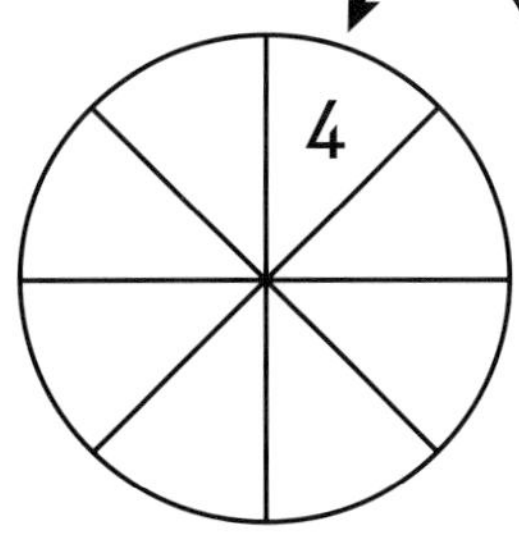

+2 onto each of these numbers.

−2 from each of these numbers.

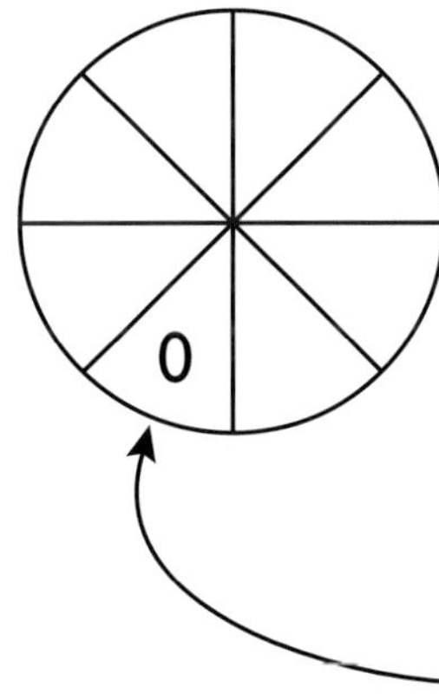

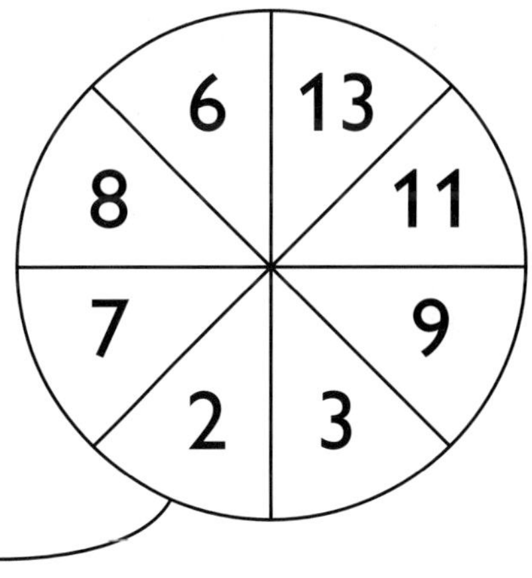

Multiplying by 10

There are 10 boxes of Easter eggs with 8 eggs in each box.

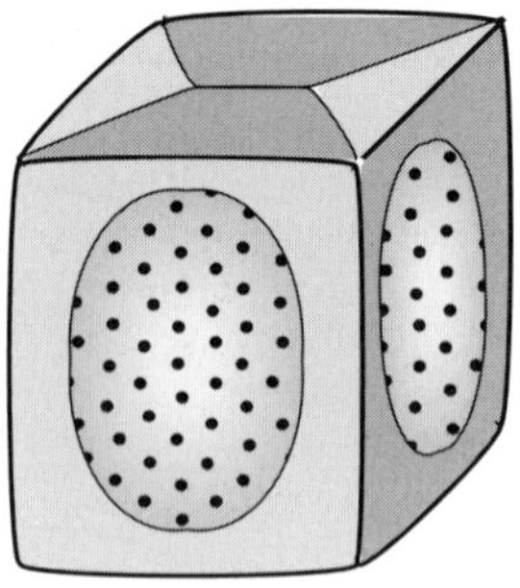

How many eggs in total?

In a football tournament 10 teams score 6 goals each.

How many goals are scored altogether by the 10 teams?

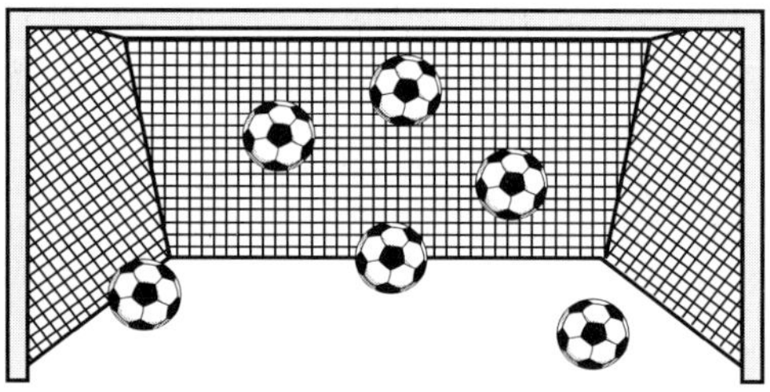

A farmer had 10 sheep in each of 10 fields.

How many sheep did he have altogether?

A wall is made up of 10 rows of 9 bricks in each row.

How many bricks make up the whole wall?

Dice game

1) Each player chooses cubes of one colour.

2) Take turns to throw two 0–5 dice.

3) Multiply the two numbers and put a cube on the answer.

4) The player with the most cubes on the cars is the winner.

5) You can have only one cube on each car.

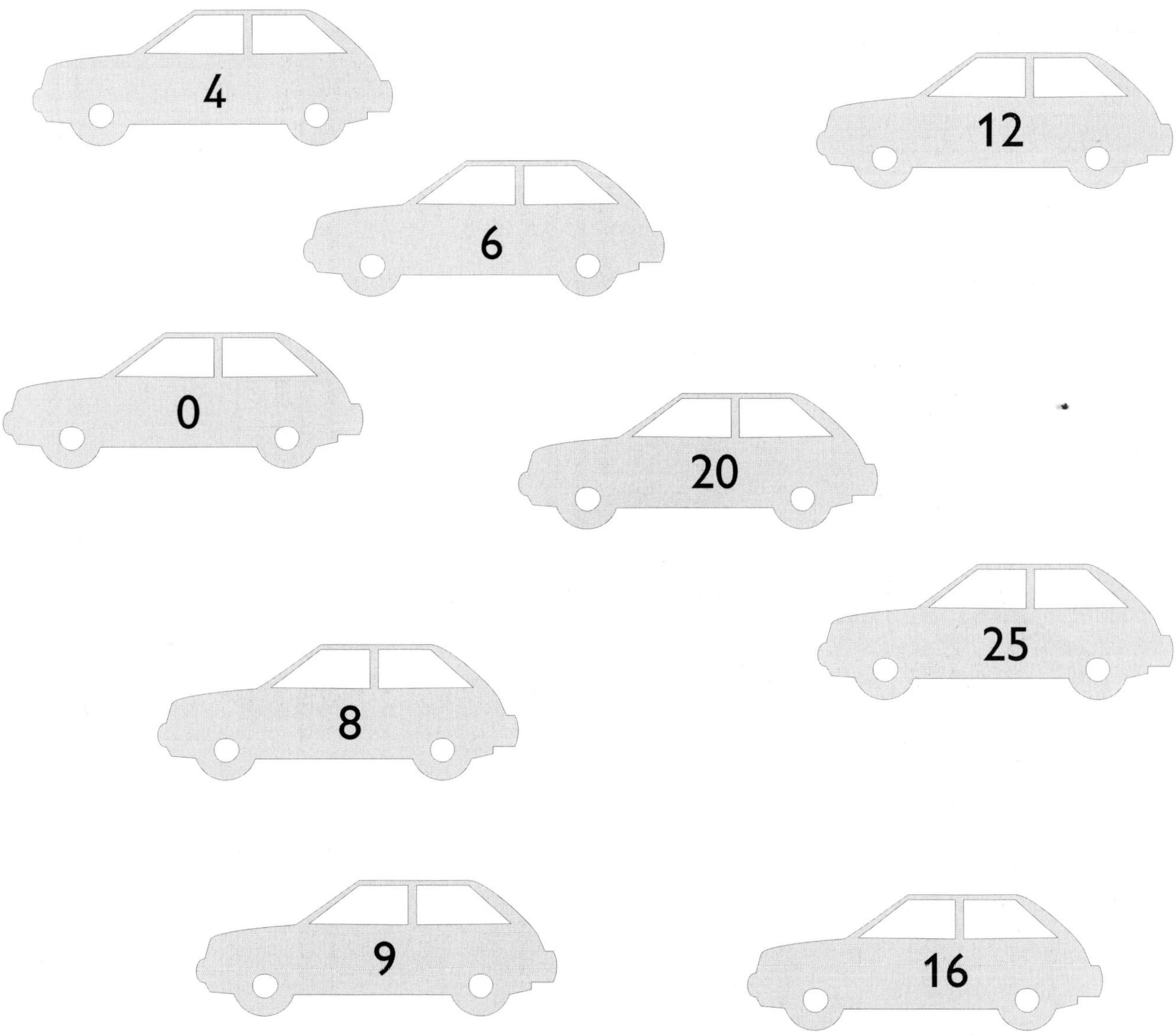

Fractions of shapes

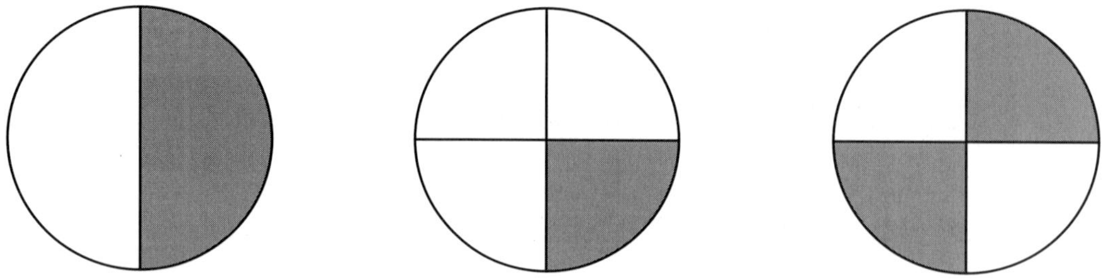

What fraction is shaded?

What fraction is not shaded?

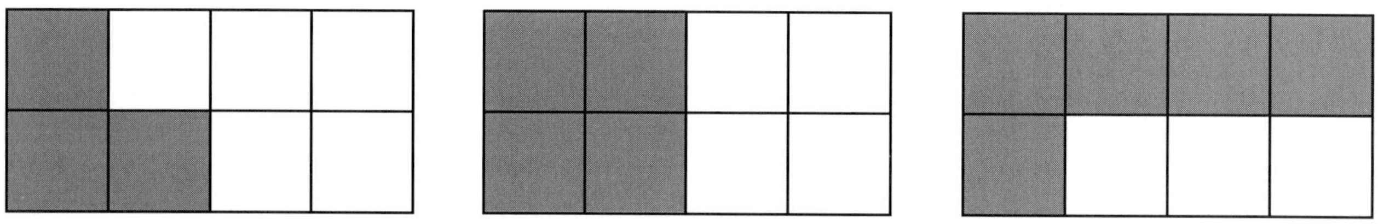

What fraction is shaded?

What fraction is not shaded?

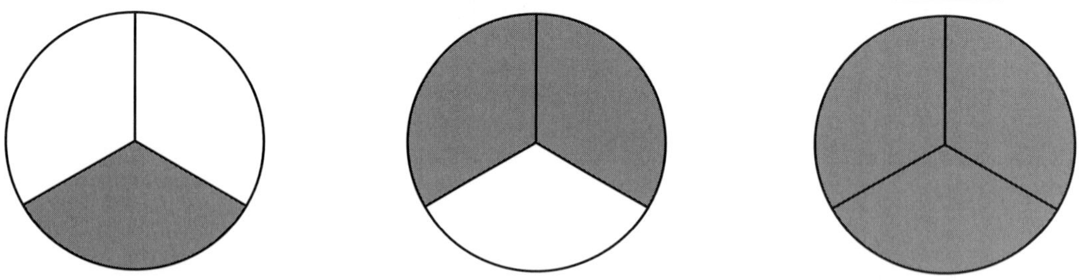

What fraction is shaded?

What fraction is not shaded?

Fractions of numbers

To find a half of 8 divide by 2.

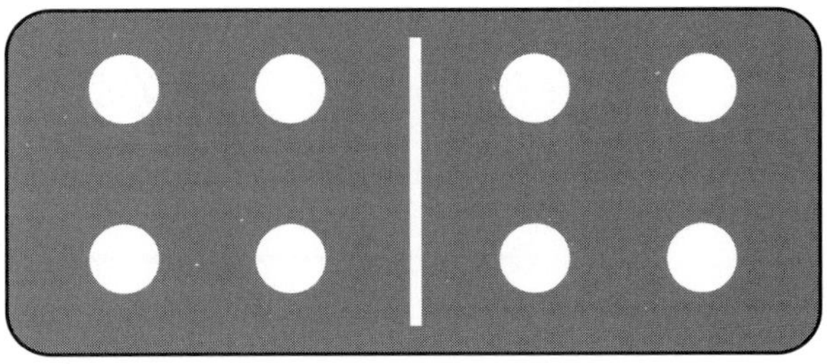

$\frac{1}{2}$ of 8 = 4

To find a half of 10 divide by 2.

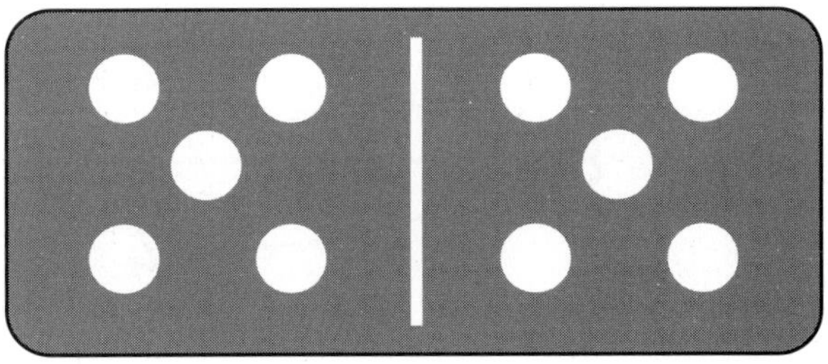

$\frac{1}{2}$ of 10 = ☐

To find a quarter of 12 divide by 4.

$\frac{1}{4}$ of 12 = ☐

$\frac{1}{2}$ of 14 = ☐ $\frac{1}{2}$ of 20 = ☐

$\frac{1}{4}$ of 16 = ☐ $\frac{1}{4}$ of 20 = ☐

There and back again

4 + 7 = 11

7 + 4 = 11

11 − 4 = 7

11 − 7 = 4

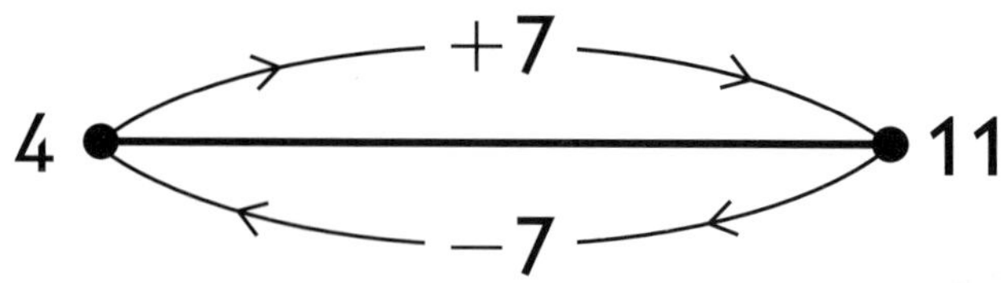

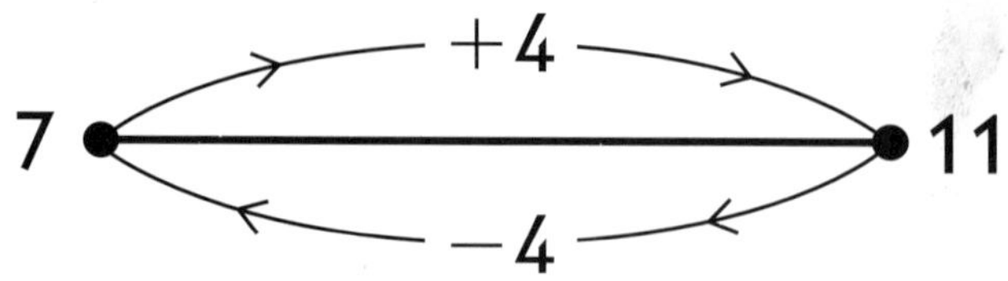

1. 4 + 8 = 12
2. 8 + 4 = 12
3. 12 − 8 = 4
4. ____________

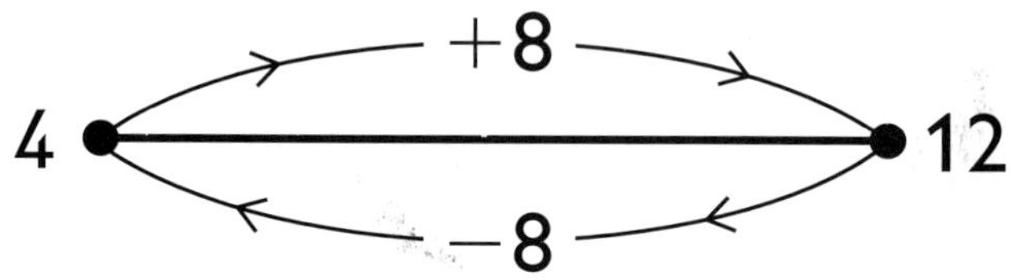

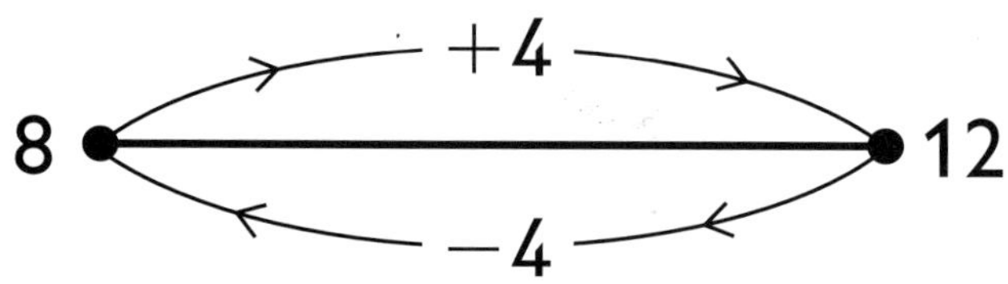

1. 9 + 6 = 15
2. ____________
3. ____________
4. ____________

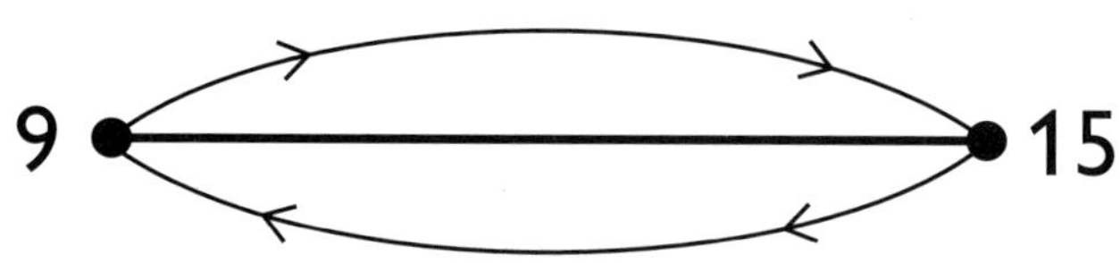

1. 8 + 7 = 15
2. ____________
3. ____________
4. ____________

Time problems

I arrive at school at  9 o'clock

and it is playtime at  10.30.

How many minutes do I have to wait until playtime?

I start P.E. at  2.30 and finish at  3.30

How long is the P.E. lesson?

I start reading at  2.00 and finish at  2.45.

How long did I read for?

I start maths at  11.00 and finish at  11.50.

How long is the maths lesson?

Graphs and charts

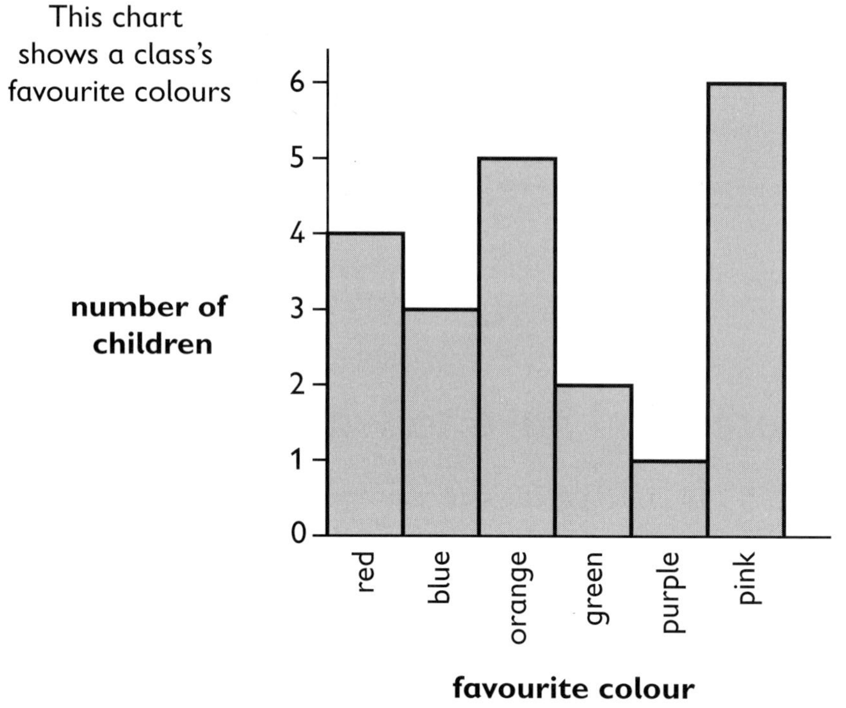

1. How many children chose red as their favourite colour? ____________

2. How many children chose green as their favourite colour? ____________

3. How many children liked red more than purple? ____________

4. How many children liked blue, red and green altogether? ____________

5. What was the most popular colour? ____________

6. How many children voted altogether? ____________

Handling data

Draw a graph for this tally chart.

Write your own questions for the graph.

Favourite football teams

Man Utd	𝍸 𝍸 III
Arsenal	𝍸 𝍸
Newcastle	𝍸 𝍸 IIII
Tottenham	𝍸
Chelsea	IIII

Decide on the scale for your graph.

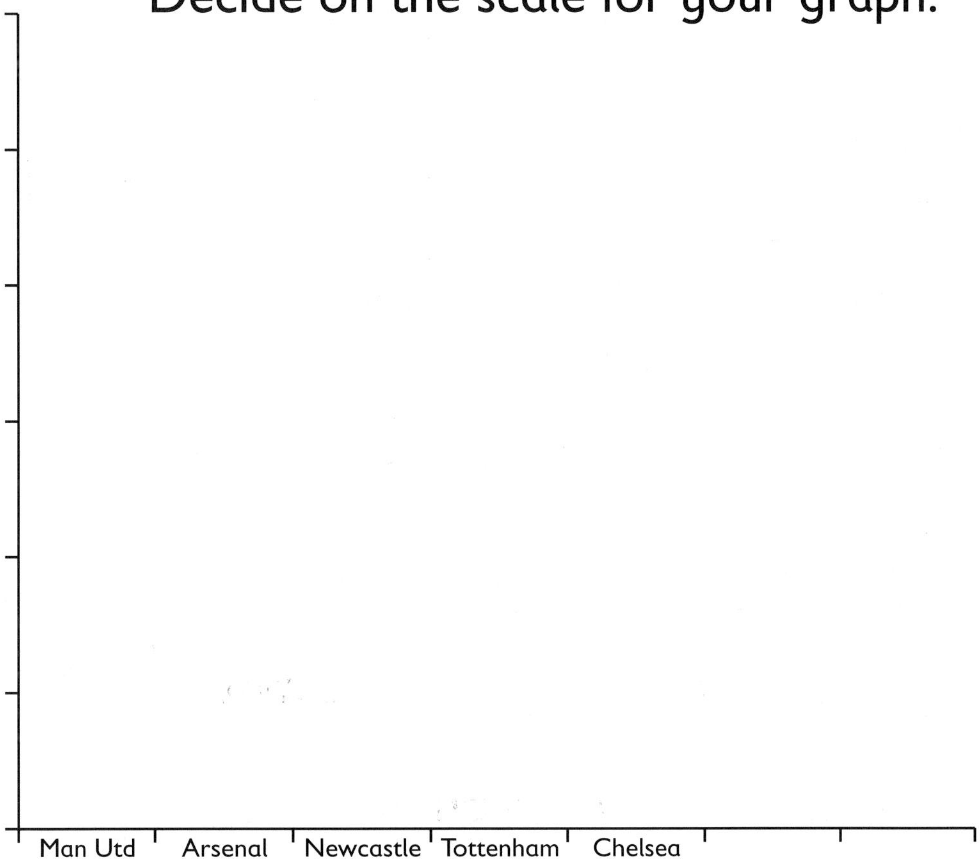

More or less

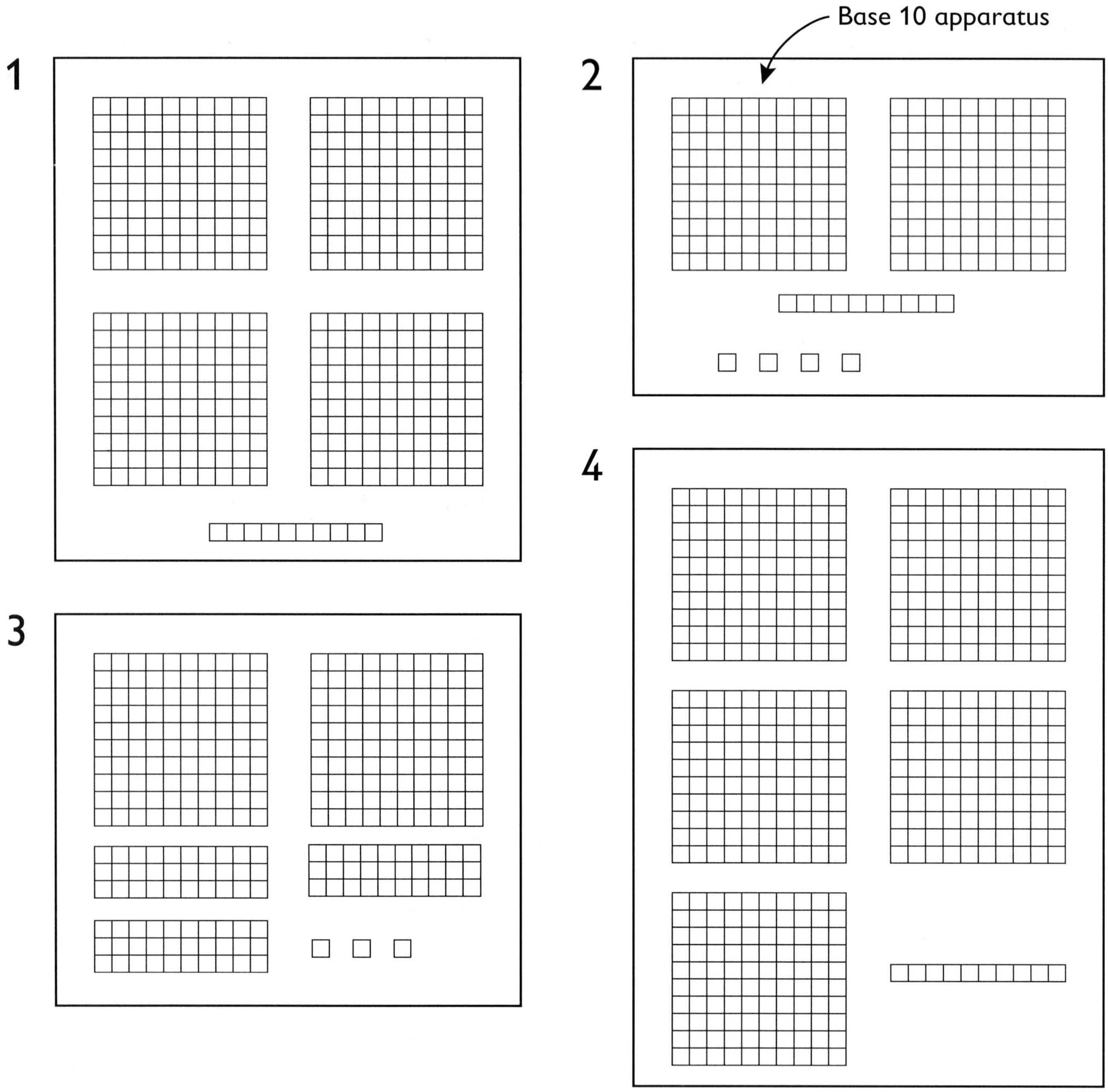

How many altogether are on mat 1 and mat 2? _______

How many altogether are on mat 3 and mat 4? _______

How many *more* are on mat 1 than mat 2? _______

How many *less* are on mat 3 than mat 4? _______

Connect three

Play with a partner
Choose a colour each for your counters.
Pick one of the squares.

1	2	3	4	5
6	7	8	9	10
11	12	13	14	15
16	17	18	19	20
21	22	23	24	25

Use any 2 of these numbers:

1, 2, 3, 4, 5, 6, 7, 8, 9, 10, 11, 12, 13, 14, 15, 16, 17, 18, 19, 20, 21, 22, 23, 24, 25, 26, 27, 28, 29, 30

Use either + or − to make the number on the square you have chosen.

Check with a calculator.

If you are right put a counter on your square.

The first to get 3 in a row wins.

Addition

1. $4 + 5 =$ ______
2. $3 + 5 =$ ______
3. $4 + 7 =$ ______
4. $6 + 5 =$ ______
5. $7 + 4 =$ ______
6. $8 + 3 =$ ______
7. $9 + 2 =$ ______
8. $7 + 3 + 2 =$ ______
9. $8 + 2 + 3 =$ ______
10. $9 + 1 + 2 =$ ______
11. $9 + 3 + 2 + 1 =$ ______
12. $4 + 6 + 3 + 2 =$ ______
13. $5 + 2 + 4 + 1 =$ ______
14. $6 + 3 + 2 + 1 =$ ______
15. $7 + 2 + 3 + 2 =$ ______

5 and a bit

Look carefully at this example:

$$\begin{aligned} 12 + 6 &= 12 + (5 + 1) \\ &= 12 + 5 + 1 \\ &= 17 + 1 \\ &= 18 \end{aligned}$$

Now try these:

$$\begin{aligned} 14 + 7 &= 14 + (5 + 2) \\ &= 14 + \square + \square \\ &= \square + \square \\ &= \square \end{aligned}$$

$$\begin{aligned} 16 + 6 &= 16 + (5 + 1) \\ &= \square + \square + \square \\ &= \square + \square \\ &= * \end{aligned}$$

$$\begin{aligned} 18 + 7 &= 18 + (\square + \square) \\ &= \square + \square + \square \\ &= \square + \square \\ &= \square \end{aligned}$$

One step

I think of a number, then subtract 12.

The answer is 26.

What was my number? ☐

I think of a number, then add 15.

The answer is 40.

What was my number? ☐

A sheep has 4 legs.

How many legs do 6 sheep have? ☐

Now work out how many legs 8 sheep have. ☐

A box holds 40 nuts.

How many nuts are left if you eat 17 nuts? ☐

How many people can have 8 nuts each? ☐

How many boxes are needed to hold 80 nuts? ☐

Money problems

PANTOMIME

Programmes 6p each

Tickets –	*Thursday*	*25p*
	Friday	*30p*
	Saturday	*35p*

a How much do 4 programmes cost? ☐ p

b How much do 6 programmes cost? ☐ p

c Find the cost of these tickets in two ways. Use a separate piece of paper.

- 3 tickets for Thursday

  ☐ p + ☐ p + ☐ p = ☐ p

  = ☐ or 3 × ☐ p

- 4 tickets for Saturday
- 5 tickets for Thursday

d What is the total cost of 3 tickets and 3 programmes for Thursday?

e What is the total cost of 1 ticket for each night?

f How many tickets can be bought for 80p each night?

Changing patterns

How are these patterns changing?

Draw the next four shapes in each pattern.

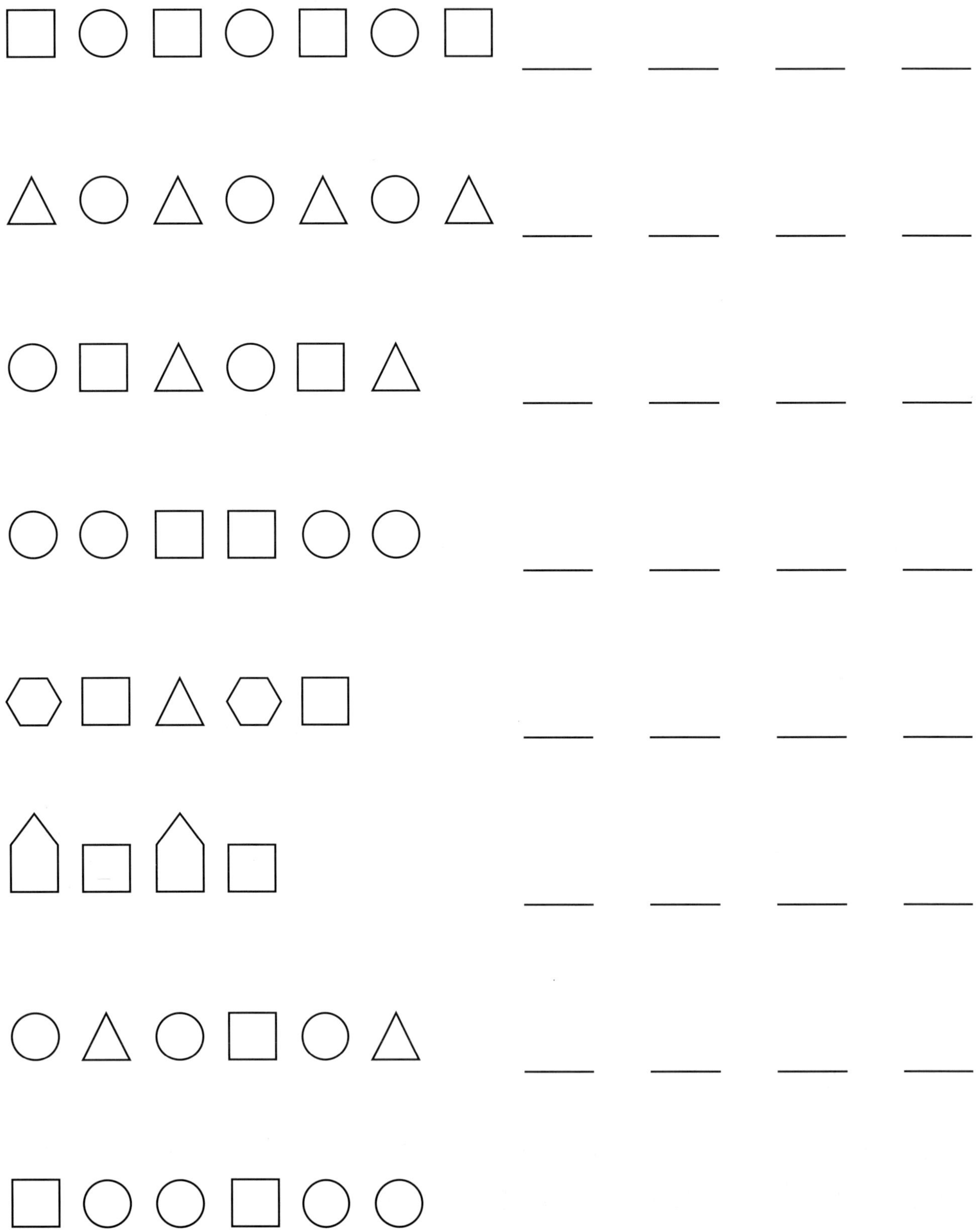

Bob's game

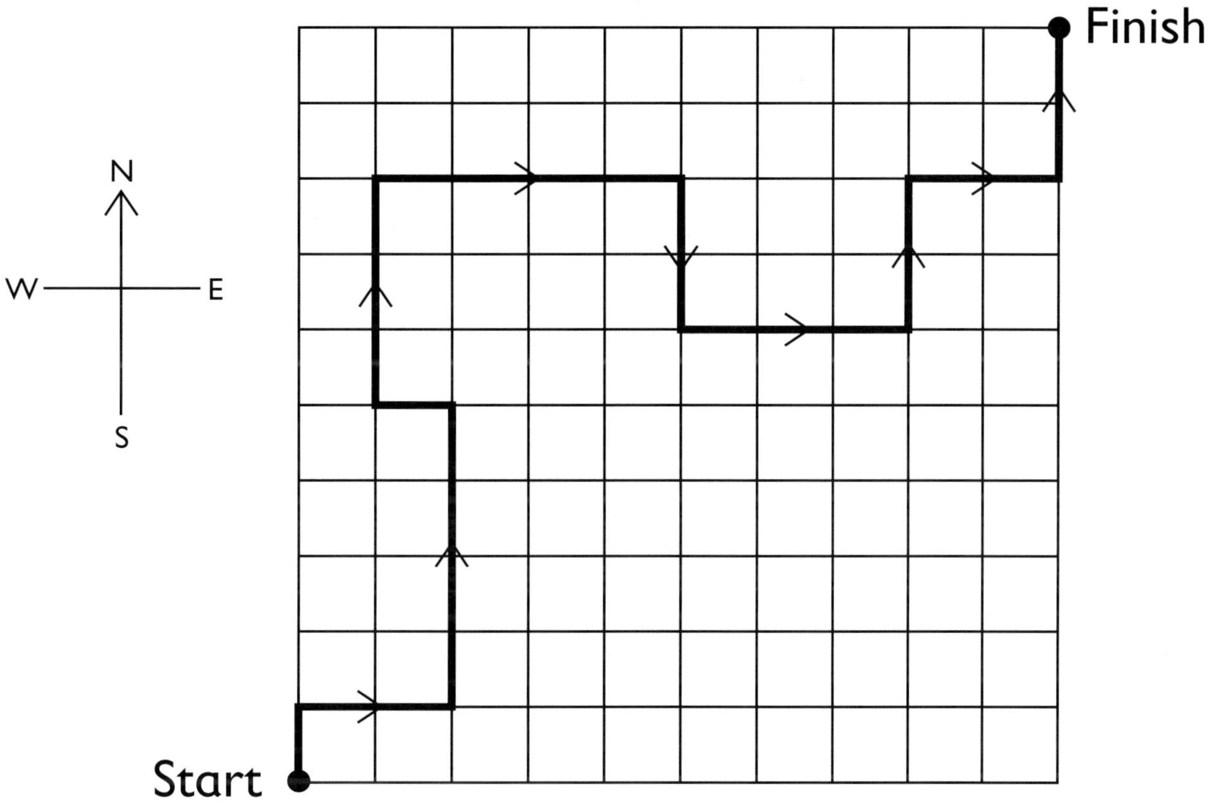

The route Bob took is:

N1, E2, N4, W1, N3, E4, S2, E3, N2, E2, N2

He can only go forwards along the lines. If he wants to go in a different direction, he has to make a right-angled turn. That is because he is on squared paper.

Draw this route on squared paper and see what shape Bob makes:

E3, N4, E5, N2, W2, S4, E3, N5, W2, N2, E2, N1, E1

Draw some more routes for him.

Write some directions for your friends. See if they can draw the route after reading your directions.

Clocks and watches

What times are displayed on these watches and clocks?

____

____

____

____

____

____

____

____

____

____

____

____

Grams and kilograms

Work these out on a separate piece of paper.

Mr and Mrs Squirrel store 1 kg of nuts for the winter.

Together they eat 150 g of nuts each month, starting in November.

How many grams of nuts are left on March 1st?

The vet is cross with Shearer the cat.

He is overweight. Shearer weighs 25 kg.

His owner puts Shearer on a diet.

He loses $2\frac{1}{2}$ kg. What is Shearer's new weight?

Later on Shearer eats too much again.

He puts on $\frac{3}{4}$ kg.

What is Shearer's weight now?

How many grams make:

1. $2\frac{1}{2}$ kg
2. 3 kg
3. $4\frac{1}{2}$ kg
4. 6 kg
5. 8 kg
6. $9\frac{1}{2}$ kg
7. $3\frac{1}{2}$ kg
8. 10 kg

Multiples

Write down the next 2 multiples in these series.

2	4	6	8		

8	12	16	20	24		

20	25	30	35	40	45		

30	40	50	70		

30	25	20	15		

50	45	40	35		

40	36	32	28		

27	24	21		

What is the next multiple of 5 after 40? ☐

What is the next multiple of 10 after 30? ☐

What is the multiple of 5 before 30? ☐

What is the multiple of 2 before 20? ☐

What is the multiple of 5 before 20? ☐

Number puzzles

John had 59 music tapes. His little brother Tom hid 12 of them. How many were left?

Ben had 46 computer games. He gave 11 of them to his friends. How many did he have left?

Paul had 75 football cards. He dropped some on the way to school. If he had 64 when he arrived at school, how many had he dropped?

James had 100 pencils and took 20 to school. He divided the rest up amongst his 5 friends. How many did they each get?

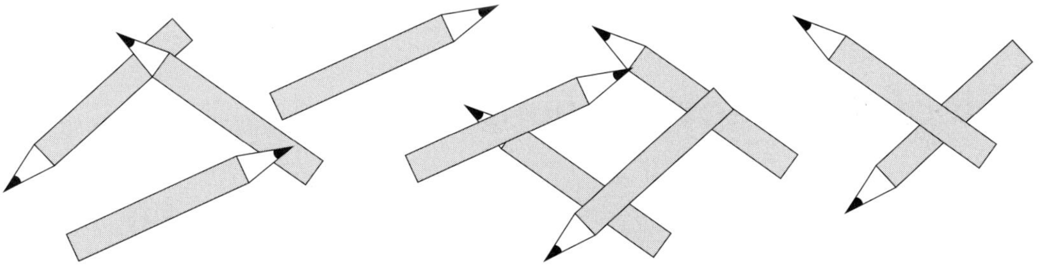

Helen collected together 25 earrings. She dropped 7 when she took them to her friend Abigail's house. Abigail gave her 11 of hers. How many did Helen have then?

Tim had 25 CDs. He swapped 5 of them with his friends and gave 3 to his Dad for his birthday. How many did he have left?

Doubles and halves

Double each number.

1. 30 ___	**4.** 15 ___	**7.** 25 ___	**10.** 31 ___
2. 21 ___	**5.** 17 ___	**8.** 13 ___	**11.** 24 ___
3. 14 ___	**6.** 26 ___	**9.** 10 ___	**12.** 18 ___

Add these *near* doubles.

1. 13 14 ___	**4.** 18 19 ___	**7.** 24 23 ___
2. 17 18 ___	**5.** 15 14 ___	**8.** 22 21 ___
3. 16 15 ___	**6.** 17 16 ___	**9.** 25 24 ___

What is half of the following numbers?

1. 10 ___	**4.** 50 ___	**7.** 30 ___	**10.** 80 ___
2. 18 ___	**5.** 60 ___	**8.** 28 ___	**11.** 50 ___
3. 34 ___	**6.** 24 ___	**9.** 36 ___	**12.** 38 ___

Divide and multiply

$$4 \times 5 = 20$$
$$5 \times 4 = 20$$
$$20 \div 5 = 4$$
$$20 \div 4 = 5$$

Can you make 4 statements from:

1. $6 \times 5 = 30$
2. $\square \times \square = \square$
3. $\square \div \square = \square$
4. $\square \div \square = \square$

1. $6 \times 10 = 60$
2. $\square \times \square = \square$
3. $\square \div \square = \square$
4. $\square \div \square = \square$

1. $10 \times 2 = 20$
2. $\square \times \square = \square$
3. $\square \div \square = \square$
4. $\square \div \square = \square$

1. $8 \times 10 = 80$
2. $\square \times \square = \square$
3. $\square \div \square = \square$
4. $\square \div \square = \square$

Number problems 1

3	4	5	7

1. Which three cards total 15? ☐ ☐ ☐
2. Which two cards have an even total over 10? ☐ ☐
3. Which two cards have an odd total over 10? ☐ ☐
4. Which three cards have an odd total? ☐ ☐
5. Which two cards have the largest difference? ☐ ☐
6. Which three cards have a total of 16? ☐ ☐ ☐

I think of a number and subtract 7. The answer is 16.

What was my number? ☐

I think of a number and subtract 9. The answer is 20.

What was my number? ☐

I think of a number and subtract 11. The answer is 17.

What was my number? ☐

Number problems 2

There are 25 books on a shelf. 12 are taken away.
How many are left on the shelf?

$25 - 12 = 13$ books left

Check: $12 + 13 = 25$

There are 30 trees in a row. 14 trees are cut down.
How many trees are left?

$30 - 14 = 16$ trees left

Check by adding □ + □ = □

Put 30 eggs into boxes of 6.
How many boxes of eggs will you have?

□ ÷ □ = □ boxes

Check by multiplying □ × □ = □

Put 42 balls into 7 nets. How many balls will be in each net?

□ ÷ □ = □ balls

Check by multiplying □ × □ = □

Share 56 sweets between 8 children.
How many sweets will each child get?

□ ÷ □ = □ sweets

Check by multiplying □ × □ = □

Copymaster 37

Equivalent fractions

1 WHOLE ONE									
$\frac{1}{5}$		$\frac{1}{5}$		$\frac{1}{5}$		$\frac{1}{5}$		$\frac{1}{5}$	
$\frac{1}{10}$	$\frac{1}{10}$	$\frac{1}{10}$	$\frac{1}{10}$	$\frac{1}{10}$	$\frac{1}{10}$	$\frac{1}{10}$	$\frac{1}{10}$	$\frac{1}{10}$	$\frac{1}{10}$

Fill in the boxes using the Fraction Wall above to help you.

$$1 = \frac{\square}{5} \qquad 1 = \frac{\square}{10}$$

$$\frac{1}{5} = \frac{\square}{10} \qquad \frac{2}{5} = \frac{\square}{10}$$

$$\frac{3}{5} = \frac{\square}{10} \qquad \frac{4}{5} = \frac{\square}{10}$$

1 WHOLE ONE							
$\frac{1}{2}$				$\frac{1}{2}$			
$\frac{1}{4}$		$\frac{1}{4}$		$\frac{1}{4}$		$\frac{1}{4}$	
$\frac{1}{8}$	$\frac{1}{8}$	$\frac{1}{8}$	$\frac{1}{8}$	$\frac{1}{8}$	$\frac{1}{8}$	$\frac{1}{8}$	$\frac{1}{8}$

Fill in the boxes using the Fraction Wall above to help you.

$$1 = \frac{\square}{2} \qquad 1 = \frac{\square}{4} \qquad 1 = \frac{\square}{8}$$

$$\frac{1}{2} = \frac{\square}{4} \qquad \frac{1}{2} = \frac{\square}{8} \qquad \frac{1}{4} = \frac{\square}{8}$$

$$\frac{3}{4} = \frac{\square}{8} \qquad \frac{2}{4} = \frac{\square}{8}$$

They're the same

Write *true* or *false* next to each statement.

$\frac{2}{4} = \frac{1}{2}$ true

$\frac{2}{8} = \frac{1}{4}$ ________

$\frac{4}{8} = \frac{2}{4}$ ________

$\frac{2}{8} = \frac{4}{8}$ ________

$\frac{1}{2} = \frac{3}{8}$ ________

$\frac{1}{5} = \frac{2}{10}$ ________

$\frac{3}{5} = \frac{5}{10}$ ________

$\frac{2}{5} = \frac{6}{10}$ ________

Use a fraction wall if you get stuck.

Bar charts

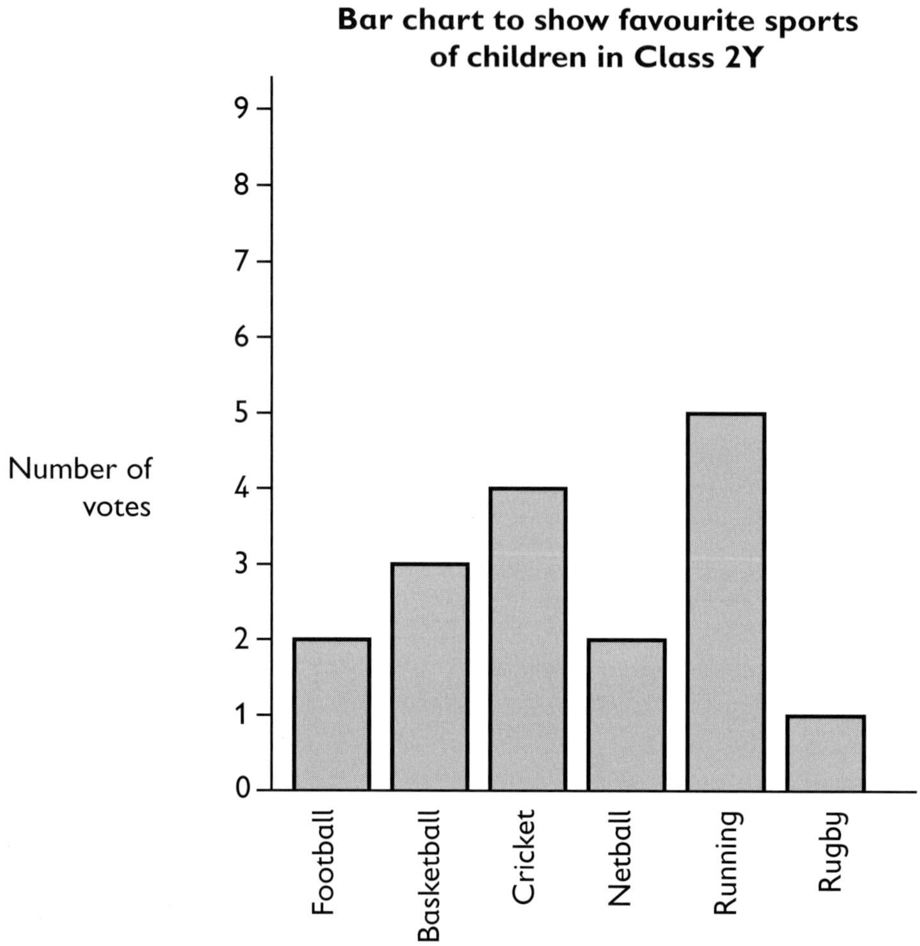

How many votes for:

football	☐	cricket	☐	running	☐
basketball	☐	netball	☐	rugby	☐

How many more children voted for running than netball? ____

How many more children voted for cricket than rugby? ____

How many fewer children voted for basketball than cricket? ____

Using a bar chart

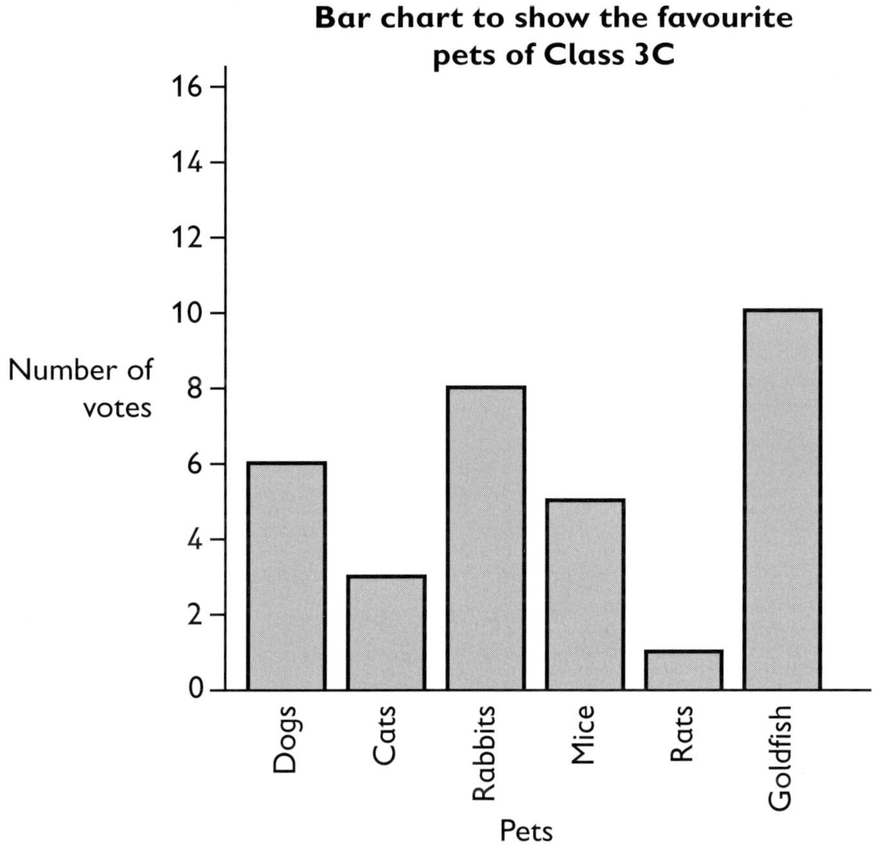

Note that the vertical axis shows 2 votes for every square.

How many votes for each pet?

dogs	___	rabbits	___	rats	___
cats	___	mice	___	goldfish	___

How many more votes:

for dogs than cats ____________________

for rabbits than mice ____________________

for goldfish than rats ____________________

for cats than rats ____________________

Numbers to 1000

Starting number		+1		+10		+100
27	→	28	→	38	→	138
24	→		→		→	
33	→		→		→	
44	→		→		→	
28	→		→		→	

Starting number		−1		−10		−100
179	→	178	→	168	→	68
197	→		→		→	
127	→		→		→	
174	→		→		→	

Kaprekar's constant

The children take three digits and form them into the greatest number they can and the smallest number they can. They then subtract (using a calculator if necessary) the smaller number from the greater. The process is then repeated using the three digits in the answer as the starting point.

1 2 3

$$\begin{array}{r} 321 - \\ 123 \\ \hline 198 \\ \hline \end{array}$$

$$\begin{array}{r} 981 - \\ 189 \\ \hline 792 \\ \hline \end{array}$$

Can you find a number with *2, 3 or 4 stages?*

$$\begin{array}{r} 972 - \\ 279 \\ \hline 693 \\ \hline \end{array}$$

Try *3 5 9.*

$$\begin{array}{r} 963 - \\ 369 \\ \hline 594 \\ \hline \end{array}$$

$$\begin{array}{r} 954 - \\ 459 \\ \hline 495 \\ \hline \end{array}$$

No changes in digits – stop.

= (5) stages until stop

Near multiples I

36 − 27
Round 27 to the nearest 10 = (30)
Take away 30 from 36 = (6)
Rounded up by 3 so add (3) onto 6 = 9

Do the same for:

49 − 37

51 − 45

55 − 46

47 + 28
Round 28 to the nearest 10 = (30)
Add 30 onto 47 = (77)
Rounded up by 2 so take away (2) = 75

Do the same for:

37 + 18

26 + 19

Use a separate piece of paper.

Near multiples 2

$3 + 29 = 3 + (29 + 1)$

nearest multiple of 10

$= 3 + 30 = 33 - 1 = 32$

$23 + 28 = 23 +$ ______
(nearest multiple of 10 to 28)

$=$ ______________________

$15 + 23 = 15 +$ ______
(nearest multiple of 10 to 23)

$= 15 + 20 + 3 = 38$

$21 + 32 = 21 +$ ______
(nearest multiple of 10 to 32)

$=$ ______________________

Copymaster 45

Money problems

Write these prices in £:

Beans	£0.30	Potatoes	£ ____
Bread	£ ____	Cake	£ ____

Write these answers in pence:

2 tins of beans ____ p

2 bags of potatoes ____ p

1 loaf of bread and 1 bag of potatoes ____ p

1 cake and 1 bag of potatoes ____ p

How much change from £1 if you buy:

2 tins of beans ____ p

1 loaf of bread ____ p

1 bag of potatoes ____ p

Check your answer

$4 + 5 = 9$ and $5 + 4 = 9$

so $4 + 5 = 5 + 4$

$6 + 5 = 11$ and $5 + 6 = 11$

so $6 + 5 = 5 + 6$

That means you can always check your answers.

$8 + 6 = 14$ CHECK! $6 + 8 = 14$ YES ✓

Work these addition sums out and check your answers.

SUM	CHECK	YES/NO
$5 + 9 =$	$9 + 5 =$	
$6 + 10 =$		
$7 + 9 =$		
$12 + 5 =$		
$15 + 3 =$		
$20 + 4 =$		
$5 + 25 =$		
$6 + 11 =$		

Reading scales – capacity

How much juice?

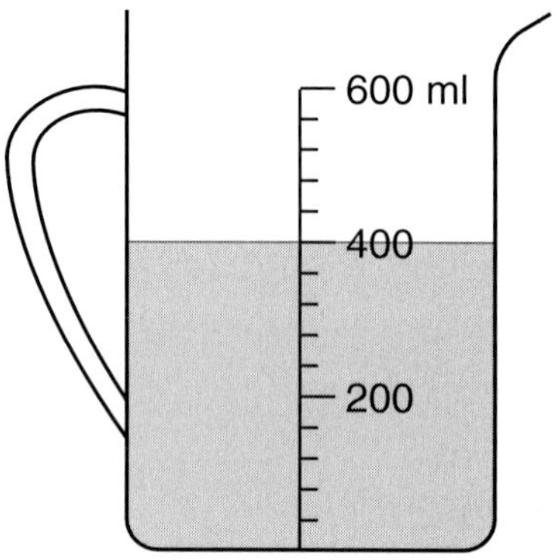

______ ml

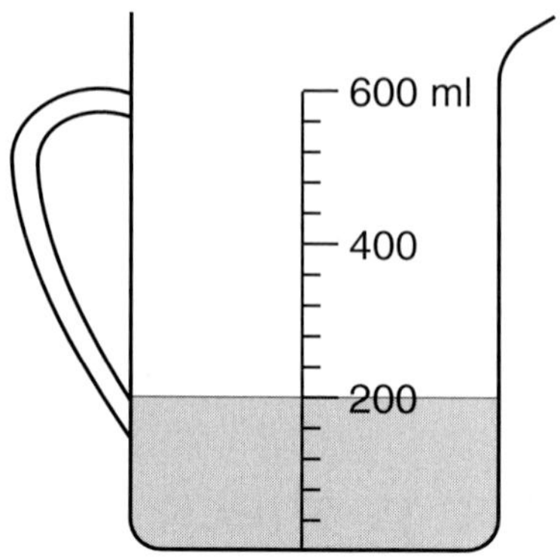

______ ml

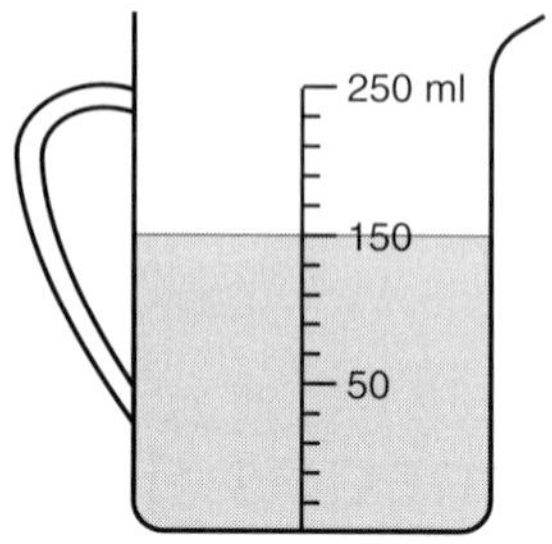

______ ml

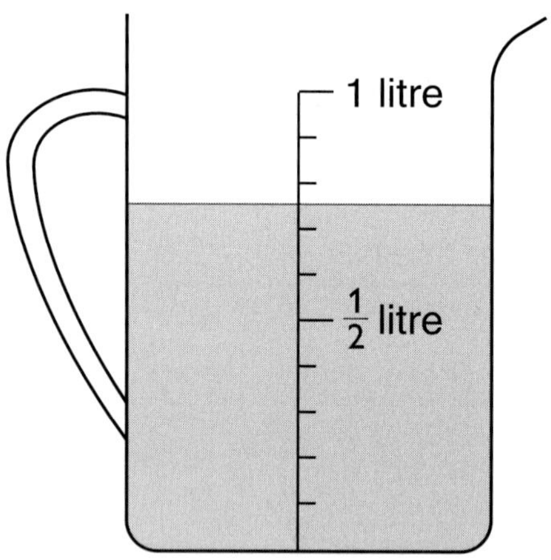

______ l

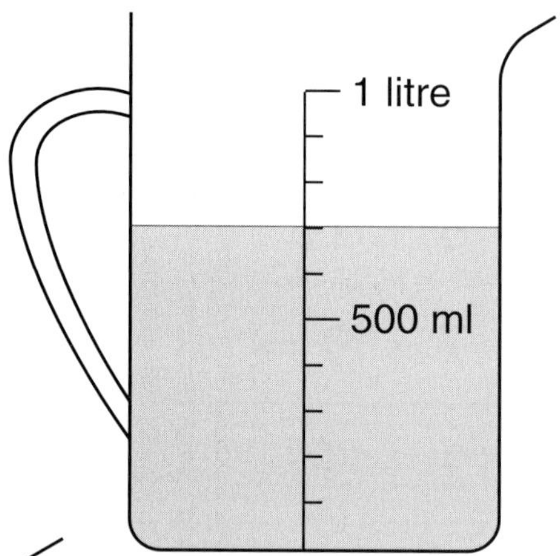

______ ml

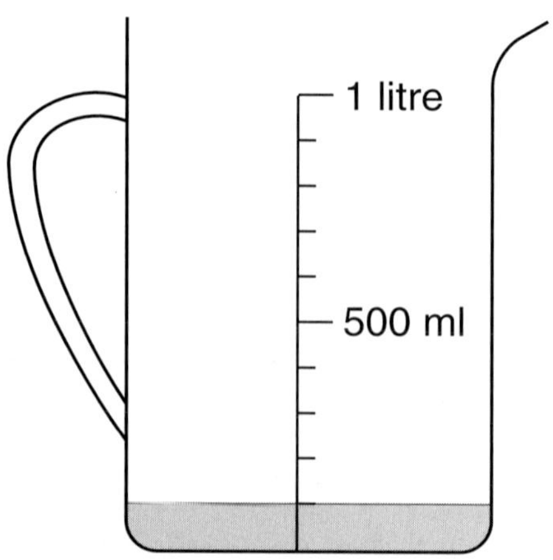

______ ml

Measurement problems

100 cm = 1 metre

1000 g = 1 kilogram

1000 ml = 1 litre

Write how many kilograms:

____

____

____

____

Write how many litres:

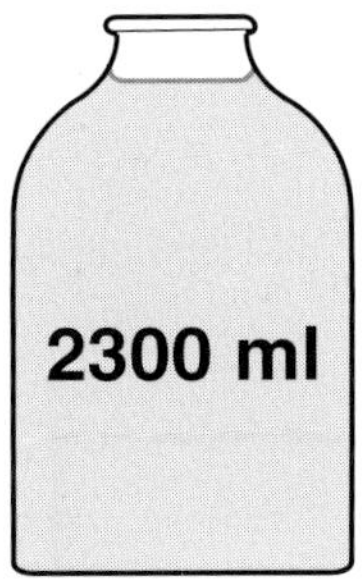

____

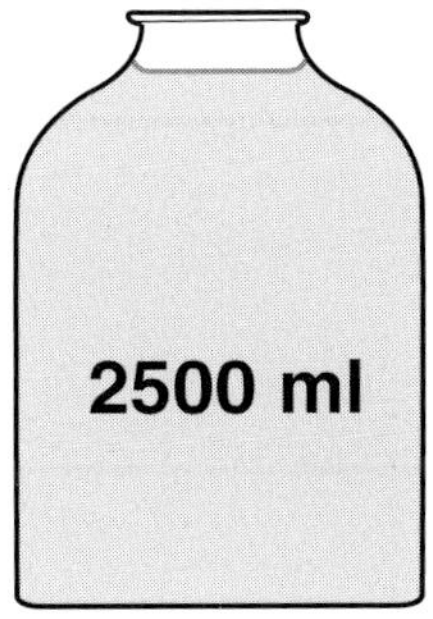

____

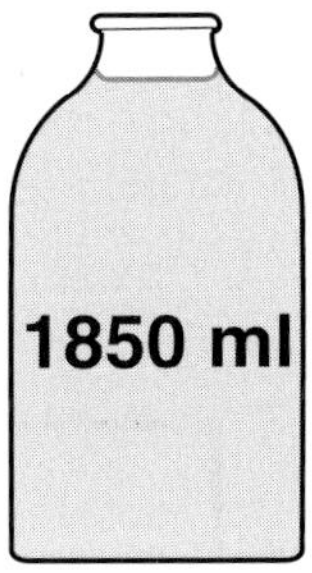

____

Write how many metres:

0 __________ 125 cm

0 __________ 85 cm

0 __________ 150 cm

Lines of symmetry

Mark on the lines of symmetry on these shapes.

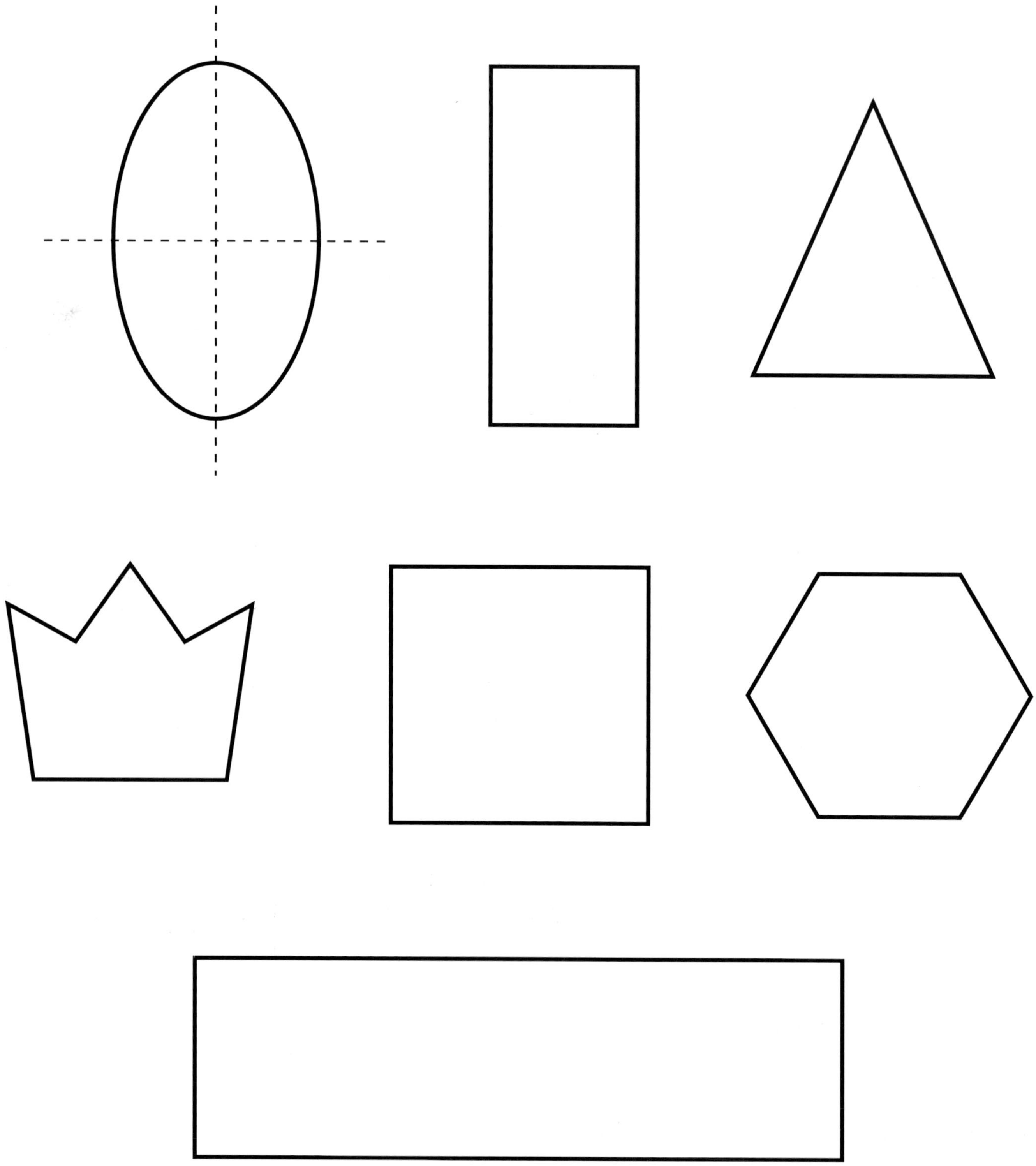

Use a mirror to check your results.

Shapes

Make the whole shape and name it.

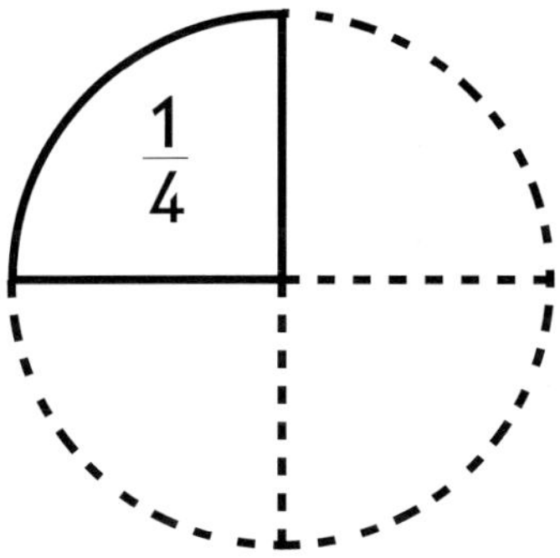

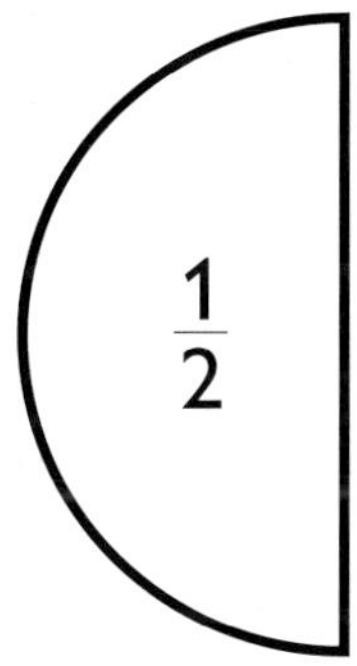

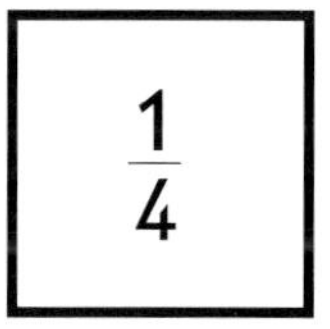

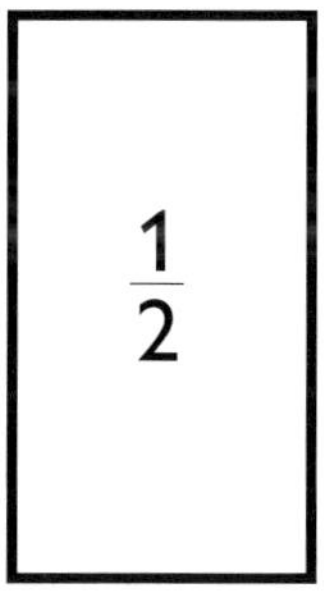

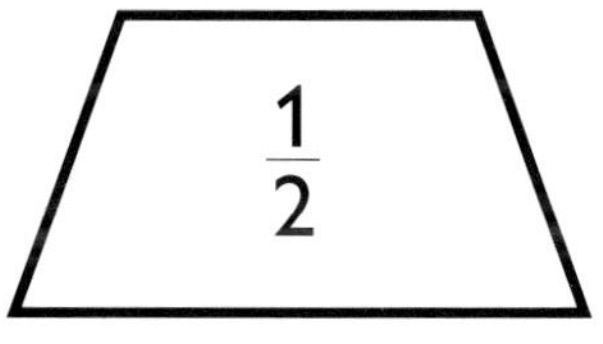

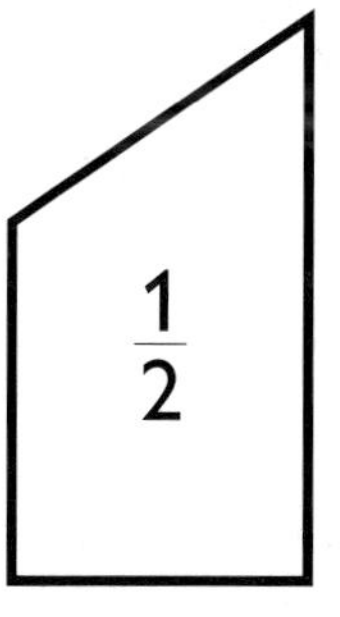

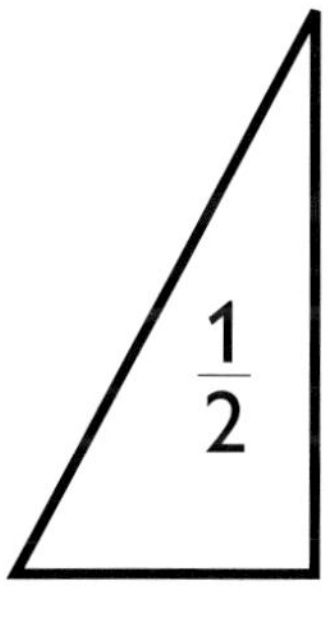

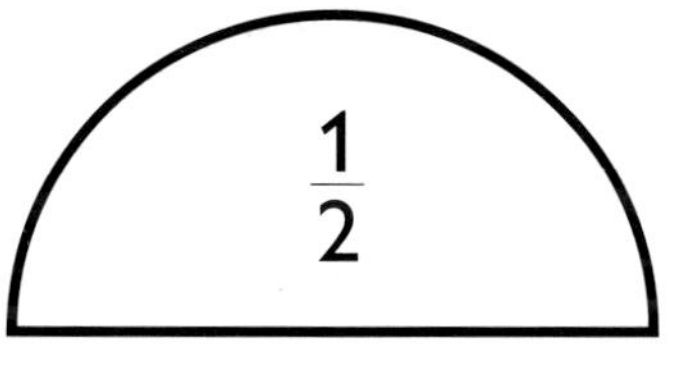

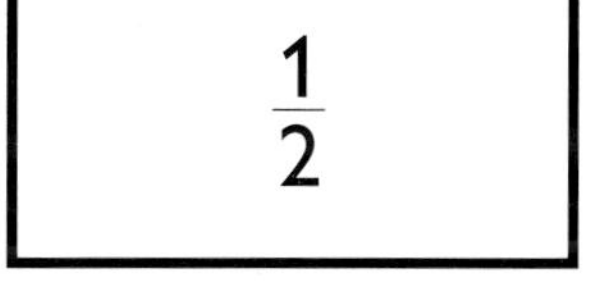

Number puzzles 1

You may use a calculator.
Use the digits 2, 4, 5, 8. Use them in pairs.
Use only the + sign.
Make as many different answers as you can.

e.g.

$$\begin{array}{r} 24 \\ 58\,+ \\ \hline 82 \\ \hline \end{array} \qquad \begin{array}{r} 25 \\ 48\,+ \\ \hline 73 \\ \hline \end{array} \qquad \begin{array}{r} 42 \\ 58\,+ \\ \hline 100 \\ \hline \end{array} \qquad \begin{array}{r} 52 \\ 84\,+ \\ \hline 136 \\ \hline \end{array}$$

What is the largest answer you can make? ☐

Choose four digits of your own
Make two of the digits the same
How many different answers can you make now?

Choose four more digits
This time make three digits the same
How many different answers can you make now?

Number puzzles

1. Each player puts a counter on Start.
2. Take it in turns to roll the two dice.
3. Work out the difference between the two numbers and move the counter to the next shape showing that difference.
4. The first person to reach Home is the winner!

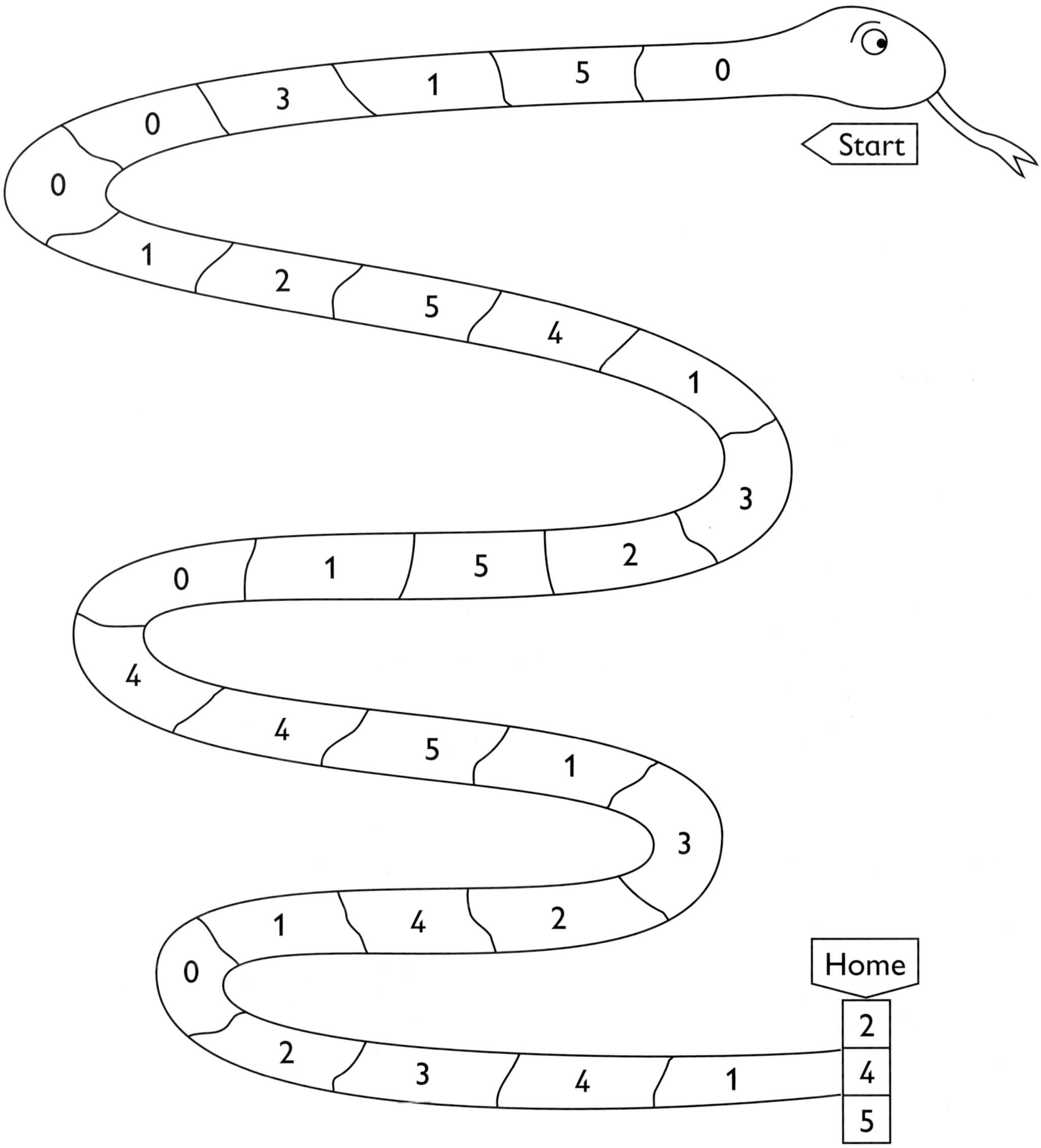

How many?

How many children can have 3 balloons?

☐ children

17 balloons

13 buns

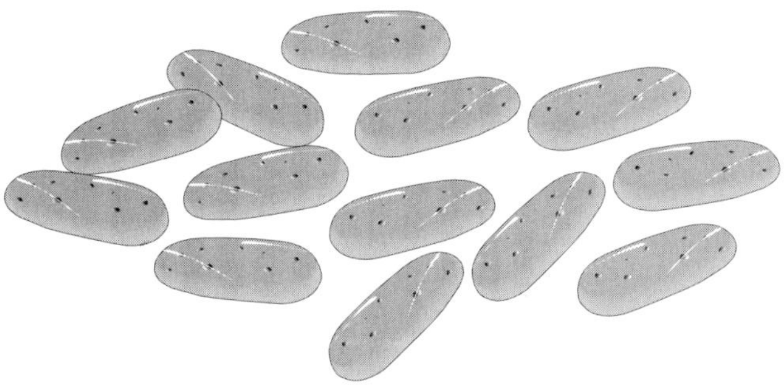

How many children can have 3 buns?

☐ children

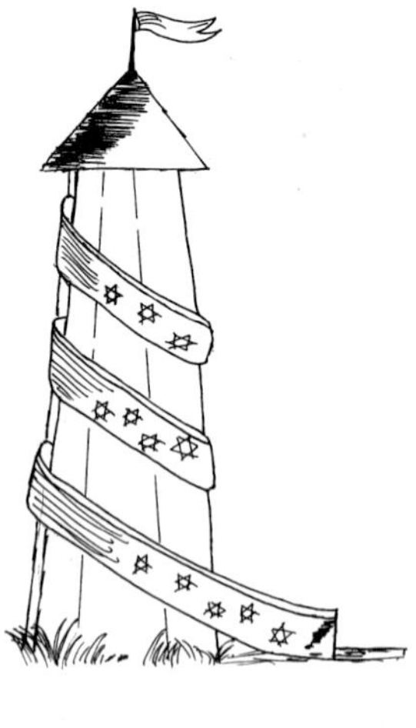

The helter-skelter costs 12p. John has 75p. How many rides can he have?

☐ rides

In the picnic area 6 people can sit at a table.
How many tables do we need for 13 people?

☐ tables

Multiplication squares

Fill in the gaps in the multiplication squares.

×	5	2	3	10
2	10			
5			15	
10				
3				

×	6	7	8	9
2				
5		35		
10			80	
3				

×	7	3	6	5
5				
2				
3			18	
10				50
4				

×	8	9	10	5
5				
2			20	
4		36		
3				

How many multiples of 2, 5 and 10 can you colour on this number square?

1	2	3	4	5	6	7	8	9	10
11	12	13	14	15	16	17	18	19	20
21	22	23	24	25	26	27	28	29	30
31	32	33	34	35	36	37	38	39	40
41	42	43	44	45	46	47	48	49	50
51	52	53	54	55	56	57	58	59	60
61	62	63	64	65	66	67	68	69	70
71	72	73	74	75	76	77	78	79	80
81	82	83	84	85	86	87	88	89	90
91	92	93	94	95	96	97	98	99	100

Divide each square into quarters:

You might need to colour in a square more than once!

More than one bit

Colour in $\frac{1}{2}$ of each of these shapes.

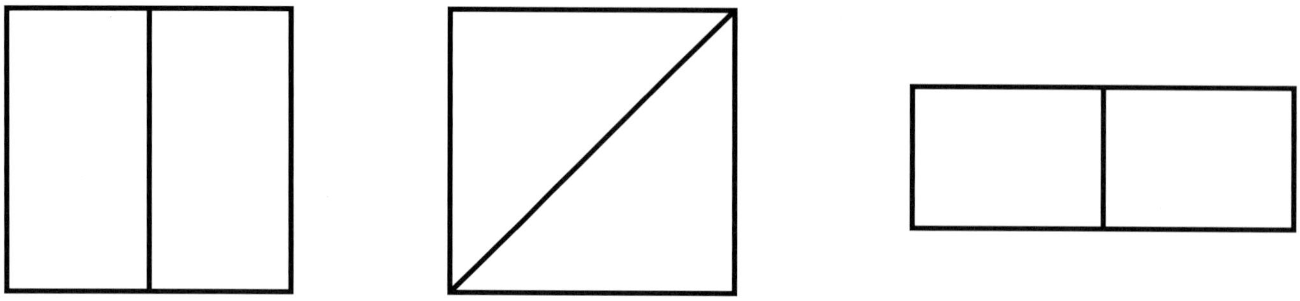

What fraction is not coloured in?

Colour in $\frac{1}{4}$ of each of these shapes.

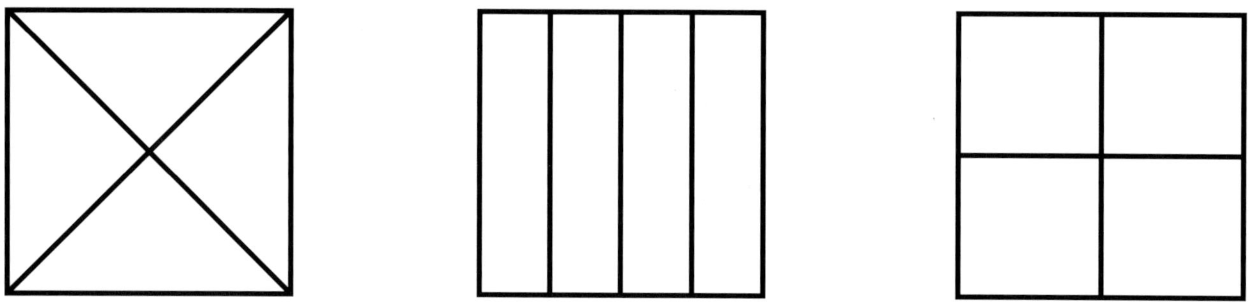

What fraction is not coloured in?

What fraction is **not** shaded in each of these shapes?

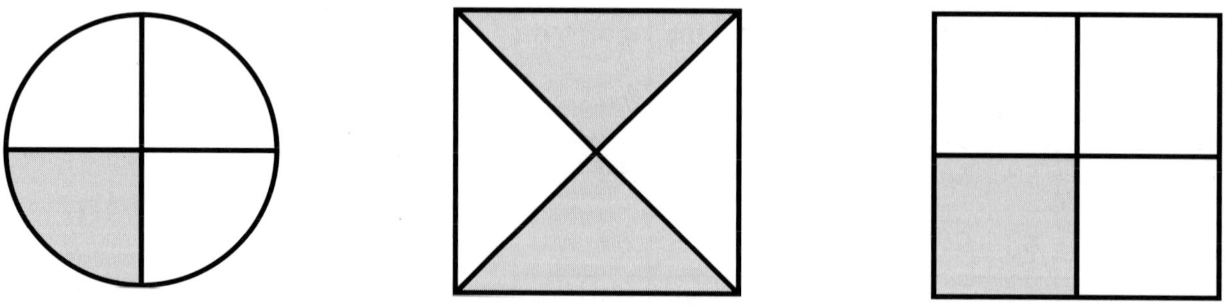

Fractions

What fraction of this bar of chocolate have I eaten? ☐

What fraction is left? ☐

What fraction of the apples have been taken? ☐

What fraction of the apples are left? ☐

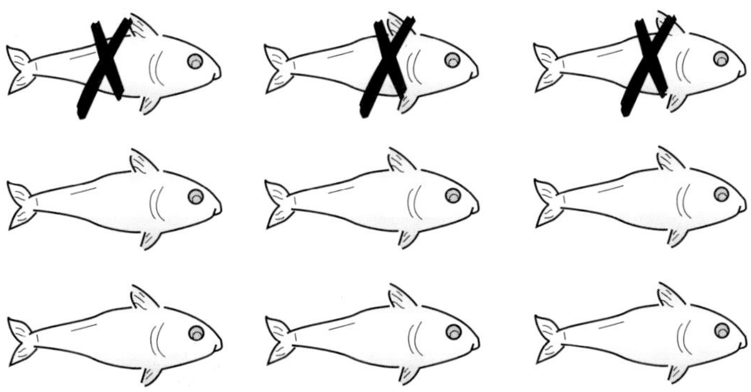

What fraction of the fish have been caught? ☐

What fraction of the fish are left? ☐

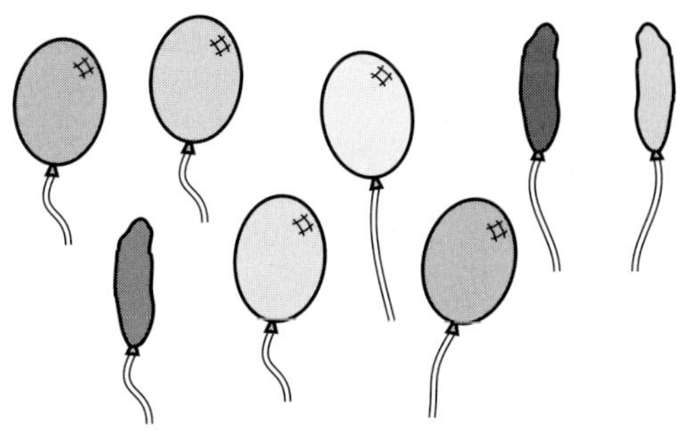

What fraction of the balloons have been burst? ☐

What fraction are left? ☐

The calendar

This shows a month of the year.

M	T	W	T	F	S	Sun
	1	2	3	4	5	6
7	8	9	10	11	12	13
14	15	16	17	18	19	20
21	22	23	24	25	26	27
28	29	30	31			

1) How many Mondays are there in the month?

2) How many Fridays are there in the month?

3) What day of the week is the 17th?

4) What day of the week is the 27th?

5) What date is it on the third Wednesday in the month?

6) What day of the week was the last day of the previous month?

7) What day of the week will be the first day of the next month?

8) What months could this be?

Time problems

Write how many hours and minutes.

1. 75 minutes ____________

2. 85 minutes ____________

3. 90 minutes ____________

4. 100 minutes ____________

5. 180 minutes ____________

Write how many days:

1. 30 hours ← more than 1 day ____________

2. 40 hours ____________

3. 70 hours ____________

4. 50 hours ____________

5. 80 hours ____________

6. 90 hours ____________

Use a calculator.

How many seconds in a day?

____

How many hours in a week?

____

How many minutes altogether in Saturday and Sunday?

____

Venn diagrams

Fill in the missing labels and in put your own numbers.

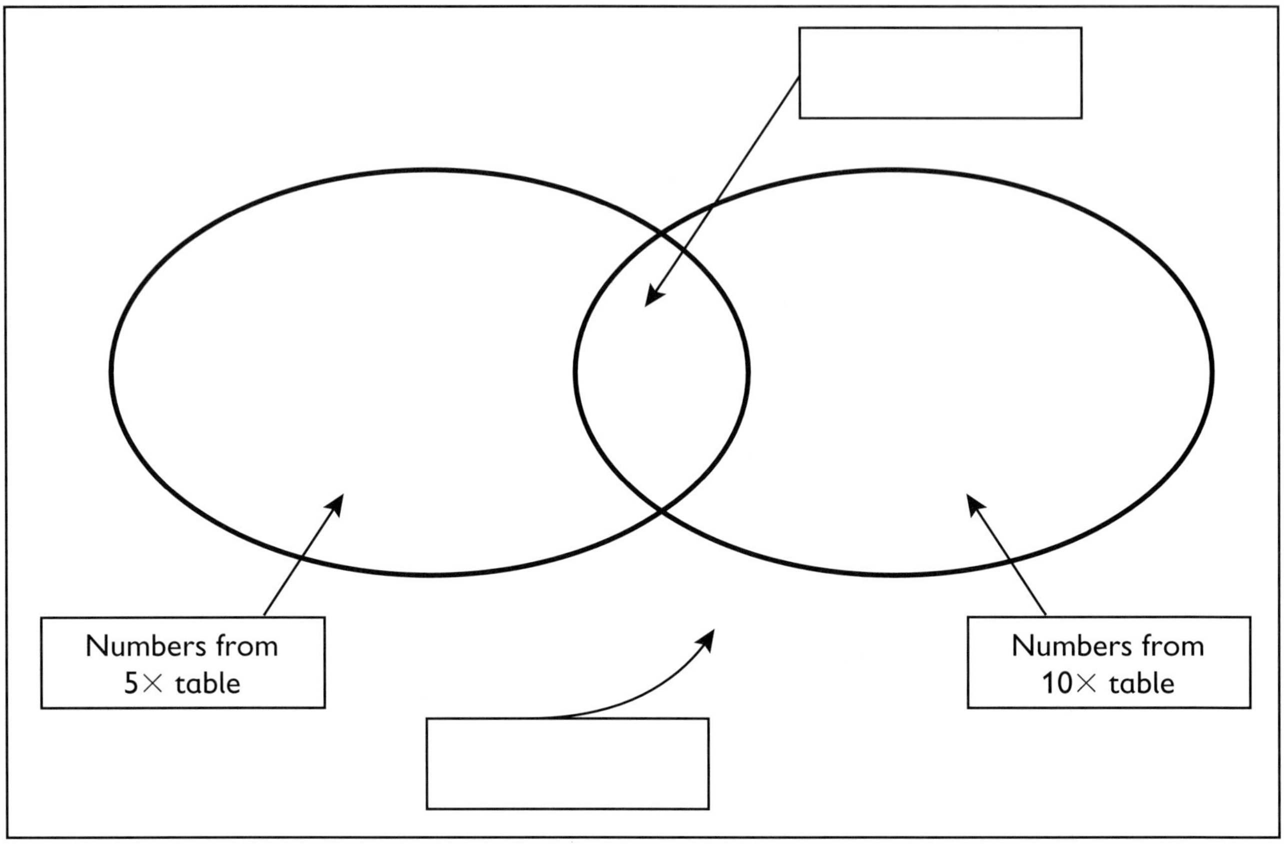

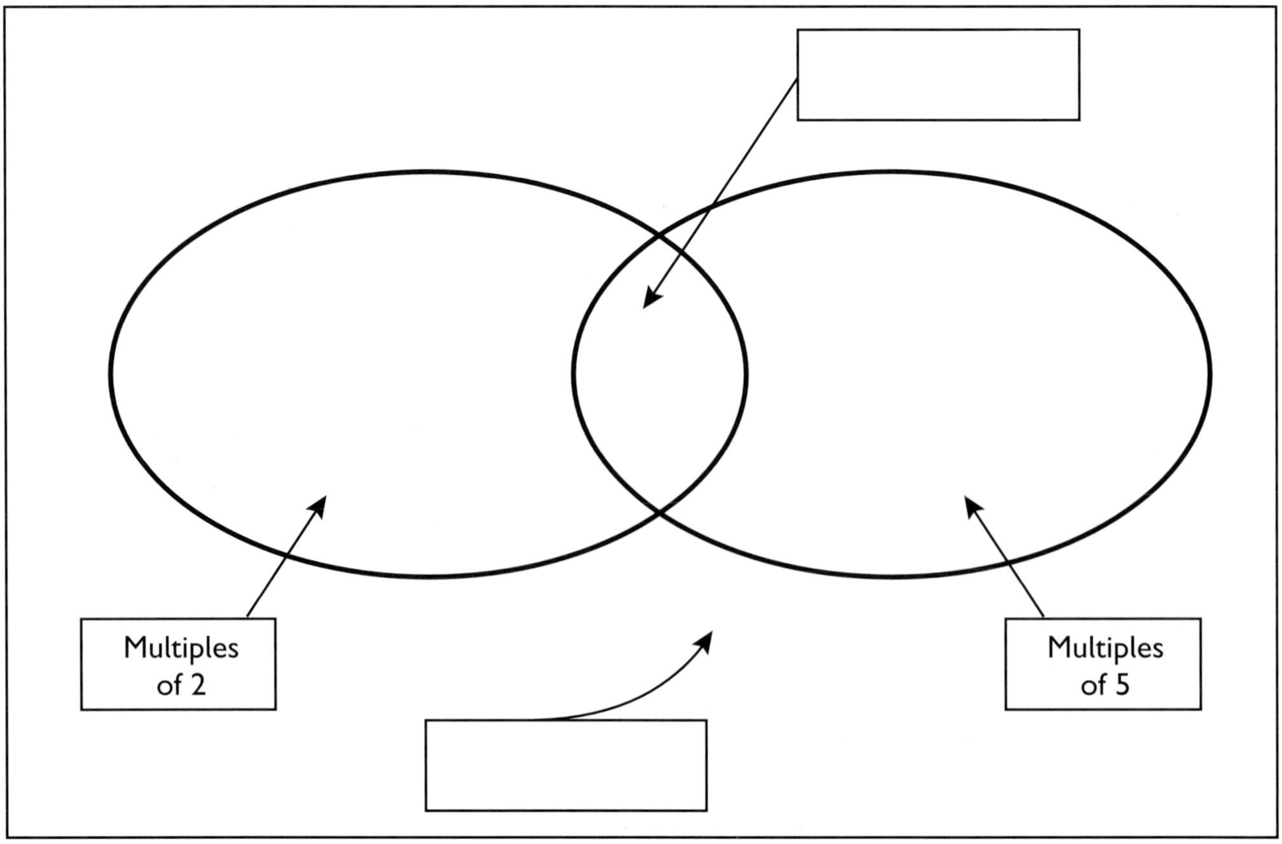

Carroll diagrams

Put these numbers in the following Carroll diagram.

6 12 18 50 27

	under 30	not under 30
even numbers		
not even numbers		

Put these numbers in the following Carroll diagram.

3 7 10 30 21 14 8

	3× table	not in 3× table
even numbers		
not even numbers		

Put these numbers in the following Carroll diagram.

2 4 11 15 5 7 8 11 22

	under 10	not under 10
multiples of 2		
multiples of 5		

Homework 1

This week we have been learning about addition and subtraction.

$18 + 5 = 23$	and	$23 - 5 = 18$
$5 + 18 = 23$		$23 - 18 = 5$

Now write 2 addition and 2 subtraction statements for:

a) $14 + 6 = 20$

1) $14 + 6 = 20$
2) ____________
3) ____________
4) ____________

b) $19 + 4 = 23$

1) ____________
2) ____________
3) ____________
4) ____________

c) $17 + 4 = 21$

1) ____________
2) ____________
3) ____________
4) ____________

d) $14 + 9 = 23$

1) ____________
2) ____________
3) ____________
4) ____________

e) $21 + 5 = 26$

1) ____________
2) ____________
3) ____________
4) ____________

This week we have been learning about money.

Use a separate piece of paper for these problems.

1. John bought a newspaper for 50 pence, a packet of sweets for 20 pence and a comic for 45 pence. How much change did he get from £2.00?

2. Sam bought a notepad for 25p, a pencil for 20p and a rubber for 10p. How much change did he get from £1.00?

3. Helen bought a doll for 75p and a game for 50p. How much change did she get from £2.00?

4. Sarah bought a ring for 60p and a magazine for 70p. How much change did she get from £2.00?

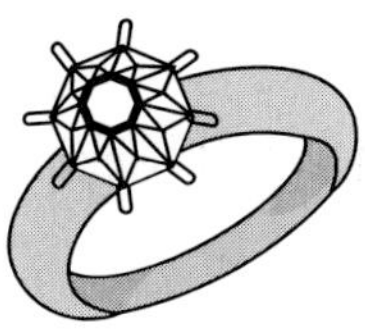

5. Zoe bought some sweets for 60p and some posters for 90p. How much change did she get from £2.00?

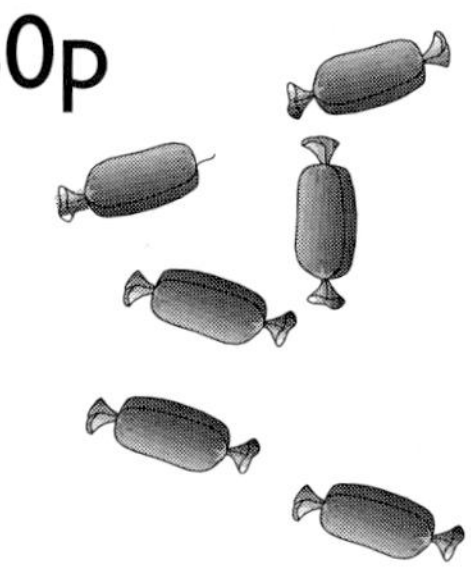

Homework 3

This week we have been learning about time.

Find the TV listings in your newspaper or from the television. Work out how long your five favourite programmes last.

1. Top of the Pops = 30 minutes
2. ______________ = __________
3. ______________ = __________
4. ______________ = __________
5. ______________ = __________
6. ______________ = __________

Write down how long it takes to:

a) Set the table for tea? __________________

b) Make your bed? __________________

c) Do this homework? __________________

This week we have been measuring length.

Estimate the measurements of the following:

The length of your little finger ____ cm

Your height in centimetres ____ cm

Your height in little fingers ____ little fingers

How long are these ropes?

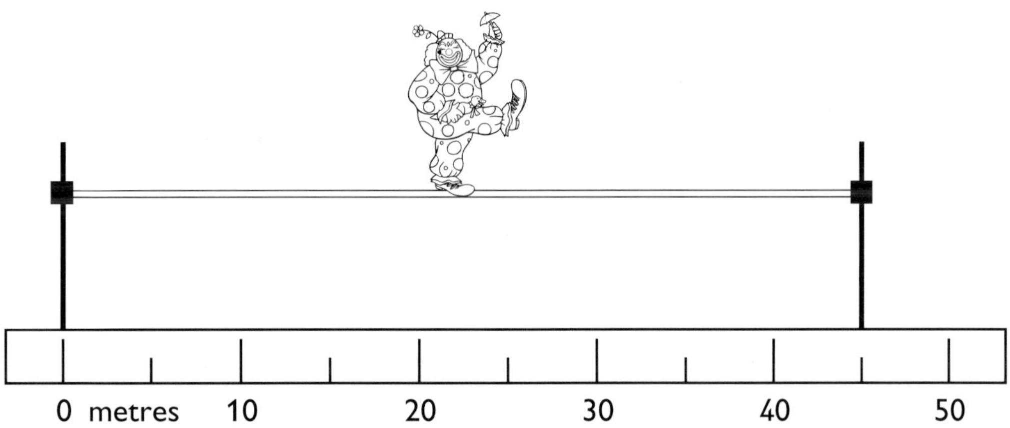

____

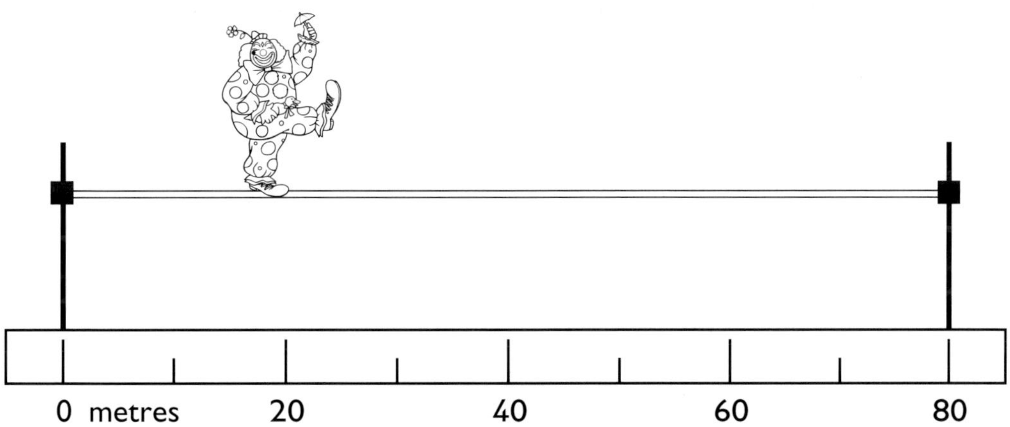

____

Homework 5

This week we have been learning about shapes.

Look for everyday items in your home.

Do any of them have right angles as part of their shape?

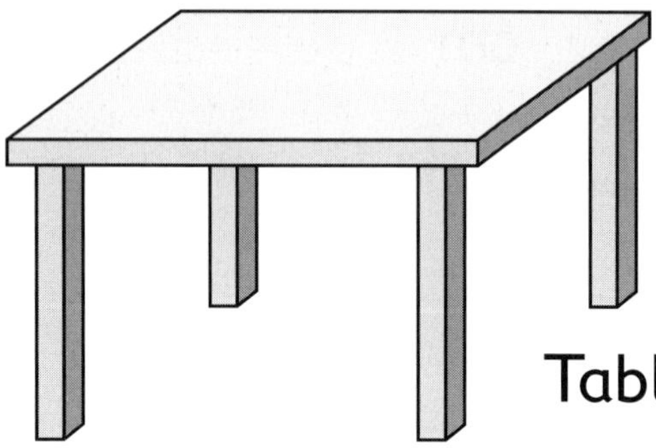

Tables

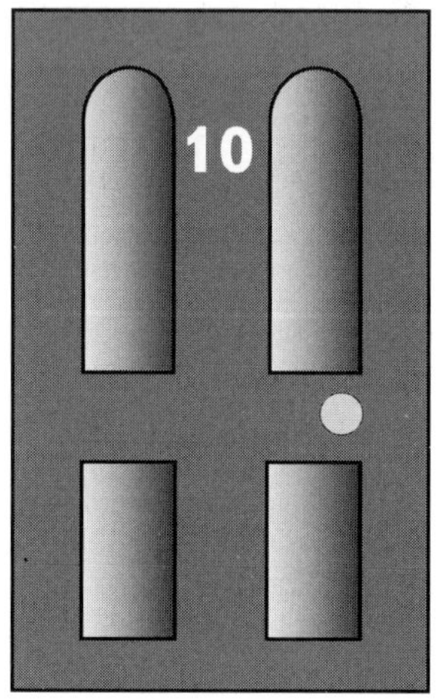

Doors

Fireplaces

Tiles

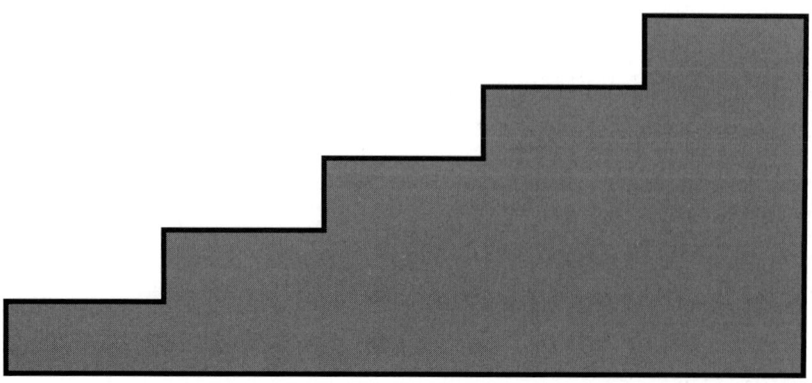

Stairs

This week we have been counting by grouping numbers.

Count the number of balls in each goal.

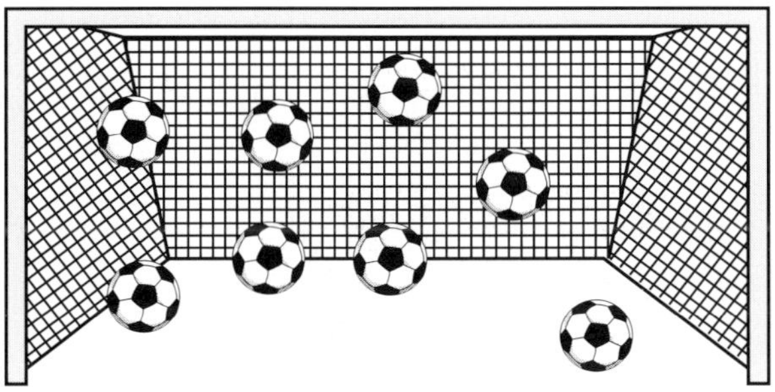

____

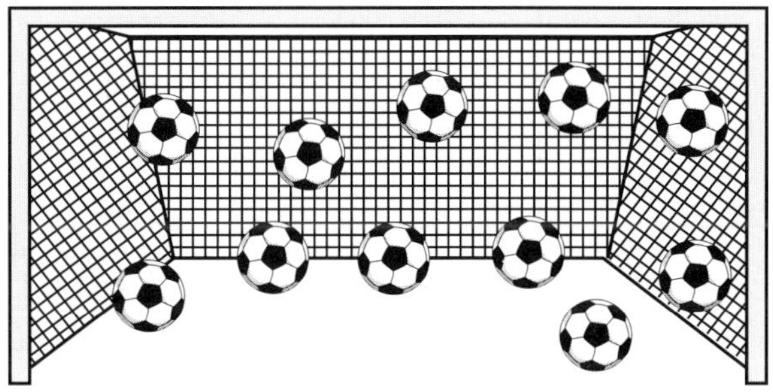

____

Circle all the multiples of 2.

Circle the balloons that are part of the 2× table.

3	4	10	5	9
2	7	11	8	
14	15	6	18	8
3	6	4	10	4

Write down the odd numbers. ________________________________

Write down the even numbers. ________________________________

Homework 7

This week we have been working on multiplication and division.

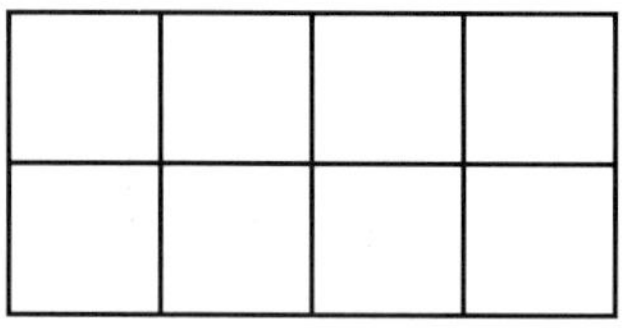

= 2×4
4×2

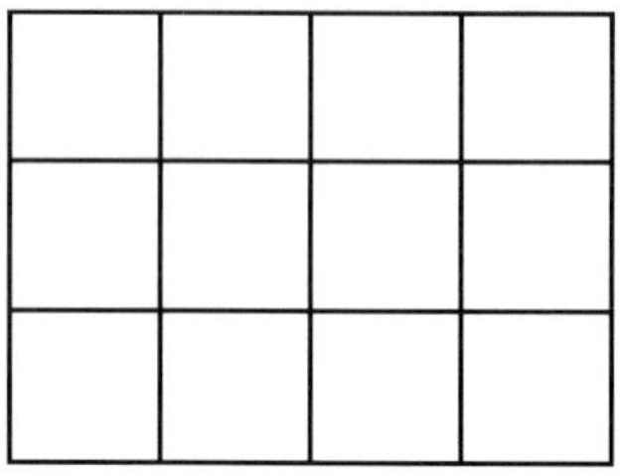

= 3×4
4×3

Write down 2 multiplication facts next to each of these rectangles.

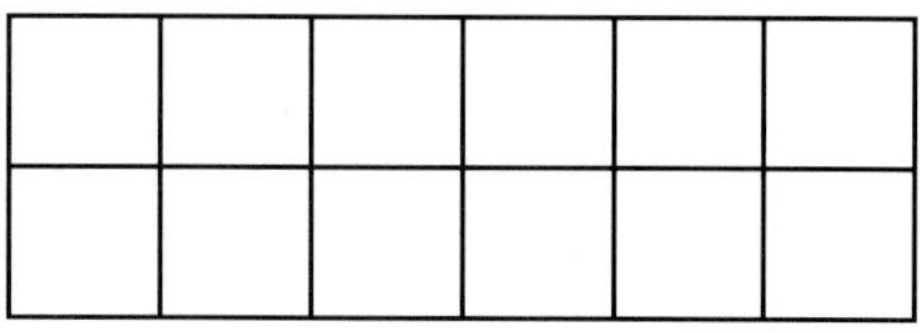

=

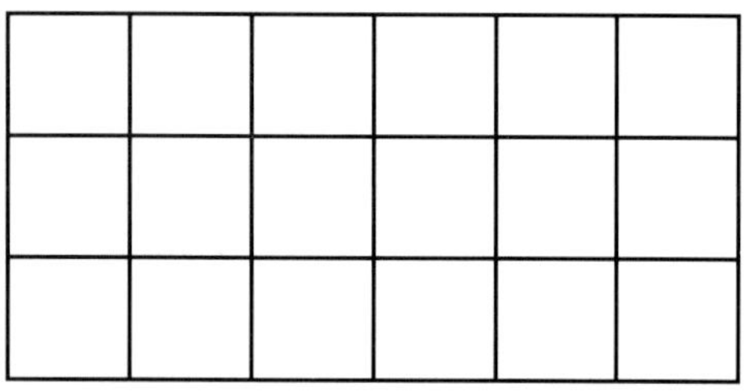

=

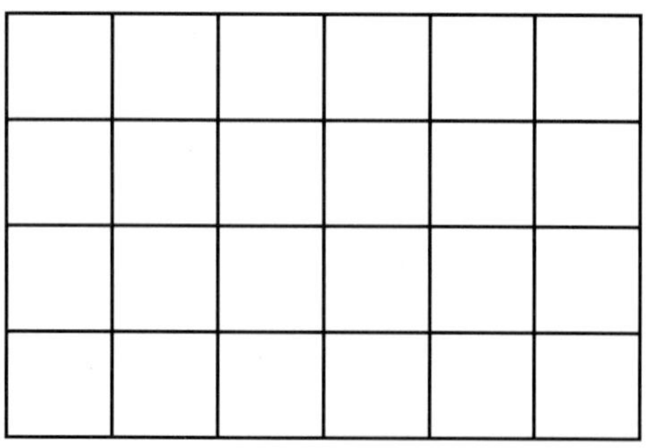

=

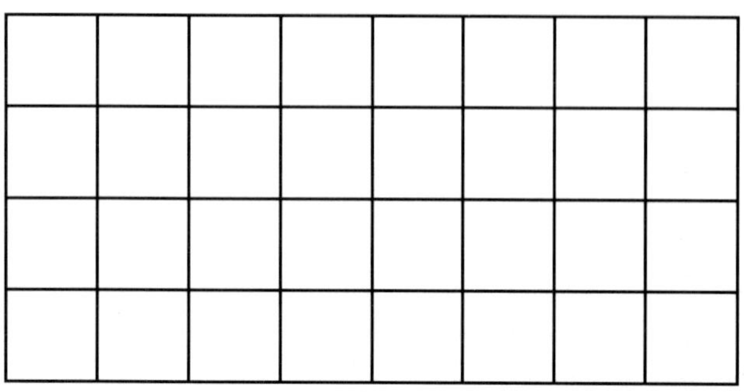

=

This week we have been working on fractions.

Find $\frac{1}{3}$ of 12 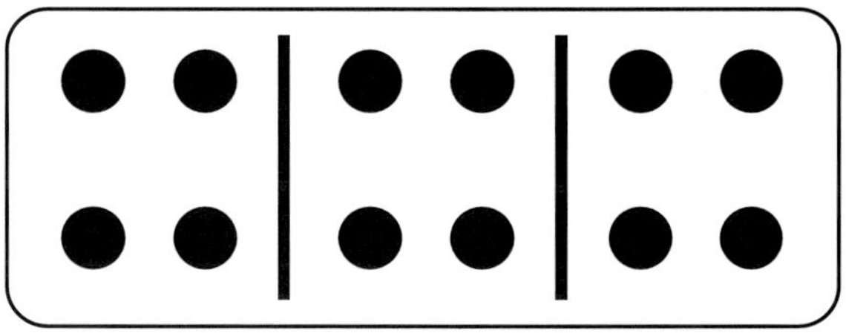 4

Find $\frac{1}{4}$ of 12 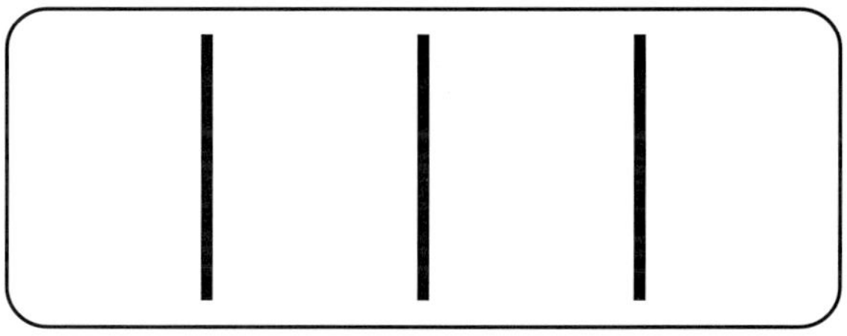

Find $\frac{2}{3}$ of 12 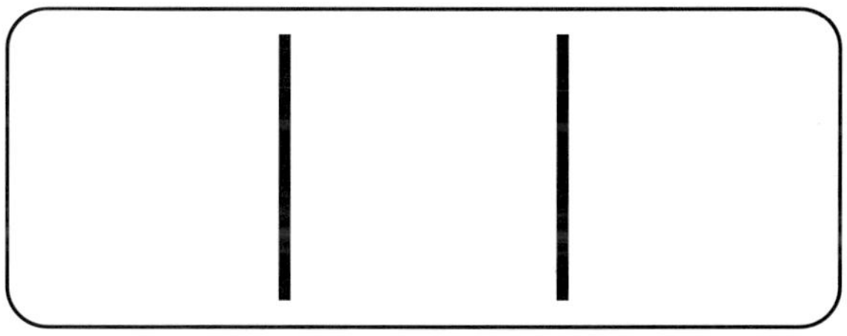

Find $\frac{3}{4}$ of 20 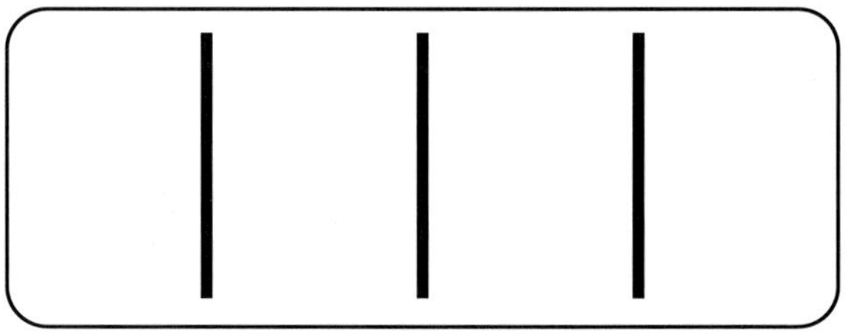

Find $\frac{2}{3}$ of 30 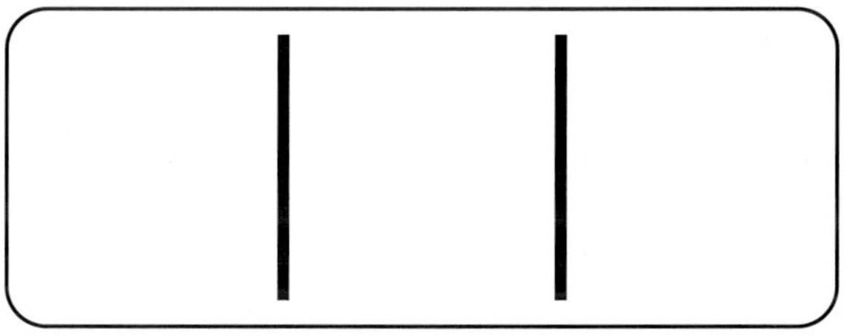

Find $\frac{1}{4}$ of 28 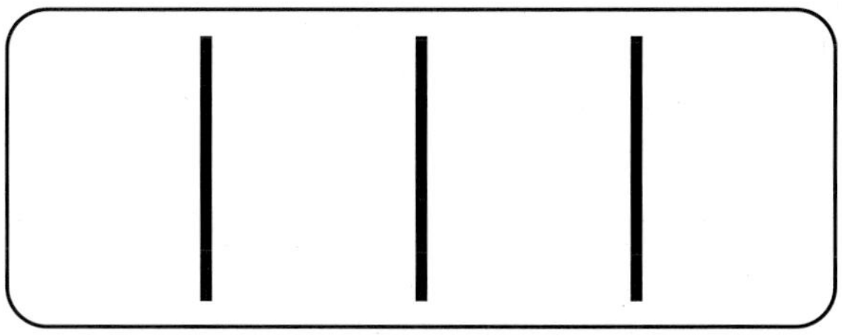

Homework 9

This week we have been practising subtraction.

How many minutes between:

2:10 and 2:35

____

4:15 and 4:30

____

3:20 and 3:55

____

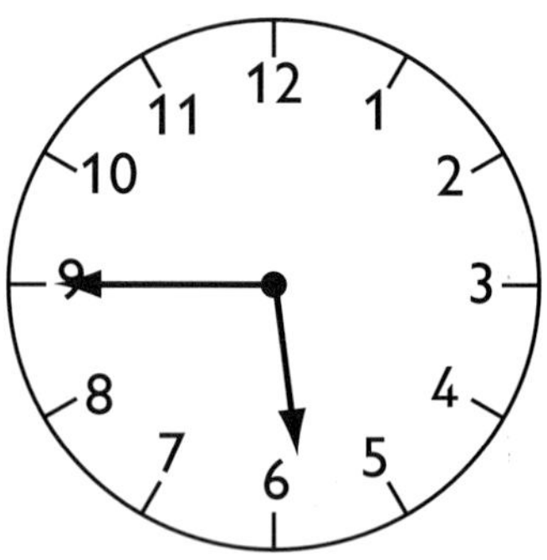
quarter to 6

and

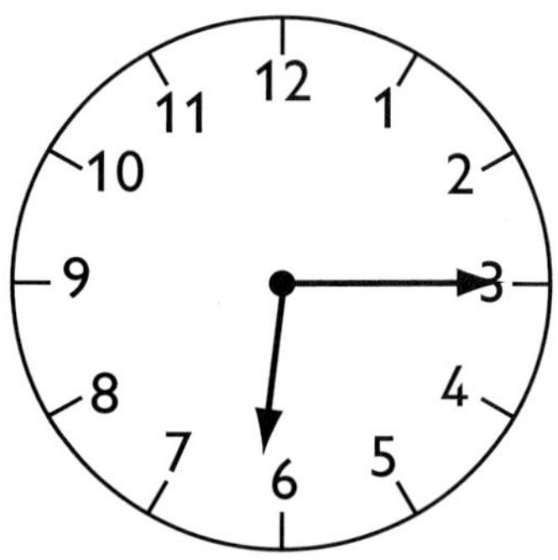
quarter past 6

____

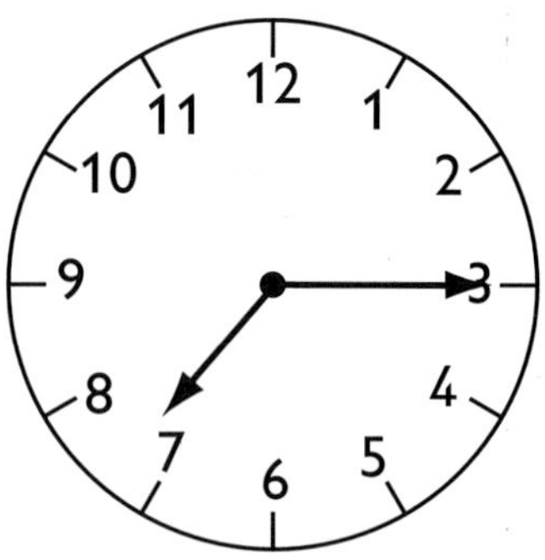
quarter past 7

and

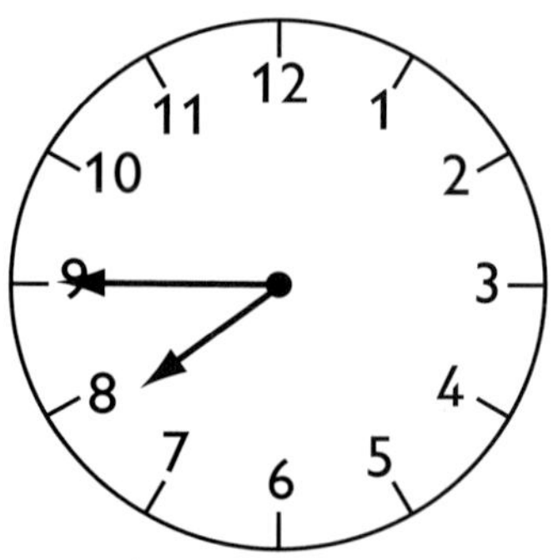
quarter to 8

____

This week we have been looking at how to handle data.

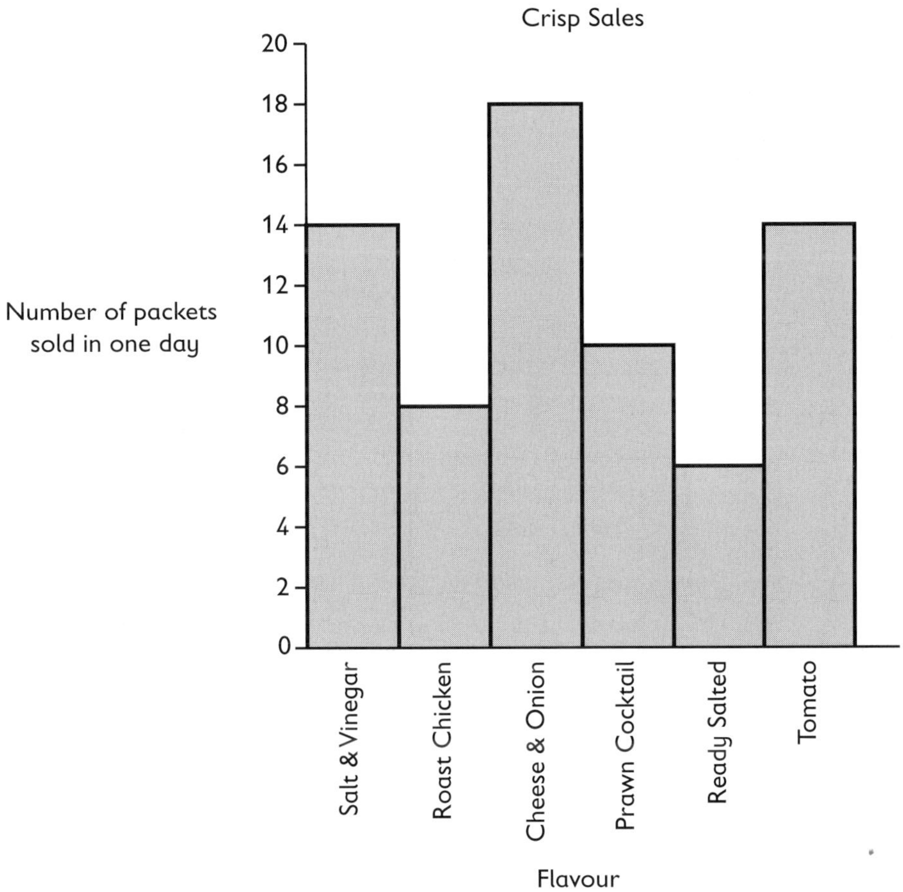

1. Which crisps sold most? __________

2. Which crisps sold fewest? __________

3. How many packs of Prawn Cocktail crisps were sold? __________

4. How many more Cheese & Onion were sold than Ready Salted? __________

5. How many fewer Roast Chicken were sold than Salt & Vinegar? __________

6. Which two flavours sold the same number of packets? __________

Homework 11

This week we have been comparing numbers and putting them in order.

How heavy is it?

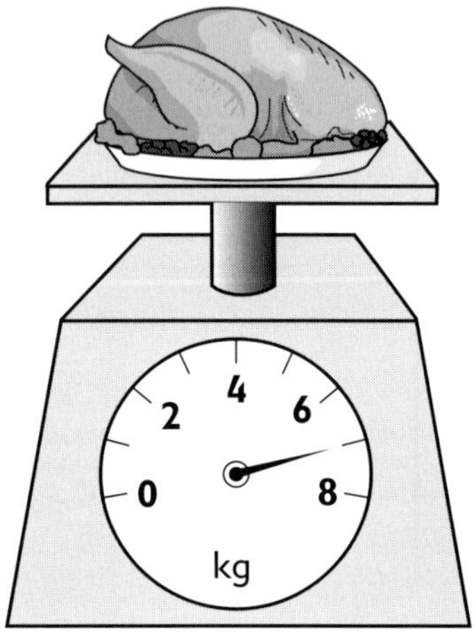

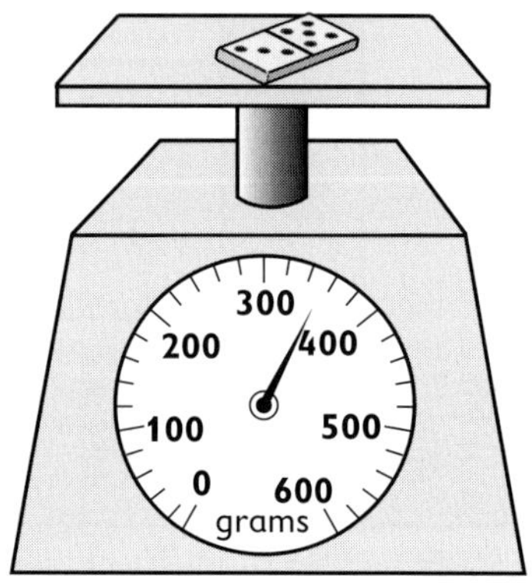

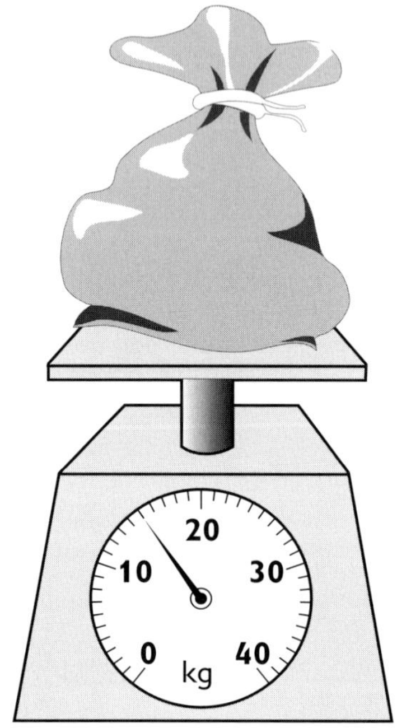

_________ kg   _________ g   _________ kg

Show the weight.

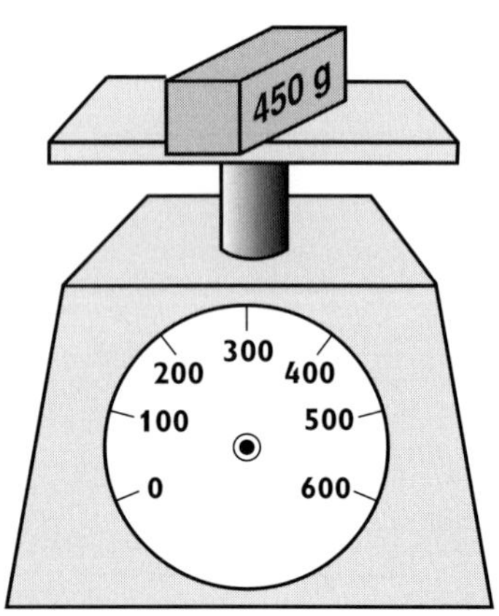

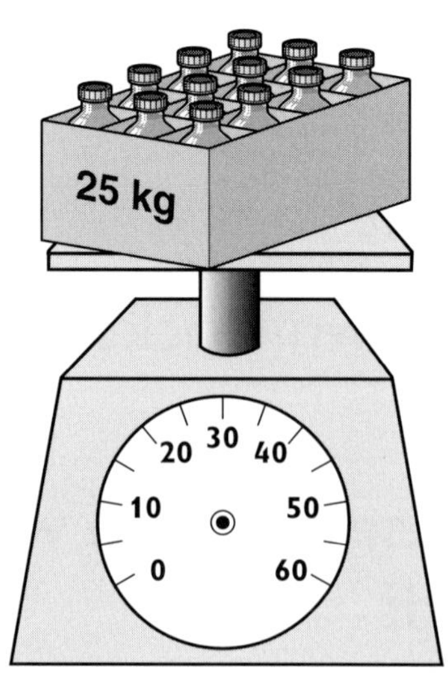

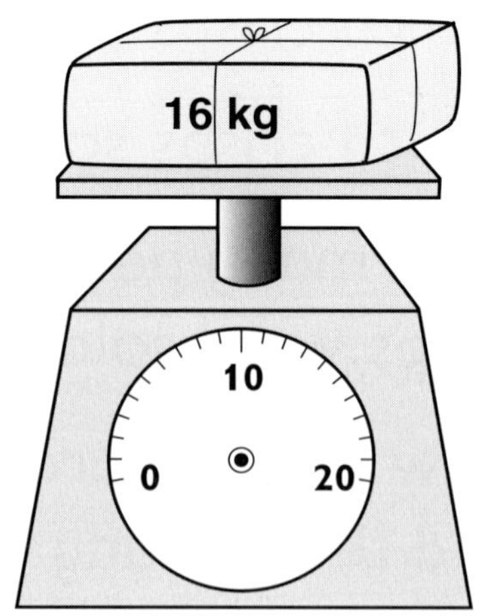

Weigh your family or friends.

Who is the heaviest? ______________________

Who is the lightest? ______________________

This week we have been practising mental addition.

Put the larger number first then add:

20 + 40 = ______________________

30 + 50 = ______________________

60 + 70 = ______________________

80 + **40 + 60** = 180
(100)

Try these

60 + 40 + 30 = ______________________

30 + 60 + **70** = ______________________

50 + 45 + 50 = ______________________

60 + 35 + 50 = ______________________

35 + 35 + 40 = ______________________

25 + 40 + 60 = ______________________

30 + 50 + 25 = ______________________

Homework 13

This week we have been solving money problems.

There is a disco at a village hall.

Refreshments

Tea	12p
Buns	18p
Orange drinks	11p
Cakes	25p

Tickets

	Adults	Child
Thur	25p	12p
Fri	30p	15p
Sat	35p	18p

Find the cost of these:

4 buns and 2 orange drinks ____________

3 orange drinks and 2 teas ____________

3 cakes and 3 teas ____________

5 teas and 2 buns ____________

Find the cost of these tickets:

3 adults and 1 child for Saturday ____________

3 children and their mother on Friday ____________

2 adults and 1 child on Thursday ____________

4 adults and 4 children on Thursday ____________

This week we have been looking at and describing shapes.

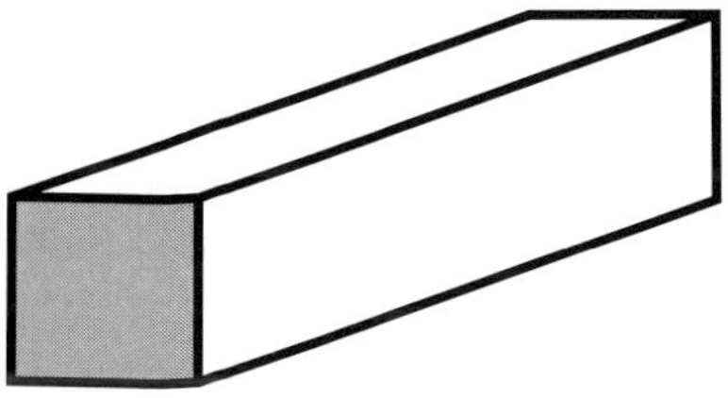

This is a *cuboid*.

What shape is the grey face?

____

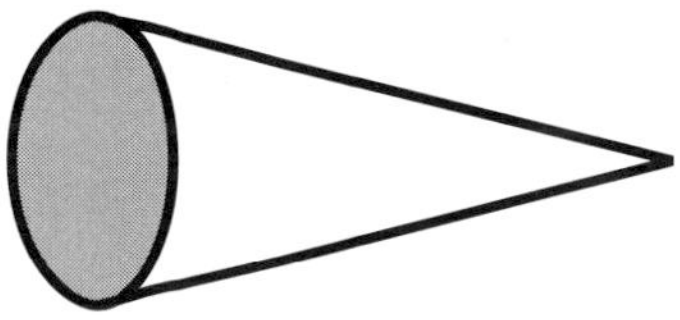

This is a *cone*.

What shape is the grey face?

____

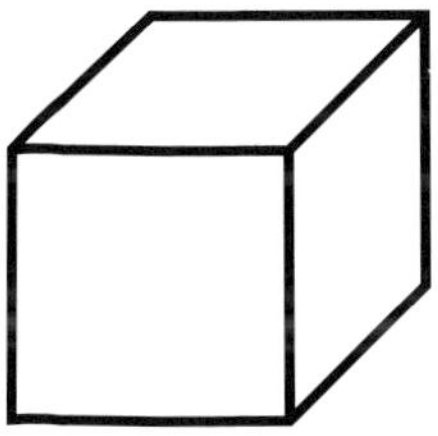

This is a *c*_________

Each face is a square.

____

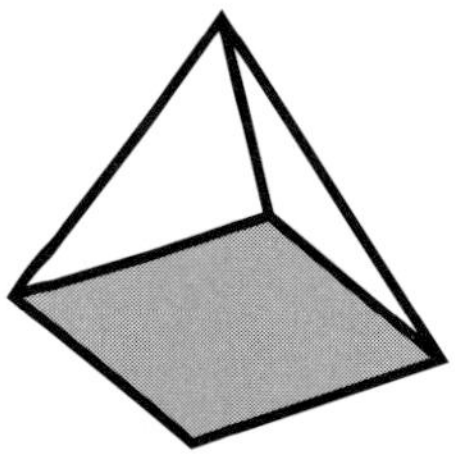

This is a *p*_________

What shape is the grey face?

____

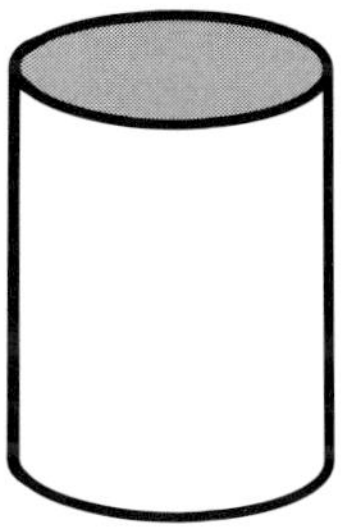

This is a *c*_________

What shape is the grey face?

____

This is a *triangular prism*.

What shape is the grey face?

____

Homework 15

This week we have been measuring mass and time.

1. Carmen's alarm goes off at 6.30 am. She gets up 10 minutes later.
   She takes 36 minutes to get ready for school.
   School is a 10 minute walk away.
   When does she get to school?

2. Linda left home to go to work at 9.00 am but got stuck in a traffic jam for 30 minutes.
   If she normally got to work at 10.15 am, what time did she arrive on this day?

3. John left school at 4 pm but fell off his bike and was delayed for 20 minutes.
   He then had to walk home, which took him 30 minutes longer than usual.
   If he normally arrived home at 4.30 pm what time did he actually arrive on this day?

This week we have been practising counting and describing simple number sequences.

1. David looked after 23 cats during his school holidays.
Two of the cats ran away.
David found the cats with 6 kittens.
How many pets did he look after then?

2. 8 football teams scored 28 goals between them.
3 of the goals were disallowed.
If Lincoln City scored 7 goals, how many goals were scored by the other teams?

3. 7 netball teams score 37 goals between them.
The best team scored 12 goals. How many goals did the worst team score if the rest of the teams scored 20 goals?

4. 10 girls bought 4 hair clips each.
2 of the girls took theirs back and bought 6 different hair clips each.
How many hair clips were bought altogether by the 10 girls?

Homework 17

This week we have been working with mental calculation strategies.

20 + 20 + 40 =

40 + 20 + 20 = 80

Largest number first

20 + 20(40) and double it = 80

Add the two 20s together to make 40 and double it

2 + 4 + 2 = 8 and times by 10 = 80

Add together the tens as single digits and times by 10

Try these in the same way on a separate piece of paper.

1. 30 + 10 + 10 = ?

2. 40 + 20 + 40 = ?

3. 60 + 10 + 10 = ?

4. 70 + 10 + 10 = ?

5. 50 + 20 + 20 = ?

This week we have been working on solving problems.

I think of a number, double it, then add 5.
The answer is 25.
What is my number? ☐

I think of a number, halve it, then add 5.
The answer is 30.
What is my number? ☐

I think of a number, divide it by 3, then add 4.
The answer is 14.
What is my number? ☐

I think of a number, divide it by 5, then add 7.
The answer is 12.
What is my number? ☐

Find the Answers

1. 50 guests, 27 chairs.
   How many chairs are needed? ☐
2. 200 aeroplane seats, 150 passengers.
   How many spare seats are there? ☐
3. 30 children, 17 pencils.
   How many more pencils do we need for one each? ☐
4. 50 children, 27 rulers.
   How many more rulers do we need for one each? ☐
5. 25 footballers, 32 footballs.
   How many footballs will not be used? ☐

Homework 19

This week we have been working on fractions and recognising equivalent fractions.

1 WHOLE ONE									
$\frac{1}{2}$					$\frac{1}{2}$				
$\frac{1}{4}$			$\frac{1}{4}$		$\frac{1}{4}$			$\frac{1}{4}$	
$\frac{1}{5}$		$\frac{1}{5}$		$\frac{1}{5}$		$\frac{1}{5}$		$\frac{1}{5}$	
$\frac{1}{10}$	$\frac{1}{10}$	$\frac{1}{10}$	$\frac{1}{10}$	$\frac{1}{10}$	$\frac{1}{10}$	$\frac{1}{10}$	$\frac{1}{10}$	$\frac{1}{10}$	$\frac{1}{10}$

Fill in the boxes using the Fraction Wall above to help you.

$$\frac{1}{2} = \frac{\square}{4} \qquad \frac{\square}{4} = \frac{2}{8}$$

$$\frac{3}{4} = \frac{\square}{8} \qquad \frac{2}{4} = \frac{\square}{8}$$

$$\frac{1}{5} = \frac{\square}{10} \qquad \frac{2}{5} = \frac{\square}{10}$$

$$\frac{1}{2} = \frac{\square}{10} \qquad \frac{2}{4} = \frac{\square}{10}$$

$$1 = \frac{\square}{5} \qquad 1 = \frac{\square}{10}$$

$$1 = \frac{\square}{4} \qquad 1 = \frac{\square}{2}$$

This week we have been looking at bar charts.

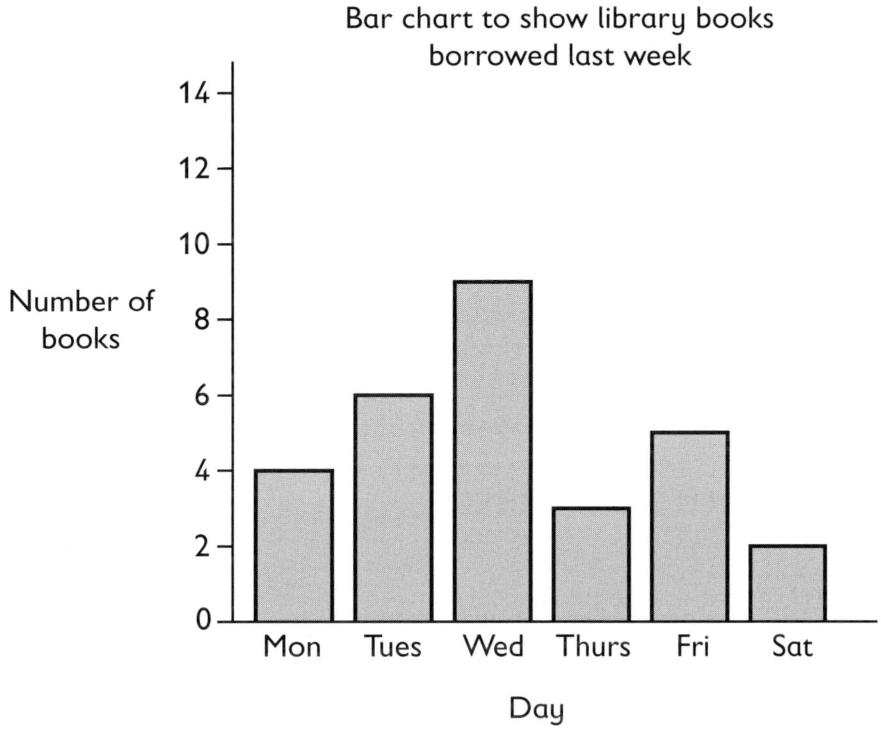

How many books were borrowed on

1. Thursday ____
2. Monday ____
3. Friday ____
4. Wednesday ____
5. Saturday ____
6. Sunday ____

On which day were:

most books borrowed? ____________

fewest books borrowed? ____________

How many books altogether were borrowed:

on Wednesday and Thursday? ____________

on Monday and Tuesday? ____________

on Thursday, Friday and Saturday? ____________

Homework 21

This week we have been comparing, ordering and rounding numbers.

Which number is the largest?

273 or 164 ______________

179 or 123 ______________

364 or 421 ______________

195 or 271 ______________

Which number is the smallest?

164 or 175 ______________

236 or 121 ______________

157 or 216 ______________

324 or 161 ______________

167 or 375 ______________

Put these sets of numbers in order, starting with the smallest.

1. 327, 165, 319, 276, 87, 217

____

2. 165, 298, 371, 245, 169

____

3. 146, 273, 169, 216, 624.

____

This week we have been working on mental addition and subtraction.

Example

19 + 2 + 5 + 8 = ?

19 + (2 + 8) + 5

(19 + 10) + 5

29 + 5 = (34)

Now try these.

1. 17 + 3 + 6 + 7 =

3. 5 + 6 + 11 + 5 =

2. 16 + 4 + 6 + 3 =

4. 9 + 7 + 3 + 4 =

Homework 23

This week we have been solving problems.

Decide if you need to use a mental strategy or pencil and paper to work out these addition sums.

$10 + 40 =$ (large number first, add up the tens, $4 + 1$, then times by 10)

$25 + 25 =$ ____________________

$30 + 25 =$ ____________________

$40 + 15 =$ ____________________

$270 + 20 =$ ____________________

$125 + 37 = 100 + 20 + 30 + 5 + 7$

$135 + 21 =$ ____________________

$120 + 52 =$ ____________________

$231 + 106 =$ ____________________

$321 + 111 =$ ____________________

$460 + 123 =$ ____________________

$500 + 106 =$ ____________________

This week we have been measuring capacity.

Carmen is ill.
She has 5 ml of medicine after every meal, 3 times a day.
She starts the medicine after tea on Monday evening.
She finishes the medicine after lunch on Friday.
How much medicine has she had?

Len buys 1 litre of fizzy lemon.
He and 3 friends each drink the same amount.
There is 200 ml of fizzy lemon left.
How much did they each drink?

Darren collects a bag of potatoes weighing 55 kg.
His family use the following amounts each day:

M	T	W	T	F	S	S
1 kg	$1\frac{1}{2}$ kg	$1\frac{1}{2}$ kg	1 kg	$\frac{1}{2}$ kg	2 kg	2 kg

How many kilograms are left at the end of the week?

Homework 25

This week we have been investigating symmetry.

Can you draw any lines of symmetry on the 26 letters of the alphabet?

A B C D E F G

H I J K L M N

O P Q R S T U

V W X Y Z

Use a mirror to help you.

Remember: A shape is only symmetrical when one side of the line is an exact reflection of the other.

This week we have been looking at properties of number.

Write a sum for each answer. The first is done for you.

You can only use odd numbers and the + sign.

5 + 3 ——→ 8
_____ ——→ 14
_____ ——→ 122
_____ ——→ 46
_____ ——→ 6

_____ ——→ 7
_____ ——→ 16
_____ ——→ 108
_____ ——→ 52
_____ ——→ 8

_____ ——→ 9
_____ ——→ 12
_____ ——→ 115
_____ ——→ 60
_____ ——→ 8

_____ ——→ 4
_____ ——→ 56
_____ ——→ 178 ⇦ For this one use a + and − sign for each one.
_____ ——→ 62
_____ ——→ 7

Homework 27

This week we have been practising multiplication and division and have been using mental calculation strategies.

1. Sam sold 8 packets of crisps to 3 classes in the Tuck Shop.
   How many packets did he sell altogether?

   ____

2. Mandy has chopped up sugar into cubes to give to her 4 horses.
   She's made 44 sugar cubes today.
   How many cubes will each horse get if she shares them out evenly? Write out the whole sum.

   ____

   ____

3. Paul eats seven sandwiches every day for four days.
   How many sandwiches does he eat altogether?

   ____

4. Make up a problem of your own.
   Use $\times$ and $\div$ operations and these numbers: 24, 6, 4, 3.

This week we have been practising work on fractions.

These are the tables tests scores for class 2X (all out of 10).

	Week 1	*Week 2*	*Week 3*
Andy	7	7	9
John	6	6	8
David	8	7	7
William	9	8	6
Sarah	8	9	5
Jane	7	10	4
Emily	9	10	3
Kieran	10	9	2
Alma	9	10	8
Ezra	8	10	7

What fraction of the class got $\frac{9}{10}$ in Week 1?

What fraction of the class got $\frac{8}{10}$ in Week 3?

What fraction of the class scored $\frac{10}{10}$ in Week 2?

Homework 29

This week we have been practising addition and subtraction and time.

1. 27 +
12
___

2. 36 +
23
___

3. 162 +
21
___

4. 64 −
12
___

5. 68 −
14
___

6. 175 −
21
___

7. Add up the number of minutes in 5 hours.

____

8. Add up the number of minutes in 3 weeks.

____

9. Add up the number of weeks in 2 years.

____

10. 36 −
24
___

11. 169 −
121
___

12. 178 −
124
___

11. Make a Time Line for your weekend.

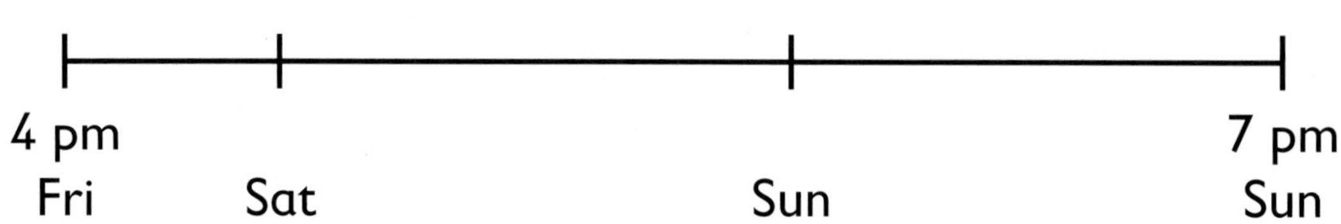

This week we have been practising handling data and have looked at Venn and Carroll diagrams.

Fill in the Venn diagram. Look at the labels carefully.

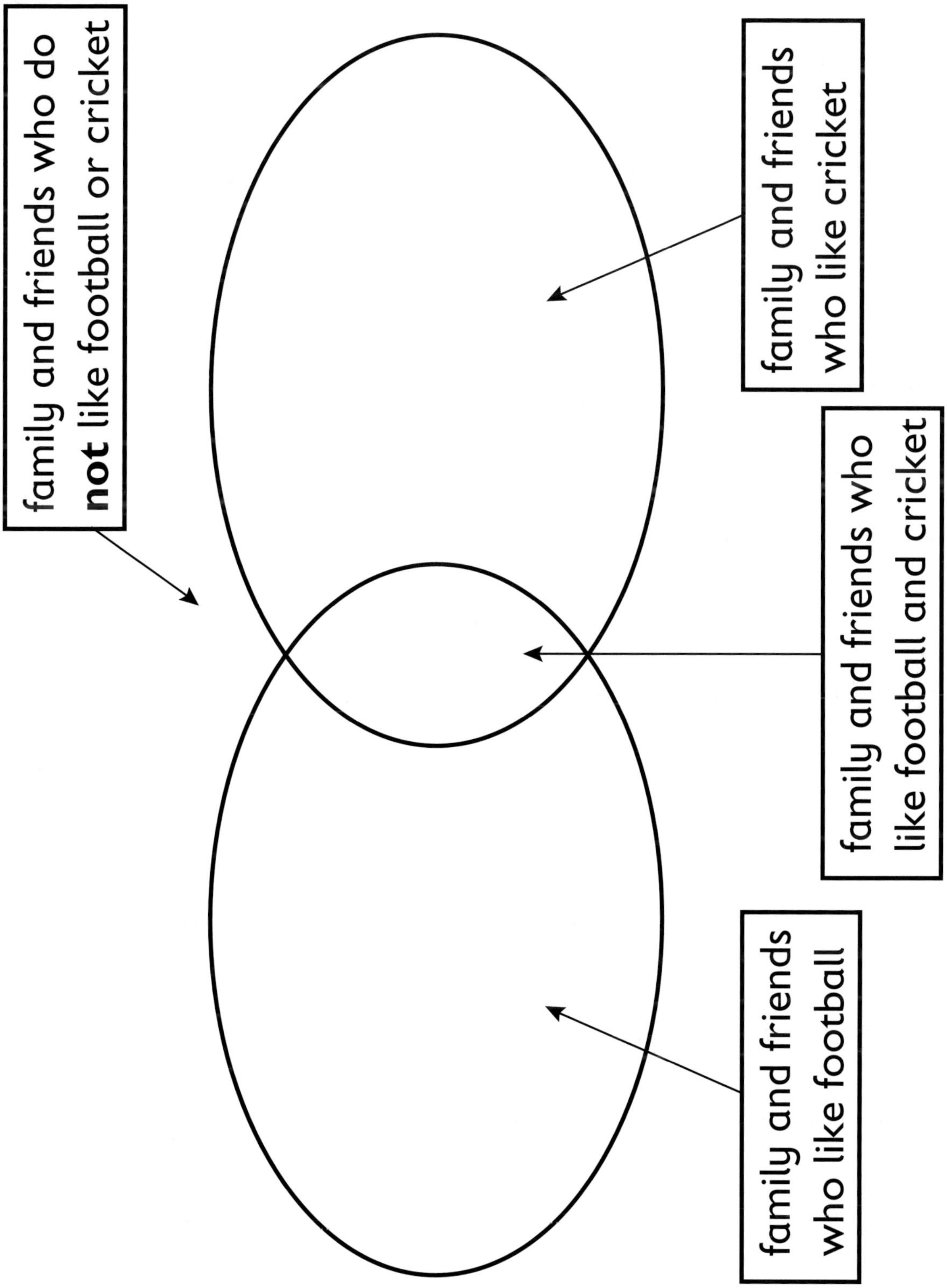

Notes

Notes